365
VEGAN
SMOOTHIES

365 VEGAN SMOOTHIES

BOOST YOUR HEALTH with a RAINBOW of FRUITS and VEGGIES

KATHY PATALSKY

AVERY

A MEMBER OF PENGUIN GROUP (USA) INC.

NEW YORK

AVERY

Published by the Penguin Group
Penguin Group (USA) Inc., 375 Hudson Street,
New York, New York 10014, USA

USA · Canada · UK · Ireland · Australia
New Zealand · India · South Africa · China

Penguin Books Ltd, Registered Offices:
80 Strand, London WC2R 0RL, England
For more information about the Penguin Group visit penguin.com

Most Avery books are available at special quantity discounts for bulk purchase for
sales promotions, premiums, fund-raising, and educational needs. Special books or
book excerpts also can be created to fit specific needs. For details, write
Penguin Group (USA) Inc. Special Markets, 375 Hudson Street, New York, NY 10014.

ISBN 978-1-58333-517-8

Printed in the United States of America
1 3 5 7 9 10 8 6 4 2

Book design by Stephanie Huntwork

ALWAYS LEARNING   PEARSON

TO GARY

CONTENTS

FOREWORD

by Gena Hamshaw,
Certified Clinical Nutritionist,
ChoosingRaw.com

Only a few generations ago, a cookbook composed exclusively of smoothies might have raised eyebrows. This is not because smoothies were a complete novelty; indeed, they had emerged as a "health drink" in the 1930s, when juice bars in California started serving blended fruit concoctions, then called "smoothees." It's because smoothies themselves weren't really acknowledged as a canvas for culinary artistry; a vehicle for one's daily serving of fruits and veggies, maybe, but no proper playground for the serious chef.

Today smoothies remain beloved among health enthusiasts, but they've slipped into the hearts of foodies everywhere: chefs, restaurateurs, home cooks, athletes, moms (and kids), students, pretty much anyone who values nourishing and delicious food. We still love smoothies because they allow us to pack a ton of fruits and vegetables into our daily routine with ease, but we also love them because they present us with endless flavor combinations, because they give us an opportunity to become acquainted with fruits we might otherwise shy away from (to this day, I'm squeamish about kiwis, but not if I blend them up), and because they're endlessly versatile. Most of us start to explore smoothies because we're looking for a breakfast option that is fast and healthy. If we're lucky, we learn along the way that these drinks are as delectable as they are sensible.

For people who eat a plant-based diet—and I don't mean just vegans, but also vegetarians, flexitarians, and anyone who simply loves fruits and vegetables—smoothies have a particularly cherished status. When I first became vegan, I was a little overwhelmed with the most emphatic recommendation of vegan chefs, cookbook writers, nutritionists, and physicians, which was to "eat more green leafy vegetables." Aside from salads, I had no idea how to incorporate the sheer volume of greens I was instructed to eat into my diet—and there were only so many salads I could eat! Then I discovered green smoothies, and everything changed. By blending a few leaves of Swiss chard, spinach, or romaine lettuce with bananas, berries, and a little almond milk, I found that I could enjoy far more greens than I had before. Over time, my taste for the vegetables increased—as did the number of combinations I was willing to try.

As a clinical nutritionist, I've seen firsthand how powerful these drinks can be in helping people adopt a healthier lifestyle. The old adage is true: Breakfast is the most important meal of the day. This is not only because it helps steady metabolism and replenish one's energy stores, but also because healthy choices made early in the day will beget more healthy choices.

Start your day with nutrient-dense, vitamin-rich foods, and you'll be less likely to turn to junk foods and stimulants for energy as the day goes on. If you're one of the many hundreds of Americans with a GI illness, you may find that blended drinks digest more easily than the equivalent amount of fruits and vegetables. If you're seeking out healthy snacks, you'll quickly learn that smoothies are far more delicious and energizing than sugary snack bars, salty, fried potato chips, or lattes. And if you've got a sweet tooth, fear not: Smoothies can make a healthy after-dinner sip feel decadent and indulgent. No matter who you are—health enthusiast, aspiring vegan, or simply an average guy or gal who's hoping to make smarter and more nutritious choices—smoothies are one of the easiest ways to get started.

It makes sense that this most approachable of healthy foods is now being given its ultimate cookbook treatment by recipe developer, writer, and all-around culinary superstar Kathy Patalsky. Kathy is one of the most talented, energetic, and creative forces in vegan and healthy food today. Her website, Healthy Happy Life, has helped many people adopt healthier and more vegetable-centric diets. As Kathy's friend and longtime admirer, I marvel at her talent as a chef and recipe developer. But what inspires me most about Kathy's work is her capacity to make vegan food feel so accessible. I'll never forget the first time I met Kathy in person. I knew she was the writer of a wildly successful blog, the webmaster of the world's only vegan food photography website, a recipe developer for various high-profile websites, and a professional photographer. In spite of these distinctions, Kathy was modest, humble, humorous, and down-to-earth. I immediately saw why her blog made veganism and healthy eating feel so accessible to so many people. It was Kathy's warm, welcoming personality, which seemed to say, "Healthy eating can be *fun*. Let me show you how."

Here, in Kathy's beautiful and informative book, you'll find smoothies for everyone. The recipes may be vegan, but you don't have to be vegan to appreciate their taste and health benefits. On offer are recipes for hardcore green smoothie enthusiasts and novice blenders alike; light, refreshing, fruity summertime sips

and hearty breakfast blends. You'll find a host of recipes that call for ingredients you already are familiar with and love—bananas, berries, flax seeds, soy milk—but you'll also find such exotic ingredients as chia seeds, hemp protein, and cacao nibs. You'll find smoothies for traditionalists and smoothies for culinary adventurers. No matter what you're hoping to find in this collection, you'll find it, along with 364 other recipes that will delight your palate and leave you eager for your next blending adventure.

You will also learn more than you ever could have hoped about different fruits and vegetables and the unique vitamins and minerals they offer. You'll learn about the best sources for vegan protein, the best sweeteners for your body, and a ton of other information about staying healthy on a vegan diet. Whether you intend to take the vegan plunge or not, *365 Vegan Smoothies* will give you the tools you need to make more nutritious choices every single day.

These 365 vegan smoothies can make your life healthier, happier, and more delicious than you've ever imagined. And they'll prove to you, once and for all, that healthy eating doesn't have to be hard. It can be as simple and accessible as plugging in a blender. With Kathy Patalsky's friendly voice, playful approach, and working knowledge of nutrition science by your side, healthy choices will feel not only well within your reach, but pleasurable, fun, and rewarding too. Get ready for a journey into the tasty and refreshing world of vegan smoothies; once you get blending, you won't want to stop!

INTRODUCTION

I was a smoothie girl from the start. I grew up in Santa Cruz, California, a beachside community that I lovingly refer to as laid-back, farmers' market–obsessed, art-infused, outdoorsy, and sunny in disposition—my version of paradise. I found myself surrounded by an eclectic mix of surfers, artists, techies, farmers, writers, musicians, athletes, and dreamers. My wellness lifestyle upbringing was, in my mind, "the norm" for American families. It was all I knew. Bike rides, hiking trips, tennis matches, beach days, picnics, and meals made from foods grown in our backyard and surrounding area farms. Mealtime was less about following a specific recipe and more about the season, ingredient origin, and inspiration.

Playful, energizing smoothies fit seamlessly into that culture and lifestyle.

I don't remember my very first smoothie, but I do remember the experience that gave me the prowess to consider myself a lifelong smoothie expert.

In my seventh-grade drama class my first big assignment was to give a ten-minute speech with the goal of teaching something new to my peers—something I considered myself an expert in.

I showed my fellow seventh graders how to make a smoothie.

Why I chose "smoothies" as my area of preteen expertise, I don't exactly remember. I *do* remember getting home from school to a quiet house, running into the kitchen, and rummaging through the freezer to scrounge for any frozen fruit we had on hand so I could craft my own creative concoctions from whatever I found. Clumsily, my tiny hands would grab at frozen strawberries, tender bananas, and big handfuls of ice. I'd drop the ingredients into our clunky plastic blender, put the lid on, and swirl! As the blender motor growled, I'd move my fingers over the buttons, switching from "pulse" to "puree" and back to "blend"—like I was playing a video game—watching my ingredients twist into a frosty spin of pink, orange, or yellow colors.

My first smoothie was probably something classic like creamy banana-strawberry. But for that anxiety-inducing drama class speech I borrowed my friend Tosh's recipe: chocolate pineapple. The recipe was one her father used to make for her. I liked it because the creative flavor combination was different from anything I had ever tried.

Ingredients: a packet of sweetened hot chocolate mix, ½ cup canned pineapple (drained), a banana, ¾ cup milk, a splash of pineapple juice from the can, and lots of ice. (Obviously, back then I was not yet vegan!)

It blended into this crazy-cool concoction of frothy, sweet pineapple-and-chocolate deliciousness. I knew it would be a hit with the class—especially since I planned on bringing little paper tasting cups to share the smoothie love.

The day of the speech I woke up extra early to pack my smoothie gear into a big brown paper grocery bag while my parents and sister soundly slept. I snuck into the dark kitchen and snatched my ingredients and supplies with the skill of a cat burglar (a tiny cat burglar with big smoothie ambitions). I didn't bother to consult my parents on my appliance borrowing activities that day. I knew they would say yes. Mom and Dad wouldn't miss it, right?

First into the bag was the enormous plastic blender. I grabbed the heavy base with both arms, plopping it in with a loud *thunk!* I wrangled the long, slinky cord and quickly stuffed it into the wrinkled brown bag like it was a wild snake. Next, I threw some ice in a plastic zipper bag, grabbed a can of pineapple, the manual can opener, a few hot chocolate packets, mini paper tasting cups, a presentation glass, and a chilled thermos of milk that I planned on storing (with my ice) in my drama teacher's mini fridge until class time. I wasn't sure the ice would hold up, but I'd manage somehow. Lifting the bag with two hands, I cringed. It was a heavy load.

Later that morning, when the bell rang signaling third period, students shuffled off to class. It was a packed house for speech day in my drama class. As I stood up in front, my eyes grew wide with anxiety at the number of eyes staring back at me from the many wooden desks snugly lining our tiny classroom. I took a deep breath and put on my game face. Smoothie time! I confidently began my speech, trying my very best to fake a cooking demo. Luckily, food is an attention-grabbing topic for teenagers. I chattered away about smoothies, then began preparing my blend. My hands shook as I put the cocoa, pineapple, and splash of milk into my tabletop blender. I flipped on the switch and the whizzing sound vibrated on the wobbly table as my smoothie spun into a frothy chocolate blend of fruit, ice, and milk. The class was very quiet as the brash blender motor echoed through the brightly lit classroom, the frosty chocolate color of the swirling blend catching everyone's eyes and stomachs.

To my classmates' glee, I announced that I had brought tasting cups for whoever wanted to try the smoothie. Every hand in the class shot up, and soon my classmates were enjoying tiny paper cups of my chocolate creation. Success! It was then that I realized that people really do just love smoothies! And people love taste-testing different smoothie flavors and combinations—especially when they feature favorite ingredients like chocolate and pineapple.

I was pleased that the speech was a hit, and from that day on, smoothies were *my thing*. I was an official expert. At the age of thirteen. And if memory serves, my teacher, Miss Chloe, gave me an A on that speech.

My smoothie-loving ways continued through high school, when I got my first job at Jamba Juice. It was called Juice Club back then in Capitola, California. It was one of the first locations of the Juice Club brand.

The first Juice Club opened in April 1990 in San Luis Obispo, California, founded by cyclist Kirk Perron. In 1995, while I was working there, Juice Club changed its name to Jamba Juice. At first, there was some resistance to the new name and logo among my friends and me. The new branding, with a glossy swirl spiral logo and deep purple colors, seemed very corporate and grand. I remember my boss telling me that "Jamba" was a word the company essentially made up, derived from the African word *jama*, which means "to celebrate." I would have never guessed that in just a few short years, Jamba Juice would become the worldwide phenomenon that it is today. All over the world people continue to embrace their love of smoothies. That same love made me want to work at Jamba Juice.

I loved that job. You walked through the glass doors and the noisy sound of multiple blenders humming would fill your ears as a wafting fresh citrus aroma crashed through your nose and mouth, coating your senses in that sunshiny smell of sweet, vibrant orange-peel citrus. There was also a sideline aroma of fresh wheatgrass and juiced carrots dancing from the wheatgrass-lined countertop. I made hundreds of smoothies a day, pouring out red, orange, pink, and chocolate-colored blends. Pumping peanut butter, filling barrels with frozen bananas, juicing carrots, and tossing in powdered juice boosts. My favorite flavor was Citrus Squeeze. I'd make my own special twist on it by piling in extra scoops of fruit, soy protein, and vitamin powder. Shot of wheatgrass (or two or three) on the side.

Smoothies were a part of life back then. Embedded into my social upbringing, like "going out for ice cream," we went "out for smoothies."

After a long, hot tennis practice, all us girls, sleeves rolled up above our shoulders, dripping in sweat, guzzling bottles filled with water, lemon, and mint, would shriek, "I need a Juice Club right now!" Proudly, I was a smoothie addict. A tall frosty smoothie, sipped slowly outside in a sunbeam, gave me immediate chilled bliss, cooling my throat and energizing my body.

These memories remind me how much joy, happiness, energy, and peace smoothies have brought me over the years. Whenever my wellness has needed a boost, I have turned to smoothies to get me back on track.

Smoothies have found a place in each of my life stages: high school, college, career, relationships, and beyond. And my smoothie tastes are always changing as my body's needs and cravings transform and evolve. I hope this book inspires you to start your own journey—or evolve on your current smoothie path.

Writing this book was a way for me to dive into the world of smoothies like never before. I discovered a long list of new favorite recipes. And to be honest, that really surprised me! There truly is always a new smoothie flavor out there for your taste buds to discover! This book goes far beyond the classic frozen fruit smoothie: You'll find frothy coolers, vibrant green smoothies, icy cool frosties, rich protein shakes, creamy grain shakes, and more.

I'm so glad you have decided to join me on this journey and see for yourself how much peace, life, joy, and wellness can be blended up into one tall, frosty smoothie glass.

Grab a glass and let's get blending!

PART 1
SMOOTHIES
101

1
WHY SMOOTHIES?

CREATING AND DRINKING A TALL, FROSTY, BEAUTIFUL SMOOTHIE is an act of pure bliss. You start by gathering a few of your favorite healthy ingredients. Then after a quick swirl in a buzzing blender those ingredients spin into a brand-new creation. A cool treat that blends up alluring and smooth, satisfying and vibrant in flavor. Sipping on a freshly blended smoothie is a uniquely refreshing experience. And when you find a flavor that speaks to your taste buds, I guarantee you will want to make that recipe again. And again! Healthy smoothies are something you'll crave, for their flavor and for the way they make you feel!

the smoothie habit

Wellness is not a sprint, but rather a very slow marathon—a lifelong journey, where you discover how your body and mind uniquely respond to food, exercise, stress, and daily challenges. Wellness requires a life-long commitment of healthy habits. Habits you enjoy and embrace and that fuel you with energy and life—rather than drain you of it. And one of my favorite healthy, happy, energizing wellness habits: the smoothie habit.

A "smoothie habit" is not a diet. Smoothies become part of your life-style. A healthy habit you come to love, depend on, and crave. Wellness is about balance. Trendy or crash diets will eventually fail because they usually encourage a negative relationship with food. Instead of depriving yourself and focusing on what not to eat, focus on what you can (and love!) to eat.

Look at your delicious smoothie as your daily boost of nutritional wellness. In one tall, frosty, juicy, colorful glass you are getting a wide rainbow of nutrients. And with 365 different recipes to choose from, you could very easily sip on a different smoothie every day for an entire year. Variety made easy.

And variety is important to nutritional wellness. With so many superfoods out there, it would be a shame to find yourself in a smoothie rut, blending the same ingredients over and over.

smoothies can change your life

Quite a statement, right? Well, it's true! Starting or nurturing a smoothie habit will increase your wellness by pumping up the number of fruits, veggies, grains, seeds, and nuts you consume. And these healthy foods will energize your mind, body, and spirit, and in turn change your life.

The foods we eat have an enormous impact on our mood, strength, energy level, weight, focus, immunity, longevity, and overall vibrancy. And whole foods—like smoothie ingredients—are some of the healthiest foods around.

I think of myself as a healthy-eating vegan, with my loyal smoothie habit one of the most powerful, wellness-enhancing aspects of my diet. Smoothies are a fast and easy way to supercharge your diet with nutrients, deliciously moving you closer to your wellness goals.

And even if you are already an experienced smoothie lover, hopefully the creative flavor combinations and ingredients in this book will inspire new smoothies to add to your proud arsenal of blended bevie recipes. Sometimes culinary inspiration is as simple as an ingredient. A flavor. A photograph. A description. An aroma. A texture.

I truly hope that my recipes and ideas inspire you. And give you the confidence and freedom to break outside your normal smoothie routine. And create a few new blends of your own!

10 REASONS TO DRINK SMOOTHIES

1 **They taste delicious.** Smoothies flat-out taste delish. Made from some of our favorite foods, like fresh fruits, veggies, nuts, and grains, smoothies serve up frosty deliciousness.

2 **They are fun!** It is fun to blend smoothies—to watch healthy, colorful ingredients whiz around in a blender and turn, almost magically, into a new creation in which the whole is greater than the sum of its parts!

3 **They are hydrating.** Your body is made up of nearly 70 percent water, and when your body is dehydrated, it can lead to fatigue, headaches, lack of focus, misinterpreted hunger, and more. Smoothies are hydrating and rich in nutrients, including electrolytes like potassium, nourishing your body with food and drink all in one.

4 **They help you eat more plants.** By adding vegan smoothies to your diet, you will consume more fruits and veggies per day— whole foods that energize and fuel your body, fight free radicals, boost your immune system, help regulate your digestion, and more. Filling up on plants means you are less likely to crave and eat those not-so-good-for-you foods. Fill up on smoothies and your refined sugar, saturated fat, and fried food cravings just may jump ship. I have found that the road to optimum wellness is paved with an abundance of fruits and veggies. Plant power!

5 **They are rich in phytochemicals.** Vegan smoothies are created using plant-based ingredients. Phytochemicals are bioactive compounds that you will find only in plants. Phytochemicals are what give certain plants their unique color, flavor, and resistance to diseases. The health benefits from consuming the more than two thousand (and counting) different phytochemicals are still being discovered and researched. Experts are finding that the benefits of a plant-rich diet range from helping your immune system and fighting free radicals to possibly even preventing cancer, heart disease, lung disease, type 2 diabetes, and other health ailments.

6 **They are rich in fiber.** Most Americans do not consume the recommended 25 to 30 grams of fiber per day. The national average is around 15 grams, according to the American Heart Association. Put that in perspective—one cup of blackberries contains a generous 8 grams of fiber; one ounce of chia seeds, 11 grams. Add in a few more whole foods and you are well on your way to increasing your fiber-per-day goals via vegan smoothies.

7 **They make breakfast happen.** Enough of the skipping breakfast routine. Smoothies provide you with a fast, easy, delicious, and healthy way to fuel your body in the morning. Many smoothies are rich in nutrient-dense carbohydrates, your body's number-one source of fuel. Crave that morning smoothie energy burst! And since smoothies are often rich in fiber, they can help kick-start your digestive system for the day.

8 **They give your digestive system a break.** The overall goal of digestion is to break down food so that it can be absorbed by your body's cells and used as needed. Smoothies are an easy way to give your body some digestive support during the break-down process of food.

Let's use a kale-citrus smoothie as an example. If you were to sit down and eat a large bowl of kale and a peeled orange (two very fibrous whole foods), you might notice that your digestive system (which starts in the mouth with chewing) kicks into high gear. But by blending the kale and orange, you are aiding your digestive system quite a bit. That smoothed-out "smoothie" texture means the blender blades have done their job by breaking down the orange and kale plant cell walls, pulverizing the foods into smaller, more liquid particles. Thanks to the blender, your teeth and stomach will have less work to do. And let's face it, the blender does a much more efficient job than your teeth in pulverizing whole foods. And a more efficient breakdown of food means you may have a better chance of absorbing more nutrients into your body as digestion progresses.

9 **They help bring you total mind and body wellness.** Delicious, nutrient-filled smoothies can help you acquire a healthier body. And starting a smoothie habit can give you some peace of mind that you are taking care of yourself. A joy-inspiring smoothie habit can also help you get off the wellness-seeking merry-go-round. Stop stressing yourself out by worrying about your diet—your journey toward mind, body, and spirit wellness may start with something as simple as grabbing a straw and sipping on a smoothie!

10 **They are fun to share.** Healthy trends rock—let's all make smoothies the new social-hour food. Instead of going out for ice cream, hop in the kitchen for a smoothie break. For the perfect light bite and quick pick-me-up, blend up a smoothie recipe and split it between two people. Or if you are both quite hungry, blend up two smoothie recipes, one for each of you.

why vegan smoothies?

Every smoothie recipe in this book is one hundred percent plant-based, vegan. Nutritional information and all. No thinking required. Vegan smoothies are free of the animal products that you often find in smoothie recipes, such as dairy milk, dairy yogurt, and honey. Dairy from animals can contain saturated fat, hormones, chemicals, and more. And for some people, digesting dairy is a taxing process.

Not only can animal products be harsh on your body, they are definitely harsh on the animals they come from. By choosing vegan plant-based smoothies, you are making a compassionate choice for animals—and a smart choice for our planet.

Not vegan? Totally OK. You don't have to be vegan to love these recipes. And blending up plant-based smoothies is an excellent way to experiment with vegan cuisine. You may be pleasantly surprised at what you *don't* miss—and how vibrant, energized, light, and satisfied you feel.

vegan substitutions for dairy

I'm making it easy for smoothie lovers. There is no reason why you would need dairy products to build a delicious smoothie, and here is how I do it with common substitutions:

dairy yogurt → **non-dairy yogurt** (such as soy, almond, or coconut yogurt)

dairy milk → **non-dairy milk** (such as almond, rice, cashew, soy, coconut, grain, or flax milk)

whey protein powder → **dairy- and casein-free protein powders** (soy, hemp, pea, or other vegan protein blends)

whipped cream → **soy, rice, or coconut whipped topping**

smoothie recipe faqs

1 **Q:** What do you mean by "healthy fats"? And aren't all fats bad for me?

A: First, when talking about fat, it is a good idea to evaluate your cognitive relationship with consuming foods that are rich in fats. If you are the type of eater who gravitates toward foods labeled "fat-free," you may need to readjust your thinking. The truth is, you *should* be including fat in your diet. And even though, calorie-wise, all fats contain 9 calories per gram, health-wise, not all fats are created equal. Some are healthier than others; thus the term "healthy fats."

Eating 10 grams of fat from butter is much less healthy than eating 10 grams of fat from walnuts. Walnuts are much higher in "healthy fats" than butter.

Healthy fats can include monounsaturated fats, polyunsaturated fats, and omega-3 essential fatty acids, aka EFAs.

Healthy fat intake plays a significant role in wellness. Everything from appetite control, brain function, mood regulation, and even weight loss may be influenced by whether or not you are consuming enough healthy fats.

Healthy fats for your smoothies include avocado, nuts, nut butters, seeds, and healthy nut and seed oils like flax, chia, walnut, pumpkin seed, and hemp.

Another important point is that some vitamins, like vitamin A (from beta-carotene), vitamin K, vitamin E, and vitamin D, are fat-soluble. This means that your body needs some fat present to properly absorb these nutrients. So adding a drizzle of flax oil, a handful of nuts, or a teaspoon of nut butter to your smoothies may actually help with total nutrient absorption.

On the flip side, should you be limiting "unhealthy" fats? Most experts agree that you should pay attention to hydrogenated fats, with their trans-fatty acids, and saturated fats in your diet. For example, the American Heart Association's Nutrition Committee strongly advises that "healthy Americans over age two limit their intake of trans fat to less than one percent of total calories."

2 **Q:** What's with all the coconut water ice cubes?

A: You will find lots of smoothies using coconut water ice cubes instead of ice. The reason for this is that coconut water cubes add nutrients and a subtle sweetness yet serve the same purpose as plain water ice cubes—to add frostiness to the texture and chill the smoothie. Substitute regular ice for the coconut water cubes if you like or if you don't have coconut water in the house.

3 **Q:** What are the different types of smoothies?

A: Not all smoothies are created equal! The term "smoothie" refers to a broad umbrella of recipes.

THE 10 TYPES OF SMOOTHIES IN THIS BOOK

1 **Green Smoothie.** A green smoothie is green in color, as it contains green ingredients. Green smoothies vary in texture and flavor but are usually a blend of fruits and veggies to optimize flavor. Contrary to what you may think about foods that are green, green smoothies are usually quite sweet in flavor from the blended fruits and veggies.

2 **Frosty.** A frosty is very similar to a smoothie; however, instead of being silky and creamy, it has a notably icy and "frosty" texture. A frosty, because of its iciness, is usually a bit colder than a smoothie and melts more slowly. However, just a like a smoothie, a frosty is vibrant in flavor and rich in whole foods, and it does not have a watered-down taste. A watermelon frosty is a good example.

3 **Frozen.** Seeking a super-light and refreshing blend? Try a frozen. Frozens are a refreshing option for hydration, as they are mostly a frozen version of a liquid drink. Think of frozen lemonade. Lots of sweet clear liquid, blended with a large amount of ice and maybe some frozen fruit to accent. Frozens are generally lower in fiber and whole foods than frosties.

4 **Whole Food Smoothie.** This type of smoothie simply contains mostly whole food ingredients. For example, instead of adding orange juice, you might add a whole peeled orange plus a splash of water to help with blending. Most green smoothies—rich in leafy greens—are also whole food smoothies.

5 **Grain, Nut, or Seed Shake.** Creamy, delicious, and packed with diverse nutrients like protein, fiber, complex carbs, and vitamins, grain, nut, and seed shakes offer your body a break from the traditional fruit-and-veggie-style blend.

6 **Protein Smoothie.** A protein smoothie is any blend that is particularly rich in protein. Maybe it contains a scoop of hemp seeds, nut butter, or protein powder. Protein smoothies usually use a non-dairy milk or water base.

7 **Shake.** A shake is a broad term for smoothies that resemble thick, creamy milkshakes—they are less icy and usually do not need any ice at all. Frozen bananas are often used in shakes, which often feature "dessert" flavors like cacao, maple, nut butter, and vanilla.

8 **Cooler or Tonic.** Coolers and tonics are the thinnest of all the smoothie varieties. They blend up to be cool, light, thin, and hydrating. Plenty of liquid and fresh chilled produce (as opposed to frozen) is often used.

9 **Cruncher.** A cruncher is any smoothie that contains an added element of crunch—vegan granola, chopped nuts, crunchy sprouted grains (such as buckwheat), puffed grains, crushed vegan cookies, and more. Cruncher smoothies are usually thick in texture so that the topping blends nicely—like a smoothie parfait. Use a spoon instead of a straw when eating a cruncher! Though you will not see many recipes for cruncher, you can alter many of my thick-textured smoothie recipes to make them crunchers. You just need to add the crunch!

10 **Basic Smoothie.** Last, if a recipe in this book does not fit one of the descriptions above, it probably falls under the wide and colorful umbrella term "smoothie." Smoothies are a blend of fresh and/or frozen fruit, maybe some veggies and add-ins, and varying liquids and ice.

Q: Is there a basic smoothie formula?

A: I would say yes if there were only one variety of smoothie. But as you will learn from my recipes, smoothies come in a wide variety of textures, colors, flavors, and temperatures. But for a "classic" frosty-creamy smoothie I like to stick close to this ratio:

I cup liquid
1½ cups frozen fruit
optional ½ cup softer fruit or veggie or liquid (such as
    room-temperature banana, kiwi, kale, or soy yogurt)
¼ to ½ cup ice

When adding leafy greens to a smoothie, I use roughly ½ cup of liquid for every 2 cups of greens to help blend the smoothie.

Q: How long do I blend my smoothie for a smooth texture?

A: You never want your smoothie to be lumpy—thus the term "smoothie." When the smoothie is a uniform color and is blending in a smooth swirl, it is done. Try not to overblend, as your smoothie will start to "melt" from the heat of the blender after a while. Serve immediately! If you are blending for a long time with no progress, either jump to a higher speed or stop and reposition the contents of the smoothie in the blender. You may have an air bubble that is caught in between the blades and ingredients.

For green smoothies, be sure to blend until the green specks turn to a uniform color. Veggie or whole food smoothies may take longer to blend than basic frozen fruit smoothies.

6 **Q:** How many ingredients are there typically in a smoothie?

A: Smoothies with just a few ingredients are nice because you can prominently taste the pure, simple, individual flavors. However, sometimes the complexity of a multi-ingredient smoothie can be quite magical and bring you to a brand-new flavor experience.

smoothie troubleshooting

1 **Q:** How do I thicken my smoothie?

A: Add more ice or more frozen fruit. If your recipe calls for frozen strawberries, try adding another scoop of them. Frozen bananas are the best quick fix to give almost any smoothie a creamy shake-like texture. Tip: A great way to ensure your recipe stays thick enough is to start by adding only half of the liquid that the recipe calls for. Then once the blend starts swirling, slowly add in the remaining liquid until your desired thickness is achieved.

2 **Q:** There are bits of unblended ingredients in my green or whole food smoothie. How do I smooth things out?

A: Try blending at a higher speed. Also try blending for a longer period of time. If it still is not smooth, add more liquid and continue blending. Water works well to loosen things up; coconut water, juice, or non-dairy milk can also be used. If none of these fixes work, you may need to upgrade your blender to one with a more powerful motor. Otherwise, adjust your recipe to include ingredient substitutions that you know your blender can handle.

3 **Q:** My smoothie is not sweet enough. What do I do?

A: A quick drizzle of maple syrup or agave syrup will help. You could also toss in some sweet accent ingredients like half a banana, a few pitted dates, some grapes or slices of pear, or even some sweet non-dairy yogurt. If needed, toss in some additional ice so you do not thin things out too much.

4 **Q:** My smoothie is too thick to drink with a straw. What do I do?

A: Enjoy it with a spoon! Or wait a few minutes. As the smoothie melts a bit, it should loosen into a more liquid texture. Or simply add a splash more liquid to your recipe to thin it out to your desired consistency.

5 **Q:** The powder, nut butter, or seeds I added stuck to the sides of my blender. How do I prevent this from happening?

A: To blend these tricky ingredients more smoothly from the start, add just the liquid and the ingredient and blend on low speed until smooth. For example, when blending matcha powder or protein powder into a smoothie, start by blending the powder and liquid on low speed until smooth, then add the remaining ingredients and continue with the recipe. If your blender allows for an ultra-low setting, add the trouble ingredients, slowly, while the liquid is blending.

6 **Q:** I have my blender on the highest speed, but my smoothie is just sitting there, not blending, what do I do?

A: There may be an air bubble caught near the blades. Turn the blender off, reposition the ingredients, and start again on low. If your machine has a plunger tool, use that.

7

Q: My smoothie always melts so quickly. How can I keep it cold longer?

A: Serve in a thicker glass or place your serving glass in the freezer for ten minutes to chill and frost it before blending and pouring your smoothie.

8

Q: My green smoothie is too grassy. How do I tweak the flavor?

A: Try adding a sweet ingredient like banana, kiwi, orange, or some simple vanilla non-dairy yogurt. Or you can add a drizzle of sweetener. Sweet accents help mellow the grassy flavor of greens.

9

Q: How do I stop or slow "smoothie splashing" during the blending process?

A: Always start your blend on the lowest speed and move slowly higher from there. Large chunks of ingredients can cause splashing, so never add a giant stuck-together clump of frozen fruit to your blend—you may damage your blender trying to break it up. Instead, allow the fruit to thaw just enough so you can easily break it into pieces.

7 smoothie myths and facts

1

Myth: If I don't like _____, I most certainly won't like it in a smoothie.

Fact: Not always true! Sometimes a smoothie can change the way an ingredient tastes so you experience it in a whole new, delicious way.

2 **Myth:** Smoothies are not really that healthy because they contain so many carbs.

Fact: Carbohydrates are our body's preferred source of fuel! The carbohydrates in smoothies are from nutrient-dense whole foods like fruits, grains, and veggies. Most smoothies are low in or free of added sugars and "empty" carbs. So even if the carb count seems high, remember that not all carbs are created equal. And remember that fiber-rich smoothies help slow the release of energy from those carbohydrates and thus help prevent nasty blood sugar spikes and crashes.

3 **Myth:** Smoothies won't fill me up.

Fact: If you want to feel satisfied from your smoothie, look for recipes that are high in fiber and contain not just carbohydrates but also fat and protein. You can also always add a small snack to your smoothie break.

4 **Myth:** Green smoothies taste overly grassy.

Fact: Green smoothies are complex in flavor. Sure, there is a little grassiness at times, but when complemented with sweet, sassy, spicy flavors, the "green" flavor becomes alluring. And despite the bright green color, sometimes you will not taste any grassiness at all! It all depends on how much of the green ingredients, and any other ingredients, you are adding.

5 **Myth:** I don't have time to make a smoothie.

Fact: Sure you do! In fact, smoothies are one of the quickest ways to fuel your body with a wide array of easily digestible nutrients. Just be sure to have plenty of smoothie ingredients on hand. A freezer stocked with frozen fruit is a must!

6 **Myth:** Smoothies are too expensive.

Fact: Some smoothie ingredients like matcha powder, goji berries, and certain nuts can get pricey, but you can choose to omit these items or just use them occasionally. You can easily make a smoothie on a budget. Foods like non-dairy milk, bananas, and many other fruits and veggies are easy to find at value prices. Buy pantry items in bulk and choose in-season ingredients for the best prices—and freshest flavors.

7 **Myth:** I don't have a fancy blender, so I can't make certain smoothies.

Fact: Most of the recipes in this book can easily be blended with a budget blender. And learning a few easy ingredient substitution tips can help as well. See my tips, beginning on page 46.

Now that you have learned some of the basics of smoothie preparation, you can see how incredibly diverse the world of smoothies is. Smoothies serve up a wide range of creative and delicious flavors, textures, temperatures, and colors. And in the next chapter, you will begin to see how smoothies also serve up a wide variety of wellness benefits!

2
THE 12 WELLNESS THEMES AND HOW TO USE THIS BOOK

IN THIS CHAPTER YOU WILL DIVE INTO LEARNING MORE ABOUT the twelve wellness themes featured in this book, and how to add a smoothie routine to your life and synchronize your smoothie habit with your everyday lifestyle. You will learn how to fit your smoothie fix into your basic meal plan, and how to use smoothies to promote wellness in specific areas of your life.

And as your wellness needs change, your smoothies can move right along with you thanks to the diversity of themes. The twelve wellness themes can help you boost your energy level, cut back on calories, increase your sense of calm, improve your digestion, make you glow from the inside out, and more!

This chapter will also introduce you to the variety of ways you can use this book as a twelve-month wellness plan. But the great thing about this book is that it is incredibly flexible to fit a variety of lifestyles. You can follow the twelve months starting with smoothie number one and take in a full spectrum of wellness benefits. Or you can hop around and start where and when you'd like, listening to your body's changing wellness needs and cravings as you move forward.

how to use this book

I know you are eager to get started, but before you dive into the details of the twelve themes, you will want to familiarize yourself with a few tips on how to use this book to maximize its value in your journey to increased wellness.

YOUR NEW SMOOTHIE ROUTINE

The beauty of wellness is that everyone is different and no one method of doing things works for everyone. You can skip around or fully commit to a front-to-back yearlong smoothie adventure. The most important part of forming any wellness habit is to say to yourself that you want to change. Once you acknowledge that you truly want to add more smoothies into your diet, the rest is easy.

Don't get discouraged by roadblocks. Life always gets in the way a little. And that's OK! There are no mistakes in this journey. Maybe you will go for a week with a smoothie every morning, then take the weekend or next week off. Totally fine! Establishing new healthy habits takes time. Sometimes years! By embracing healthy vegan smoothies today (just by reading this book), you are well on your way to adopting a smoothie habit and moving toward your wellness goals.

WHEN AND HOW TO ENJOY SMOOTHIES

You can enjoy a smoothie as a meal replacement, a tasty snack, or a side beverage. As you become more familiar with smoothie making, you will become more in tune with your own body and when it craves its smoothie fix. I have learned that there is no wrong time to drink a smoothie! Craving a chocolate-banana protein shake at two a.m.? Green smoothie for dinner? Go for it!

My two favorite times to enjoy a smoothie:

1 In the morning. Breakfast smoothies energize and get you started on the right wellness track for the rest of your day.

2 As a late-afternoon pick-me-up, around three or four p.m., to stay satisfied until dinnertime or to fuel up for an evening workout.

WHEN NOT TO ENJOY A SMOOTHIE

Right before strenuous exercise. Depending on the type of smoothie you are consuming, you want to allow enough time for your body to ease into digestion. And everyone is different. Some people might be fine running a mile after just drinking a large smoothie, while others may want a good hour to digest that smoothie, and yet others may prefer a smoothie as an after-workout refueling sip instead.

TOO MUCH OF A GOOD THING?

You could easily enjoy one or two smoothies every day as a snack or meal replacement if you like. However, you do want to make sure that if you are using smoothies as meal replacements, you are still meeting the calories and nutritional requirements for your body type and lifestyle. And since everyone's needs are different, you may want to consult with your doctor to gain more insight.

I find that most long-term smoothie drinkers will replace one meal a day with a large smoothie, usually breakfast or lunch, then snack lightly around that meal if they are still hungry. Nuts and seeds make great healthy snacks to complement a smoothie.

As a long-term smoothie drinker, I find that smoothies are a dependable afternoon pick-me-up for some easy energy. If you usually reach for a coffee beverage in the late afternoon, consider switching to a smoothie break instead! Try it for a week and see how you feel. Make it enticing by choosing your favorite smoothie flavor. Maybe almond butter–banana or chocolate with raspberries!

SERVING SIZE

Each smoothie recipe makes about two servings, sometimes more or less, depending on your produce and how accurately you commit to measuring. Sharing is optional.

If you drink the entire smoothie yourself (as I very often do), the nutritional content given is based per recipe, not per serving.

If you drink the entire smoothie yourself (as I very often do), the nutritional information will be as shown.

INGREDIENTS: BOOST IT!

Each recipe has an optional "boost it" ingredient following the main recipe. These are add-in ingredient suggestions that can work to boost the wellness value or flavor profile of your smoothie.

NUTRITION FACTS DISCLAIMER

The provided nutritional information is to be used as a guide. Calculations are estimates, since ingredient brands and produce varieties will vary greatly.

12 months of smoothies

This book is divided into twelve sections, each devoted to a different area of wellness. You can start at month one or you can go directly to the themes or smoothies that interest you most. As your needs change, the recipes you choose can change as well. However, you do not need to start with January—any month is a great month to start your wellness journey. You can easily start on a new wellness theme each month; just know that the number of smoothies given per section may not align perfectly with the number of days in your current calendar month. Feel free to fill in extra days with any smoothie you'd like to make or skip one at the end of your month as the case may be.

If you don't have a specific area of wellness you want to target, you are perfectly welcome to jump around however you choose. A different random smoothie every day is OK. Simply adding these nutrition-infused recipes to your diet is a great way to expand upon your general wellness. You can also jump around based on the specific ingredients you may crave or have on hand. Refer to the index if you need help finding a smoothie with a specific ingredient.

WELLNESS THEMES DISCLAIMER

Ingredients and recipes featured as wellness month enhancers are guide foods—and their effect on wellness will vary from person to person. There are many variables that play a role in your wellness within the twelve themes. Always consult a doctor and/or dietician first about your personal wellness, medical conditions, and dietary needs. Always consult your doctor with any health questions, reactions, or concerns you may have regarding the ingredients and recipes. Recipes are not meant to cure, treat, or diagnose health issues or diseases. The information I am providing is based on both factual nutritional analysis and personal experience.

month 1: detox smoothies

Favorite detox ingredients: apples, cayenne, ginger, lemons, apple cider vinegar, pineapples, cucumbers, celery, bananas, grapefruit, coconut water, chia seeds, aloe vera juice, beets, watermelon, cantaloupe, carrots, kale, spinach, kiwis, blueberries, spirulina, and oats.

Detox smoothies are a great way to support your body's natural cleansing mechanisms by removing toxins and stimulating renewal. Detox smoothies may be warming and spicy, electrolyte-rich, low-calorie, zesty, enzyme-rich, hydrating, alkalizing, and rich in cleansing fiber and/or rich in green foods, which are usually quite dense in nutrients and nurturing to the body. Nutrients to pay attention to include fluid-balancing potassium and water-soluble vitamins like vitamin C and B-complex—these need to be replenished more frequently, especially when you are drinking a lot of liquids.

Detox is possibly the most important stage in any wellness journey. It represents a starting point. You are detoxing not just in a diet/foods-you-eat sense but in an emotional and physical sense too. Now is the perfect time to really analyze your current state of wellness and set realistic goals and a roadmap for how you plan to achieve those goals. Your goals can be as simple as improving your diet by adding one smoothie a week—or as multifaceted as including goals for exercise, stress management, work/life balance, and more.

Our modern-day environments and activities produce plenty of wear and tear on our bodies via stress, pollution, poor dietary choices, lack of sleep, and overindulgence in alcohol, processed foods, and more. Detox is your chance to start over and begin rebuilding your body from the inside out through plant-based, nutrient-dense foods. Detox is a time to revamp, rethink, and break through any wellness roadblocks in your life.

Tune in to the signals from your body and honestly assess what you are putting into it. Alcohol, refined sugar, refined carbohydrates like white flour, caffeine, dairy, and other animal products if you are not vegan, chemicals in the form of artificial sweeteners and colors, and other wellness robbers can be minimized during this stage.

Detox can actually make you feel worse before it makes you feel better. Yup. Compare it to when you get a deep tissue massage and the massage therapist tells you to drink plenty of water for the next few hours and days to help flush out the toxins that may have been released into your system from the massage stimulation. Those freed toxins could make you feel kind of crappy before they exit your body. So try not to be discouraged if you feel especially tired or grumpy the first few days or weeks of your journey. Embrace the power of positive thinking. Thank goodness for our body's natural detox systems.

Staying hydrated by drinking plenty of purified or spring water or coconut water is the best detox habit you can practice. Hydration encourages your body to stay in a productive detoxification mode. Listen to your body's natural cues for hunger and thirst. Detox is a time to get reintroduced to and reacquainted with your body and become reawakened to the awesome, magnificent machine that it is. Listen, learn, and practice being present in the moment—especially when you are eating and drinking.

month 2: energizing smoothies

Favorite energizing ingredients: apples, bananas, beets, oats, buckwheat, cashews, açaí berries, blueberries, pomegranates, cherries, carrots, grapes, spirulina, matcha green tea, kale, soy, peanuts, mangos, and pineapples.

Now that your body has detoxed and purified to a more neutral state, you are probably ready to embrace your newfound feeling of clean and infuse your cells with some energy. Energy smoothies can bring you vitality and life. They are rich in vitamins, nutrient-dense carbohydrates, and electrolytes. Fiber, protein, and healthy fats will help sustain your energy. Perky, spicy, sweet, and zesty flavors will infuse your smoothies this month.

Nutrients to pay attention to include B-complex vitamins, which help your body convert food to energy, as well as vitamin E and iron. Electrolyte-rich smoothies are helpful in keeping your body well hydrated, as a dehydrated body can lead to fatigue. These smoothies are also high in vitamin C, iron, copper, potassium, zinc, folic acid, and magnesium.

month 3: slim-down smoothies

Favorite slim-down ingredients: watermelon, cantaloupe, strawberries, blueberries, goji berries and other berries, aloe vera juice, grapefruit, peaches, hemp seeds, apples, cucumbers, buckwheat, lemons, cayenne, pomegranates, coconut water, almonds, spinach, parsley, bell peppers, melons.

If you are looking to lose some weight or just maintain your weight, this month is for you. Slim-down smoothies are (mostly) low in calories, sugar, and fat and are often high in fiber to help curb hunger and cravings. Spicy, stimulating ingredients like cayenne and ginger may give your metabolism a boost. I have also squeezed in a few sweet-treat smoothies during this month to offer you an alternative to indulging in high-calorie desserts.

Nutrients to pay attention to when trying to slim down include chromium and magnesium, which help regulate blood sugar levels and in turn control hunger. Since you may be cutting back on fat during this month, you should still be aware of getting enough fat-soluble vitamins including vitamins A, D, E, and K. Also make sure you are getting enough B vitamins, including folic acid.

But drinking smoothies is not enough to slim down or maintain a fit physique. Be sure to boost or maintain a healthy exercise program. Consult your doctor about what fitness activities are ideal for you. You will also want to pay attention to the rest of your diet and tune in to food portion sizes. Eating fiber-rich, nutrient-dense plant-based/vegan foods at every meal may infuse you with vitality and help curb unwanted cravings. Ask your doctor or dietician how many calories you should be consuming for healthy weight loss or to maintain your weight.

month 4: strengthening smoothies

Favorite strengthening ingredients: pumpkin seeds, hemp seeds, blackberries, blueberries, cacao, cashews, almonds, peanuts, pistachios, soy, kale, spinach, chard, cherries, buckwheat, broccoli, oats, avocados, and plant-based protein powders.

Building and strengthening your muscles, bones, and joints involves making sure you are getting enough protein, calcium, vitamins A and D, and other essential nutrients like magnesium, manganese, copper, zinc, potassium, and thiamine. Various complete protein ingredients like soy and hemp will be highlighted in strengthening smoothies. Magnesium helps in calcium absorption, and iron and vitamins C and E are also important when building strength.

Aside from smoothies, you can consult your doctor about starting a strength-training program to fit your body's needs. Strong bones and muscles will help keep your body feeling and looking fit from the inside out.

month 5: calming smoothies

Favorite calming ingredients: avocados, mint, chamomile, lavender, bananas, mangos, cashews, peanuts, coconut, spinach, non-dairy yogurt, buckwheat, vanilla, cinnamon and other soothing spices, aloe vera juice, matcha green tea, oats, cucumbers, açaí berries, blueberries, other assorted berries, and whole grains.

Everyone needs a little Zen in life. These smoothies will help you cool down and chill out.

Stress, which affects us mentally and physically, can be a roadblock in our wellness goals. It can interfere with our sleeping and eating patterns and make us feel run-down. Since stress (both good and bad stress) is a normal part of life, being able to turn to healthy habits that calm and center us is important. A smoothie habit—rich in calming smoothies—may be your ticket to Zen.

If you have trouble with digestion during times of stress, watching your intake of foods rich in insoluble fiber may be helpful. Also try boosting probiotics and drinking more water. Hydrating smoothies may help ease digestive stress.

Featured calming nutrients include B-complex vitamins and vitamin C, as they can easily be depleted during times of stress, as well as calcium and vitamin A, which may aid in healthy nerve function. Other helpful nutrients include magnesium, vitamin E, copper, and ingredients that are rich in complex carbohydrates and tryptophan, which is known for its calming effects. Complex carbohydrates help stimulate the production of serotonin in the brain to improve and calm your mood. Calming herbs like peppermint, lavender, and chamomile also serve a naturally mellow purpose.

month 6: brain-boosting smoothies

Favorite brain-boosting ingredients: walnuts, almonds, chia seeds, hemp seeds, flax seeds, açaí berries, kale, spinach, blueberries, blackberries, avocados, pomegranates, green tea, virgin coconut oil, and nut and seed oils.

Mental health via a smoothie! Feed your brain what it craves, including complex carbohydrates for energy and essential fatty acids for wellness. And no, you don't need fish oil to get your omegas. Vegan ingredients like açaí berries, avocados, walnuts, and flax and chia seeds are delicious sources of healthy fats. Brain-boosting smoothies also feature antioxidants like vitamins C and E and the mineral copper. Reducing inflammation and increasing antioxidant intake via the foods you eat may improve brain function and prevent age-related deterioration.

Fun fact: The brain is made up of nearly 60 percent fat!

month 7: healthy-digestion smoothies

Favorite healthy digestion ingredients: non-dairy yogurt, bananas, papaya, pineapple, ginger, chia seeds, buckwheat, oats, aloe vera juice, coconut water, mint, lemon, radishes, kale and other dark leafy greens, apples, soy, blackberries and other assorted berries, and fermented foods.

So much of our wellness and immunity is based on the health of our digestive tract—some studies say up to 70 percent of our immunity is in our gut! Drinking smoothies that keep it healthy, happy, and running smoothly are important for overall wellness.

This month's smoothies will be full of fiber, probiotics, digestive enzymes like bromelain and papain, and tummy-soothing ingredients like bananas and aloe vera juice.

A note on fiber: Fiber needs will vary from person to person. And while some may find that adding more fiber to their diet improves digestion, others may find that it disrupts it. It all depends on how much fiber you are currently including in your diet (and meals outside smoothies) and how your personal digestive system handles fiber. Ask your doctor about your personal fiber needs, food allergies or intolerances, and overall digestion wellness.

Healthy digestion smoothies feature vitamins A and B_6, zinc, thiamine, fiber, probiotics, natural digestive enzymes like bromelain and papain, soothing ingredients like aloe vera juice and folate, and vitamin B_{12}, which may help support a healthy digestive tract.

month 8: healthy-heart smoothies

Favorite healthy-heart ingredients: apples, beets, soy, oats, buckwheat, pomegranates, grapes, tomatoes, watermelon, cantaloupe, spinach, kale, other dark leafy greens, garlic, hemp seeds, chia seeds, flax seeds and oil, kiwis, strawberries, blueberries, cherries, other berries, almonds, walnuts, Brazil nuts, oranges, coconut water, bananas, cacao, and whole grains.

According to the American Heart Association, heart disease is the number-one cause of death in the United States. So taking care of your cardiovascular system is important for wellness.

Healthy cholesterol is an important part of heart health, and cholesterol levels are based roughly on two things: genes and lifestyle, including diet, i.e., the foods you eat! Unfortunately, you can't do a lot with the genes you were given, but you do have control over the foods you put into your body.

The sixteen-year Oxford Vegetarian Study, published in 1999 in the *American Journal of Clinical Nutrition*, showed that "vegetarians generally had lower LDL cholesterol levels and lower death rates." Most vegans, me included, are walking examples of how switching to a plant-based diet can lower your bad (LDL) cholesterol levels while raising your good (HDL) cholesterol.

Plant-based smoothies are wellness wins for heart health, as they are usually low in calories and fat; high in fiber, water content, and potassium; rich in phytochemicals, vitamins, and minerals; and low in sodium.

Healthy-heart smoothies feature the nutrients potassium, omega-3 fatty acids, magnesium, fiber, copper, thiamine, phosphorus, resveratrol (found in grape skins), and B-complex vitamins. Iron, calcium, and vitamins A, C, E, B-complex, and K are important for a healthy heart and healthy veins and arteries, as well as for wound healing and blood clotting.

month 9: anti-aging smoothies

Favorite anti-aging ingredients: blueberries, strawberries, grapes, raspberries, soy, citrus fruits, chia seeds, flax seeds, peaches, açaí berries, pomegranates, cantaloupe, carrots, kale, spinach, mangos, Brazil nuts, walnuts, matcha green tea, and cacao.

Slow down the aging process without the use of lasers, creams, or expensive and potentially dangerous medical procedures. Rebuild, repair, and keep your body feeling youthful from the inside out with vegan smoothies that are rich in free radical–fighting nutrients.

Anti-aging smoothies feature vitamins A, C, E, B-complex, D, and K, selenium, magnesium, copper, potassium, fiber, calcium, and plenty of protein to maintain muscle mass, plus healthy fats to help absorb fat-soluble vitamins.

month 10: mood-boosting smoothies

Favorite mood-boosting ingredients: avocados, bananas, oats, pumpkin seeds, flax seeds, hemp seeds, sunflower seeds, cacao, walnuts, pistachios, vanilla, cinnamon, kiwis, lemon, cherries, cayenne, mint, almonds, ginger, raspberries, blueberries, spinach and other dark leafy greens, and other whole grains and citrus.

"Get happy" smoothies include a blend of carbohydrates, healthy fats, and mood-balancing nutrients. Mood-boosting smoothies work to boost serotonin in your brain to help banish a grumpy mood and hopefully put a smile on your face.

Mood-boosting smoothies often have bright and perky colors and flavors to inspire a positive spirit. This month you will taste plenty of cheerful citrus, brightly colored fruits, and zesty flavors.

Highlighted nutrients include omega-3 fatty acids, energy vitamins like B-complex, and plenty of complex carbohydrates mixed with some fat and protein to keep your serotonin levels at a mood-boosting level. Tryptophan, folic acid, iron, and vitamins C and D may help you maintain an energized, balanced mood. Chromium and magnesium help regulate blood sugar. Healthy fats and complex carbohydrates can also help regulate blood sugar levels as you enjoy your smoothie. Low and unstable blood sugar levels can lead to a depressed, cranky mood and make you feel lethargic and worn down. Stable energy levels are key for feeling perky and cheerful.

month 11: immunity-boosting smoothies

Favorite immunity-boosting ingredients: lemon, garlic, spinach, kale and other dark leafy greens, pineapple, papaya, kiwis, oranges, grapefruit, strawberries, mangos, coconut water, non-dairy yogurt, bananas, açaí berries, bell peppers, beets, cayenne, flax seeds, and pomegranates.

Whether you are fighting a bad cold or just want to stay in tip-top condition, these smoothies will boost your body's natural immunity. Ingredients rich in antioxidants like vitamins A, C, and E, probiotics, electrolytes, copper, iron, zinc, magnesium, selenium, and stimulating spices like ginger and cayenne will be highlighted.

And don't forget to wash your hands, get plenty of rest, and find ways to manage stress—these factors also affect immunity.

month 12: beauty smoothies— beauty from the inside out!

Favorite beauty ingredients: cherries, peaches, oranges, apricots, beets, matcha green tea, strawberries, spinach, kale, and other dark leafy greens, bananas, kiwis, pineapple, mangos, flax seeds, chia seeds, almonds, walnuts, açaí berries, pomegranates, cacao, plums, and avocados.

Beautifying from the inside out means adding strength to your hair, skin, nails, and internal tissues, muscles, joints, and bones. Vitamin C helps support collagen and antioxidants A, C, and E will help combat free radicals, which can weaken your cells. Beauty smoothies also feature fiber, electrolytes, and minerals such as copper, zinc, and selenium, and healthy fats and potassium to help you get that smoothie "glow."

Stay hydrated, get plenty of beauty sleep, and avoid overindulging in caffeine, sugar, alcohol, chemicals (in the foods you eat and the beauty products you use), and overly processed foods during this beautifying month. You may want to supplement your beauty plan with an exercise routine to build and maintain bone and muscle mass. Reducing or managing the stress in your life can also help you stay beautiful from the inside out.

3

IN THE KITCHEN: TOOLS, TIPS, AND SMOOTHIE INGREDIENTS

BEFORE YOU DIVE INTO THE RECIPES, IT IS A GREAT IDEA TO review some information on blending tools and smoothie ingredients. The information in this chapter covers basic concepts, such as choosing a blender, and more advanced tips, such as choosing superfoods and even making your own plant-based milk from scratch.

So although the process of blending a smoothie may sound like an easy task, by learning a few tips and tricks you are more likely to have smoothie success each and every time you blend.

In this chapter I also want to give you some insight into the ingredients you will find in my recipes. Some ingredients, like bananas and strawberries, may sound quite familiar, but others, like chia seeds and coconut water, may be new to you.

And as you experiment with new ingredients, you are sure to have a few questions about how to best use them in smoothies, as well as why they are healthy to begin with. This chapter answers all those questions and more! You can skim the list of ingredients as you choose and refer back to it as you progress through the recipes with possible ingredient questions.

The list of ingredients is also a great motivator to remind you why the foods in the recipes are so valuable to your health. By reading about the basic nutritional qualities of spinach, for example, you may feel extra inspired to seek out a green smoothie recipe to blend up and enjoy!

tools

Essential: A blender.
Preferred: High-speed blender like a Vitamix or Blendtec.
The most important tool for your smoothie journey is a blender. You don't *need* a fancy blender to make a smoothie; however, some of the smoothies in this book do require the use of a high-quality or high-speed blender to help pulverize the ingredients properly.

If you are a smoothie lover, I highly recommend that you invest in a high-speed blender. You can use it not only for smoothies but also for everyday cooking. If there is one new kitchen appliance you save up for or splurge on this year, make it a rock star blender. The wellness and health you will infuse into your life will be worth the price in the long run.

If you use a basic blender, you can make simple ingredient substitutions as needed to facilitate blending. For example, instead of blending a whole orange in a Vitamix, you can substitute orange juice and adjust other ingredients as needed.

Other helpful tools include:

Plunger, such as the Vitamix tamper plunger, which can be inserted in the top lid to help remove air pockets and move around large clumps of ingredients while blending.

Spatula for scraping the sides of your blender when pouring thick shake-like smoothies.

Nut milk bag for preparing homemade nut milk (see pages 43–44).

Citrus juicer and or fruit/veggie press for making homemade fresh-pressed juice.

Freezer bags and bowls for freezing ripe bananas and other fresh fruit ingredients.

ingredients tips

BUYING INGREDIENTS

You will be able to find most of the ingredients for these smoothies at your grocery store (including Whole Foods) or health food store. And you can always look to the Internet to find specialty items. If you cannot find certain ingredients, don't fret; there are more than enough healthy foods available in an average grocery store for you to be able to blend up a wide variety of the recipes in this book. You can always experiment with making smart substitutions when needed.

If fresh produce is not available to you, frozen produce is always a great substitute, but never use canned fruit for fresh or frozen. It just will not suffice.

KATHY'S INGREDIENTS TEST

The most important variable in your smoothie is the quality of your ingredients. So you really want everything from your frozen fruit to the brand of soy milk you use to be the best-tasting, highest-quality option—within reason in terms of your budget and geographical location, of course. Remember this trick: The ingredients you put in your smoothie should be just as delicious as if you were to eat them on their own.

The test: Take a nibble or sip of each ingredient before blending. As you do this test for different brands and varieties of produce, nibbling, blending, and tasting along the way, you will acquire a more developed smoothie-making palate. You will know what tastes bad, good, and amazing (to your taste buds) when it comes to smoothies. You will also realize that your personal taste preferences play a big role in choosing which smoothie ingredients you like best.

When it comes to frozen fruit, you may find that your own fresh fruit freezes up to be just as flavorful as packaged frozen fruit, or more so. I have gotten in the habit of buying fresh in-season fruit (and veggies) and simply sticking them in plastic baggies or freezer-friendly bins and freezing them myself. If you try this trick, be sure to chop the ingredients into a small blendable size before freezing. You don't want to freeze items with peels or rinds left on—remember to remove those first. Also try to remove bitter seeds from citrus. Ingredients that freeze well include berries, bananas, melon, tropical fruits, grapes, peeled citrus, and any veggies or fruit you can thickly slice, dice, or chop, like cucumber, peaches, and even avocados!

There *are* plenty of high-quality—even organic—frozen fruit brands out there, many of which I do love and use. But there are also brands that you can tell do not always use the highest-quality fruit. So when in doubt, freeze yourself! Here are some tips to do just that:

FREEZER FOODS

Frozen foods add frostiness, chill, and body to a smoothie. But don't limit yourself to store-bought varieties. Use plastic bags or freezer-friendly containers to store your own. You want to store the fruit exactly as you will be adding it to the blender. That means no peels, stems, or bitter seeds should go into the freezer. And prep chopping is a must. My favorites:

Frozen bananas—Slice peeled ripe bananas and freeze. Bananas are used often, so stock up on them! Frozen bananas are the secret ingredient for creating creamy shake-like smoothies that are naturally sweet and appealing in texture.

Frozen cucumbers—Dice the cucumbers (skin on) and store in the freezer. Use organic cucumbers when possible and try to stay away from cucumbers that have a waxy skin.

Frozen watermelon—Watermelon can add a unique frosty texture to creamy blends! It is one of my favorite secret ingredients. Remove the flesh from the rind, cube, and freeze. Most melon freezes quite well; try cantaloupe and honeydew too.

Frozen grapes—Pluck grapes from their stem before freezing. If the grapes are oversized, you may want to slice them in half. Wash grapes before freezing.

Frozen kiwis—Peel and slice into cubes before freezing.

Frozen citrus—Peel and roughly chop or segment citrus, including grapefruit, oranges, and tangerines. Remove the seeds before freezing if you like, but it's not necessary.

Other frozen fruit—You can freeze pitted cherries, blueberries, strawberries, peeled avocados, mangos, and more.

What not to freeze? Foods that do not freeze well include leafy greens (they are too delicate) and some apples and pears (they can become very mealy upon freezing).

ORGANIC INGREDIENTS

I am a big fan of organic produce for smoothies. Pay attention to buying organic for foods that have a thin (or no) skin, like berries, apples, leafy greens, and grapes. Organic is not as important for foods that have a thicker skin, like oranges and bananas. I personally try to buy organic when possible, not only for nutrition and taste but for environmental reasons as well.

THAWING TIP

Melon gets very hard in the freezer and can be a tricky blend, even for a high-speed blender. My thawing trick is to add the desired amount of melon to a bowl or blender, then douse it with hot water. Quickly drain the water. The heat and liquid will thaw the outside of the melon, but the inside stays frozen. This trick can also help break apart frozen-together cubes of melon or other fruit.

FARMERS' MARKET PRODUCE

There is nothing more inspiring than strolling through your local farmers' market and picking out fresh in-season ingredients for your smoothies.

Complete dietary wellness includes being able to understand where your food comes from. Plus, fresh local produce may taste better, as it usually spends less time in transit from farm to blender.

TIP

Buy seasonal foods like berries at the farmers' market and freeze them yourself to enjoy in months to come.

CREATIVE ICE CUBES

If you think ice cubes come in only one flavor, "water"—think again! Get creative with frozen cubes by trying juice cubes, coconut milk cubes, and more. Also, if you know a recipe calls for a certain liquid and ice, you can instead freeze some of that liquid and omit the ice. This will give you bolder flavor in each sip. Many recipes call for coconut water ice cubes. This is mainly for nutritional purposes, since coconut water contains nutrients like potassium that plain water does not have. Make coconut water ice cubes by pouring coconut water into ice cube trays. And by coconut water, I am referring to clear coconut water, not the thick, opaque, creamy white stuff known as coconut milk. Coconut water is the clear liquid inside a fresh young coconut. You can find it in most grocery stores from a variety of brands. If a recipe calls for coconut water ice cubes and you do not have them, simply use ice cubes made from water. Easy.

Other creative cubes include chamomile tea, green tea, coconut milk, fruit juice, soy yogurt, coffee, espresso, lemon or lime juice, non-dairy milk, or aloe vera juice.

TIP

Create a frosty shake without using ice cubes: Freeze the base liquid into cubes and use them instead so you don't water down the flavor of the shake. For example, when you're making a frosty chocolate soy shake, freeze chocolate soy milk into cubes and then blend with a few splashes of liquid and any additional fruit or other ingredients.

SALT

Sometimes a pinch can enhance flavor! Especially in smoothies using grains, raw nuts, and silken tofu. All of the recipes that need salt for enhancing flavor call for it in the recipe.

NUTS

Always use *raw* nuts (as opposed to salted and roasted ones) in your smoothies unless specified otherwise. When blending nuts, use a high speed on your blender to fully pulverize them.

ADD-INS

Follow my recipes exactly—or not: you always have the power to add, remove, or change ingredients in any recipe. Creativity is encouraged!

STOCKING YOUR SMOOTHIE PANTRY

If you are a baker, you know there are a few ingredients your pantry needs. Flour, baking powder, salt, spices. Well, here are your smoothie pantry essentials, with a few nonessentials thrown in as well for variety. You do not need to buy all of these ingredients at once, but keeping some of them on hand will allow you to blend up a wide variety of smoothies anytime you choose.

Non-dairy milk (almond, soy, rice, coconut)
Assortment of frozen and fresh veggies and fruits, especially
   frozen bananas
Açaí berry products (frozen açaí smoothie packs or açaí powder)
Superfood seeds (chia seeds, flax seeds, hemp seeds)

TIP

Blend your liquid and nuts first before adding more delicate ingredients like fruit and ice.

STORAGE TIP

You can freeze nuts, because they have a high fat content. This prolongs their life and even adds chill to your smoothies. Bring nuts to room temperature first if you are going to soak them.

Omega-3 fatty acid–rich oils (hemp, pumpkin seed, flax,
    or a blend)
Raw cacao powder and cacao nibs (or dairy-free cocoa powder)
Protein powder (hemp, soy, or a vegan protein blend from
    brands like Vega)
Liquid sweeteners (maple syrup and/or agave syrup)
Liquid boosters (apple cider vinegar, aloe vera juice)
Coconut water (and trays for coconut water ice cubes)
Cayenne and cinnamon
Green boosters (spirulina, wheatgrass powder)
Superfood powders: matcha green tea, maca, açaí, pomegranate
Unsweetened coconut flakes
Assortment of raw unsalted nuts (almonds, cashews, pecans,
    Brazil nuts, walnuts)
Raw unsalted nut butter (almond, peanut, walnut, cashew)

SUPERFOOD PANTRY: 20 INGREDIENTS

This is a list of my twenty favorite superfood ingredients. They broadly
support wellness and are generally easy to find. With so many ingredients used in this book, this list helps you focus on a few foods that are
wellness superstars. (And my personal favorites!)

Dark leafy greens (kale, spinach, chard)
Protein or multinutrient powder (plain, chocolate, and vanilla
    work best)
Açaí products (açaí powder, açaí juice, or frozen açaí smoothie
    packs)
Bananas
Raw cacao powder and cacao nibs
Melon (my favorites: watermelon and cantaloupe)
Chia seeds

Flax seeds and oil

Almond or peanut butter

Soy milk and soy yogurt, vanilla flavor

Whole grains (buckwheat and rolled oats)

Coconut water

Citrus (a wide variety, including sweet fruits like oranges
and sour fruits like lemons)

Kiwis

Pineapples

Grapes

Red and purple berries (strawberries, blueberries, blackberries,
raspberries)

Hemp seeds

Walnuts

Matcha green tea powder

NON-DAIRY MILK

I use vanilla soy milk most often in my recipes; I find it the most appealing plant-based non-dairy milk alternative because of its creamy texture and mild, smooth flavor. It is also widely available in stores.

But as you move through recipes, you can easily switch up the non-dairy milk varieties you choose for your smoothies. Try almond, grain, rice, and more. You can even expand your smoothie horizons by making milks at home. Below are a couple of recipes to try.

Most homemade nut and seed milks require the use of a nut milk bag to strain the pulp and smooth out the texture. Nut milk bags are optional, but they are a wonderful addition to any wellness kitchen. If you do not strain your milk, the texture will be slightly or very gritty and fibrous. If you are blending the nut or seed milk into a fibrous smoothie, you probably will not notice the grittiness, but if you are drinking the milk plain, you probably will want to strain it through a nut milk bag to ensure a silky texture.

homemade vanilla bean hemp milk

Makes about 4 cups

3 cups purified water

½ cup raw shelled
  hemp seeds

1½ tablespoons liquid
  sweetener, or to taste

A few pinches of
  ground cinnamon

½ vanilla bean,
  chopped, or
  ½ teaspoon pure
  vanilla extract

Salt to taste

Combine all the ingredients in a blender and blend on low at first to get things moving, then increase the speed to high and blend until the mixture is frothy and opaque white. If it seems watery, keep blending or add a few more seeds for richer, creamier milk.

Use in smoothies as is or, for a silky milk, strain the milk through a nut bag to remove the hemp pulp.

homemade nut milk

Makes about 4 cups

FOR SOAKING

3 cups purified water

½ teaspoon salt

1 cup raw nuts
  (almonds or cashews
  work best)

FOR BLENDING

About 3 cups chilled
  purified water

Salt to taste
  (try ¼ teaspoon)

Sweetener to taste (try
  2 tablespoons agave
  syrup or maple syrup)

⅛ teaspoon pure vanilla
  extract (optional)

Pour the first 3 cups water into a large bowl and add the salt. Add the nuts and soak in the salted water overnight.

Drain the soaking liquid and rinse the nuts well.

Add the rinsed nuts and 1½ cups of the remaining water to a blender and blend until smooth. Add some of the remaining water to thin out; continue to blend and add fresh water until you have a creamy milk.

Strain the nut milk through a nut milk bag to remove the nut pulp.

Rinse the blender and return the strained milk to the blender; add the salt, sweetener, and vanilla, if using, and blend on low to combine.

Store in a covered container in the fridge and use within 3 days. Natural settling may occur, so shake before using if needed.

Homemade Cashew Milk

technique tips

WATER IT

You can always thin out a smoothie by adding water. This is especially pertinent information when blending up whole food and green smoothies. Coconut water is also a nice neutral liquid to add when needed to thin a blend.

SMOOTH BLEND

There is nothing worse than sipping on a smoothie that is bumpy, lumpy, and filled with bits of unblended ingredients. If this happens to you, simply toss your smoothie back in your blender for a quick fix. Keep blending until smooth.

What probably happened was that you didn't blend long enough, you had an air bubble, or your speed was too low—or all three. Start smoothie blending on low until large chunks smooth out and then move to a higher speed to finish, making sure all is smooth, frosty, and blissful. Stop when you see a smooth swirl—overblending can cause your frosty smoothie to melt.

5 TIPS FOR WORKING WITHOUT A HIGH-SPEED BLENDER

1 **Chop, chop!** Whether it's frozen fruit or fresh veggies, chopping before blending is my best tip for blending ease. With hard veggies and fruit like apples, carrots, and beets, you can also try grating them before adding them to your blender.

2 **Sub with juices.** If a recipe calls for a whole orange, but your blender simply cannot handle that item, sub with a few splashes of juice instead. Experimentation will be key to discovering how much to substitute to achieve your desired smoothie consistency.

Add more blendable fruit or ice if needed in addition to the juice.

3 **Add more liquid.** Liquid always eases a blend. So if you are having trouble with a recipe in your blender, add a few more splashes of liquid to get things moving.

4 **Go low to high.** Use my blending rule: Start on a low speed until things get moving, then end on a high speed to fully pulverize the ingredients.

5 **Juice it.** Maybe you don't have a high-speed blender but do have a juicer. If so, this is great news because most of the ingredients you may have trouble blending (thick leafy greens, whole oranges or apples) can be juiced! You will just need to add some more whole blendable ingredients like frozen fruit or ice to make up for lost fiber from juicing.

SUBSTITUTIONS

The fabulous thing about smoothies is that they are very forgiving when it comes to making slight ingredient substitutions. When a recipe calls for a certain variety of juice or milk—say, orange juice or soy milk—you have complete power to change these out for different varieties.

Here are a few basic substitutions for common ingredients:

Greens—Other leafy greens (kale, spinach, chard, and more)
Citrus—Other sweet citrus (oranges, tangerines, mandarins, grapefruit)
Berries—Other berries
Creamy texture—Bananas, mangos, and avocados sub well with each other since they all have a creamy texture. Soy yogurt and silken tofu are also worthy creamy texture substitutes.
Roots—Beets and carrots sub well, as do apples and jícama.

Sweeteners—You can choose whatever sweetener you prefer (agave, stevia, maple syrup). Maple syrup has the most distinct flavor. You can also use sweet foods like dates, pears, and grapes.

Protein powders—Vegan protein powder can come from a variety of sources: soy, pea, hemp, sweetened vitamin-boosted blends, and more. Find a brand that you come to crave and that contains all the nutrients to fit your wellness goals. I like plain and vanilla and chocolate flavors best. If a recipe calls for protein powder and you do not have it, you may want to decrease the liquid a splash.

Ice—Coconut water ice cubes can easily be subbed with regular ice. If you are out of ice, experiment with strawberries or frozen melon for added frosty texture.

Açaí—Açaí comes in a variety of forms—juice, powder, and frozen smoothie packs. All varieties can be used interchangeably with a bit of creativity. Experiment to become more familiar with them and learn which flavors and textures you like best.

Soy yogurt—Other non-dairy yogurts, like rice or almond yogurt, or silken tofu.

Nut butter—Other nut or seed butters.

Coconut flakes—Try raw coconut meat if available. A splash of coconut milk can also add similar flavor.

Grains—Other grains or dry ingredients like nuts or seeds.

Seeds—Chia seeds sub well with flax seeds, as they both have a thickening quality. Larger seeds like pumpkin and sunflower sub well for each other. Hemp seeds are unique because of their fluffy, light texture. Rolled oats actually make a nice non-seed sub for seeds, as they are both dry and absorb liquid.

Whole food smoothies—If you need to make whole food substitutions, go with your instincts. One large orange will produce about ½ cup of juice plus fiber. So add that amount of juice plus maybe another tablespoon of blendable fruit like banana or frozen berries.

SEED AND NUT SOAKING

It is sometimes easier to blend nuts and seeds into smoothies if they have been soaked until softened first. Soaking overnight is ideal. Place nuts or seeds in a bowl with salted water (just a pinch of salt) to cover by about an inch, place a lid or dishtowel over the bowl, and leave on the countertop to soak overnight. Drain the soaking water and rinse well with fresh water. Soaking and rinsing nuts can help remove pesky enzyme inhibitors that can interfere with digestion and nutrient absorption.

Quick-soak method to soften nuts: Soak in hot salted water for as long as time allows—a few minutes is a good start—then rinse as usual. For example, if you quick-soak raw cashews or raw pumpkin seeds in hot water before blending, your smoothie may be a bit silkier.

wellness tips

ON FIBER

One of the benefits of a smoothie-rich diet is the addition of soluble and insoluble fiber.

Soluble fiber can dissolve in water and turns into a sort of "gel" in your digestive system—slowing down the absorption of calories—thereby possibly aiding in the regulation of blood sugar. Insoluble fiber stays intact through digestion, absorbing water as it moves through your system—adding bulk to stools—thereby acting as a possible aid to constipation or irregularity.

Sources of soluble fiber include oats, bananas, and sweet potatoes. Sources of insoluble fiber include potato skins, whole grains like wheat, hemp seeds, apple peel, and the tiny seeds in berries. Most leafy greens and raw vegetables contain some amount of insoluble fiber.

While fiber is generally a great thing, too much fiber—especially if your body is not used to it—can be a nuisance and make you quite uncomfortable in terms of digestion. It can possibly even lead to inflammation.

The good news is that smoothies may actually be helpful to people with weak digestion, as those smoothie blades help break down whole food fiber. Ask your doctor about your personal fiber needs and digestion constraints, as fiber needs vary and your tolerance for fiber can change over time. Instead of going from 10 grams of fiber to 35 grams overnight, increase it gradually. This may keep you from experiencing uncomfortable fiber side effects like bloating, indigestion, and flatulence. Give your body time to adjust to your new healthy habits. You can always modify smoothie ingredients to suit your fiber needs.

NON-DAIRY MILK NUTRITION

The nutritional content in this book is based on using fortified non-dairy milks, aka plant milks. Drinking fortified plant milks, which are made from healthy ingredients like beans, nuts, seeds, and grains, is an easy way to boost intake of vitamins D and B_{12}, calcium, and more. Read the labels, because the type and amount of nutrients in different brands will vary greatly. Some are fortified to closely mimic the nutrients found in dairy milk, while others are minimal in additional ingredients and fortifications. If you want to obtain some key nutrients found in dairy milk, look for non-dairy milks fortified with vitamin B_{12}, calcium, and vitamin D. The great news is that by drinking plant-based milks instead of animal-based dairy, you will not be ingesting lactose and you will be avoiding certain hormones, chemicals, and the saturated fat found in dairy. In addition to getting the nutritional benefits of plant-based milks, you will be exercising a compassionate choice in using a milk that is cruelty-free.

smoothie ingredients: the detailed list

Before you dive into making some amazing vegan smoothies, you may be curious to learn more about the ingredients featured in the recipes. Some ingredients like blueberries and bananas may be quite familiar to you, but others like coconut milk, chia seeds, and açaí may be more of a mystery. It's helpful to read this chapter front to back for some nutritional inspiration, and you will want to come back to it as a reference tool as you begin your smoothie-blending journey.

Health note: When trying new ingredients, be sure to consult your doctor. Your doctor will also be able to answer any questions you may have about ingredient use, health benefits, safety, and prescription medication interactions.

Açaí berries—Açaí is a dark purple berry, native to Central and South America. Most commonly you will find açaí in the form of açaí juice, açaí frozen smoothie packs, and freeze-dried açaí power. Açaí has a creamy rich texture and very deep purple color. The flavor is mildly sweet in a chocolate-meets-blackberry sort of way. The rich texture blends up a decadently creamy smoothie.

Açaí berry is rich in antioxidants, fiber, essential fatty acids, amino acids, micronutrients like resveratrol, polyphenols, flavonoids, and minerals like magnesium and potassium. The rich antioxidant content makes it a superb free radical–fighting, energizing, heart-healthy, and anti-inflammatory ingredient. The essential fatty acids are useful in improving brain function and heart health.

Agave syrup—Agave syrup is a natural sweetener from the agave plant. Agave can be purchased in deep amber or light amber colors. You can also find raw agave, which is not heated and less processed. Raw agave is a popular vegan sweetener for raw-foodists because maple syrup (the most popular alternative) is heated during processing. Agave syrup has a very neutral flavor that makes it a perfect natural vegan substitute for refined sugar. It dissolves easily into liquids. Refined sugar can be vegan, but sometimes it is refined with animal products, something called bone char. Your sugar is vegan if it is organic: all certified organic sugar is actually vegan, because the animal products used to refine sugar are not certified organic, so their use would not allowed.

There has been some controversy about how healthy agave syrup is and whether claims about its low glycemic properties are actually true. As with any sweetener, use it in moderation.

Algal oil—Algal oil is a more recent discovery in the essential fatty acid supplement sector. Instead of supplementing your essential fatty acids using fish oil (which obviously is not vegan), you can choose algal oil, derived from microalgae (which fish eat). I do not include algal oil in many smoothies, but if you are looking to add more omega-3 fatty acids to your smoothies, you might want to ask your doctor about algal. More research is being acquired about this relatively new plant-based supplement.

Almonds—Ah, almonds, a wonder nut if ever there was one. You can purchase almonds in raw or roasted form, but for smoothie purposes, use raw unsalted almonds. Soaking raw almonds overnight in salted water allows them to more easily blend into smoothies or be used in making fresh almond milk.

You can also use almonds in smoothies in the form of almond butter. You can choose from raw or roasted, salted or unsalted, creamy or chunky, sweetened or unsweetened. For maximum purity and nutrition, go with raw, unheated varieties. My preference for flavor is unsweetened, salted, raw almond butter.

Almonds are rich in calcium, iron, riboflavin, folate, and vitamin E and minerals including manganese, phosphorus, magnesium, and copper. Almonds are also a good source of protein and fiber. They contain a good amount of fat—with just a small amount coming from saturated fat. Since most fruit and vegetable smoothie ingredients are very low in fat, the fat content in almond butter helps round out the nutrient content so that your appetite can be curbed and you stay satisfied for a longer period of time. Almonds blend surprisingly well with fruits like bananas and apples and leafy greens like spinach and kale.

Almond milk—Almond milk is a variety of non-dairy milk. It is made from the "milk" of almonds and is soy-free. Store-bought almond milk is creamier than rice milk but generally not as creamy as soy milk. Fresh, raw almond milk can be made at home with a high-speed blender, and this is the healthiest (and most delicious) way to drink it.

You can use almond milk rather than soy milk as your non-dairy milk of choice in any of my smoothies. However, nutritional information, flavor, and texture will change. Almond milk is not as high in protein as soy or hemp milk, but it does offer a wide range of nutrients like vitamin E, magnesium, zinc, and calcium, plus some protein and healthy fat. Purchase fortified almond milk for even more nutrients per sip.

For smoothies, plain or original flavors add a neutral creamy taste; vanilla adds more sweetness. You can also find "light" versions of almond milk as well, some with as few as 35 calories a cup. These varieties are usually low in sweeteners and have a thin texture and mild flavor. It is a good idea to taste a few brands and varieties before deciding on which one appeals to you.

Aloe vera—Aloe vera juice is a tangy clear liquid that you can buy at most health food or vitamin stores. Aloe is a natural soother and healer, well known as a topical remedy, most commonly used for wound healing and sunburn treatment. Aloe vera juice heals and soothes from the inside out.

Aloe juice has such a tangy intense flavor that it is best when diluted in liquids like water or added to smoothies. When aloe is added to a smoothie, you can barely taste it. I usually add 1 teaspoon per 16-ounce smoothie.

Aloe juice is known for a wide variety of health benefits including strengthening the white blood cells and immune system, aiding and supporting digestion, and even reducing inflammation and supporting healthy joints. Aloe is also used to help neutralize stomach acid and soothe internal tissue, further aiding in digestion.

Apples—Apples come in a variety of colors and are wonderful when added whole to smoothies. They add texture, flavor, and fiber.

Apples are rich in vitamin C and potassium. As apples are rich in natural sweetness, they work well as a sugar substitute. They are also rich in natural fiber and pectin, and help tone and add body to a smoothie.

Quick tip: If you have trouble blending a whole apple for your smoothies, try grating it.

Apple fiber has been shown to help reduce LDL (bad) cholesterol levels and even support HDL (good) cholesterol levels. Green apples contain the most pectin, making them a good digestive cleanser for detox. Apples with brightly colored red skins contain the phytochemical lycopene and anthocyanins, both of which are important for a healthy heart and may even protect against some cancers.

Apple cider vinegar—Apple cider vinegar is an amber-colored liquid that is made from fermented apples. It has been used to treat everything from poor digestion to low energy, and it may even aid in weight loss.

Though it is usually added to salad dressings and marinades, apple cider vinegar is a perky smoothie ingredient. It adds a slightly zesty flavor, similar to a spritz of lemon juice.

Apple juice—Apple juice made from 100 percent apples is rich in natural sweetness. Processed, from-concentrate apple juice is not recommended for your wellness smoothies. Farm-fresh apple cider is my favorite apple juice variety for smoothies.

Apricots—Apricots are a velvety peach-colored tree fruit. Apricots are not terribly juicy, so they can help add fiber and body to a smoothie but not much liquid. They have a zesty sweet flavor—the natural sugars develop as apricots ripen and soften. Ripe, juicy apricots are preferred for blending into smoothies.

Apricots are rich in fiber, vitamins A and C, and potassium. They are also a good source of tryptophan.

Arugula—Arugula is a tender leafy green with a slightly spicy and zesty flavor. It has a crisp yet silky bite. Arugula is easy to add to green smoothies and can be used in place of other greens like kale, spinach, and chard.

Arugula is rich in vitamins A, C, and K and folate, and in the minerals calcium, magnesium, manganese, and potassium. Arugula, like most leafy greens, is low in calories.

Avocados—The avocado is an oily, tender, green-fleshed tree fruit. Avocados are delicious when blended into smoothies because they add body and flavor. They supply a "creamy" texture to your smoothies. They are a worthy substitute for creamy bananas. Avocados blend well with both sweet and grassy flavors.

Avocados are rich in healthy fats (monounsaturated fats and essential fatty acids). They are a good source of vitamins C, E, K, and B$_6$, folate, and pantothenic acid. Avocados are rich in the minerals copper and potassium. They are also a good source of fiber and are rich in tryptophan.

Bananas—Bananas are one of the most commonly used ingredients in smoothies. Bananas have a creamy, blendable texture and a clean, sweet flavor. They can be used fresh or frozen. Frozen bananas blend to create a thick, almost "milkshake" texture. Bananas are best when used in a ripe state—when more of the flesh has turned from starch to sugar. Starchy (underripe) bananas, which create a bitter, slimy, or sticky-textured smoothie, should be avoided.

Quick tip: Slice bananas into thin rounds before freezing. This makes the blending process much easier. A large, frozen whole banana is more of a blending challenge. Store sliced bananas in freezer-friendly bins or plastic baggies. Never place unpeeled bananas in the freezer—they will be nearly unusable in their peel-on frozen state!

Bananas are rich in fiber, carbohydrates, vitamins C and B$_6$, and folate and in the minerals magnesium, potassium, and manganese.

Bananas have been known to soothe tummy aches and support the digestive system. Their rich potassium content helps maintain the body's water balance and a healthy heart. Easily digested bananas, rich in energy-yielding carbohydrates, are an excellent energizing ingredient for smoothies.

The natural sweetness of bananas allows you to skip or reduce the amount of added sweetener to your smoothie so you can pass up the empty calories. The dessert-tasting qualities of banana make it an excellent treat food.

When a recipe calls for a banana, use one average-sized ripe banana at room temperature. Recipes that specifically call for frozen bananas do so to add thickness and frostiness to your smoothies.

Basil—Basil is a tender green herb with a strong sweet aroma. Sweet green basil is a lovely herb to add to smoothies in the same way that mint is used. It adds complex flavor while accenting sweet, grassy, or tart ingredients.

Basil is rich in vitamin K, which helps in blood clotting.

Beets—Beets are round or heart-shaped firm root vegetables. They come in a wide variety of colors, from deep red to pink and even golden orange. Beets have a thin, rough exterior and are quite firm inside, yet are very juiceable.

Beets are delicious eaten raw, as they are rich in natural sweetness. Beets are well known for their intense color. When slicing into a beet, you will notice the highly concentrated plant pigments. Just a few drops of beet juice can stain a glass of white soy milk to pink.

Beets can be added to smoothies in the form of juice (you will need a juicer to make fresh beet juice) or they can be added whole. Whole beets are a tricky veggie to blend and usually require the use of a high-speed blender. To ease blending, finely dice your beets or grate or shred them with a vegetable grater. You may want to strain some of the beet fiber after blending.

Beets are rich in fiber and carbohydrates. They are also rich in vitamin C and folate and the minerals manganese and potassium. The rich pigments in beets are associated with their intense phytochemical concentration. Beets contain a group of phytochemicals called betalains, which fight free radicals and aid healthy cell renewal.

Bell peppers—Bell peppers are crisp and juicy, with a light and zesty flavor that is mildly sweet. You can buy bell peppers in a variety of colors, including green, orange, yellow, red, and even purple and white. Bell peppers add water and a mild zesty-sweet veggie flavor to smoothies.

Bell peppers are rich in vitamin C and low in calories.

Blackberries—Blackberries produce a deep purple juice and have noticeable tiny seeds, but the seeds are tiny enough to suck through a smoothie straw.

Blackberries are a super-berry, as they are very high in free radical–fighting antioxidants. They are rich in fiber and vitamins C and K and the minerals copper and manganese. Manganese is known as the good-mood mineral. Blackberries are also rich in the phytochemicals anthocyanins and phenolics, which are associated with anti-aging and increased memory function.

Black pepper—Black pepper is made from ground peppercorns. You can buy whole peppercorns to grind yourself or pre-ground black pepper. Fine pepper is great for adding to smoothies; it easily blends into liquid. Black pepper has a spicy, vibrant flavor that can be used to accent smoothies.

Pepper has more than peppy flavor—it also may aid in digesting nutrients, boost metabolism, and even act as an anti-inflammatory ingredient.

Blueberries—Blueberries are tender, blue-colored berries with a thin silky skin and very tiny (usually unnoticeable) seeds. Ripe, fresh blueberries should be juicy and almost pop in your mouth—avoid mushy or wrinkled fresh berries. Blueberries have a slightly creamy texture with a pure, perky sweetness. They can be used both frozen and raw in smoothies. Wild blueberries contain a slightly higher amount of antioxidants per serving.

Blueberries are rich in antioxidants like vitamin C, fiber, manganese, and vitamin K. The antioxidant capacity of blueberries makes them a powerful free-radical fighter. They can also aid the immune system. Blueberries are one of the most popular superfoods you can find, so seek them out in both fresh and frozen form.

Quick tip: Buy organic blueberries when possible, since their thin, delicate, edible outer skin offers less protection from harsh pesticides than, say, a banana or orange.

Brazil nuts—Brazil nuts are large sand-colored nuts with a dark brown thin skin. Brazil nuts are crunchy and creamy in texture because of their high fat content. You can blend Brazil nuts into smoothies or chop them and sprinkle over the tops of shakes.

Brazil nuts are rich in selenium and can help fight free radicals to aid the immune system.

Brown rice syrup—Brown rice syrup is a sticky, thick sweetener made from brown rice. You will notice that it has a thicker consistency than agave or maple syrup. You can use brown rice syrup to replace either agave or maple syrup in any smoothie.

Buckwheat—Buckwheat groats are diamond-shaped and light tan in color. Buckwheat is similar to a grain but technically is more of a seed. It is actually wheat-free—despite its name—as well as gluten-free.

Buckwheat is a nutrient-rich ingredient used to make creamy, rich, satisfying grain and seed shakes. It can easily be added to smoothies in either soaked or sprouted form. Buckwheat sprouting is an easy process but does take a commitment of a few days. For the recipes here, I will be using soaked and rinsed buckwheat for convenience.

Soaking buckwheat is simple. Soak the groats in enough water (add a pinch of salt to the water if you like) to cover them. You can soak them for as little as twenty minutes or as long as overnight. Drain the water and thoroughly rinse the groats before blending into your smoothies.

Buckwheat is rich in fiber, calcium, and all eight essential amino acids, which makes it a nice protein source. The fiber in buckwheat is beneficial to digestion and heart health. It may also keep you full longer and aid in stabilizing blood sugar, which is important for energy and weight loss.

Cacao nibs—Crunchy dark brown cacao nibs are bits of the cacao bean. They have a bitter flavor with bold notes of chocolate. Even if you don't enjoy the intense flavor of raw cacao nibs on their own, you may enjoy them blended into creamy sweet smoothies.

Cacao nibs are rich in "chocolate" antioxidants, as they are made from the purest form of cacao—the bean itself. Cacao is rich in magnesium and antioxidants. Some studies show that cacao may be beneficial in a wide number of wellness areas, including heart health, energy, and mood, and the rich antioxidants may fight free radicals for anti-aging benefits.

Cacao powder—Cacao powder is made by cold-pressing cacao beans into a paste. The oil is extracted and a powder is formed. Look for cacao that is vegan and raw, meaning processed at very low temperatures to preserve the nutrients. Cacao powder carries similar benefits to cacao nibs.

Cacao powder can be added to a wide variety of smoothies to create chocolate-infused, blissful blends. Cacao blends very well with bananas, berries, avocado, nuts, soy, hemp and other seeds, and grains.

Cantaloupe—Cantaloupe is a juicy, sweet, orange-fleshed melon that is low in calories and hydrating. It is excellent blended into smoothies in its fresh state, or freeze cantaloupe cubes for a frosty melon beverage.

Cantaloupe is rich in fiber, potassium, and vitamin A.

Carrots—Carrots are crunchy root vegetables, bright orange in color, though some varieties can be purple, red, or black. They can easily be blended into smoothies using a high-speed blender, or you can juice carrots for a fresh carrot juice smoothie. Tip: Try grating carrots to make blending easier.

Carrots give smoothies a sweet veggie flavor and a rich orange color. Carrots are high in fiber and vitamin A.

Cashews—Cashews are buttery, cream-colored nuts with a creamy bite. They are one of the softest nuts when properly soaked, so they blend very well into creamy smoothies and shakes. Soaking cashews is easy: Submerge them in water, add a pinch of salt, and allow them to sit for at least four hours or preferably overnight. Store in the fridge and use within about two days of soaking. When ready to use, drain, discard the soaking water, and rinse well. Soaked cashews may take on a slightly purple hue—this is normal.

Cashews are rich in iron, protein, vitamin K, copper, zinc, phosphorus, manganese, and magnesium.

Cayenne—Cayenne powder is a fine red powder made from cayenne chiles. Cayenne is a wonderful add-in to smoothies since it gives a spicy flavor with just a few pinches. Cayenne powder is a dried spice, so it is easy to keep on hand, and a jar will last you a good while.

Cayenne increases blood flow and is a warming spice. It may also stimulate digestion and raise body temperature. Studies have shown that spices like cayenne may boost metabolism slightly after being consumed. They may also give a boost to the immune system, or even aid in illness symptoms like congestion.

Chamomile—Chamomile blossoms are tiny daisy-like flowers. They have a sweet aroma similar to apples. The fresh or dried blossoms are most commonly used for brewing tea, but here they are blended right into creamy, calming smoothies. You can find fresh, organic chamomile blossoms at some farmers' markets, or you can grow them yourself in an herb garden.

Chamomile is a calmness-inducing ingredient: It is known for its ability to relax nerves, soothe an upset tummy, fight insomnia, calm anxiety, and ease muscle tension.

Chard—Chard is a dark green leafy green. It has a sturdy celery-like vein with thick, velvety, buttery wide leaves. Rainbow chard has colorful stems that appear orange, red, and purple in color. Chard is delicious added to green smoothies; you can use it as a substitute for most any leafy green, including spinach and kale (which show up more commonly in my recipes). Do not be afraid to add the thick veins to your smoothie if you have a high-speed blender—those thick veins contain healthy fiber.

Chard is rich in vitamins A, C, and K, magnesium, and manganese. It is also a good source of fiber and iron. This healthy leafy green has a zesty, grassy, slightly sweet taste.

Cherries—Cherries are a perky red tree fruit. They are sweet and juicy with a shiny outer skin and a hard pit and stem. The pit and stem should always be removed before adding the fruit to a blender. You can also use cherry juice, which has a deep red color.

Fresh cherries are rich in vitamin C, potassium, and fiber. They may work as a natural anti-inflammatory.

Chia seeds—Chia seeds are tiny seeds similar in appearance to poppy seeds; they are a dark blue-purple black color, and there are white varieties as well. They are one of the most concentrated sources of healthy omega-3 fatty acids. They can absorb up to thirty times their weight in water, making them super-hydrating. They are high in fiber, and their soluble fiber helps clean the intestines by binding to debris in the digestive system and carrying it out of the body.

Chia seeds are rich in calcium, phosphorus, and manganese. And they contain 4 grams of protein per ounce!

Chocolate—See **Cacao powder**.

Cinnamon—Cinnamon is a brown-colored spice made from a dried tree bark.

Cinnamon is both stimulating and warming; its aroma can cast a calming and soothing effect and may evoke the smell of baked goods and sweet treats. Cinnamon pairs well with creamy ingredients like soy and almond milk, banana, and coconut.

Citrus—see **Grapefruit**, **Lemons**, **Limes**, and **Oranges**.

Cocoa powder—See **Cacao powder**.

Coconut—Coconut is a multifaceted ingredient, as you will find that it comes in many forms. Dried coconut flakes (unsweetened for use in smoothies) add texture and light coconut flavor, while creamy coconut milk adds richness and bold coconut aroma. Fresh young green coconuts have silky white coconut flesh—also called coconut meat—as well as fresh coconut water. Coconut is a tropical ingredient and pairs well with a wide variety of flavors.

Coconut milk is rich in iron and manganese; it is also very high in saturated fat.

Coconut water—Coconut water comes from the inside of a fresh young green coconut. It has a mild flavor and is slightly cloudy white or gray in color. There are various brands of coconut water available in stores; for smoothies use unsweetened coconut water. Or you can crack your own coconut to yield fresh, raw coconut water, though this takes a bit of effort. For convenience and safety, it is easiest to buy packaged coconut water or whole coconuts that have already been sliced open, since opening a coconut with a sharp knife requires some skill. Some juice bars offer raw, unheated coconut water, which is especially delicious.

You will find coconut water ice cubes used frequently in this book. They are made by simply filling ice cube trays with coconut water and freezing them. The cubes are mild in flavor but carry added nutrients.

Coconut water is very rich in potassium as well as manganese, magnesium, and vitamin C. Because of its high potassium and electrolyte content, coconut water has been called "nature's sports drink."

Cranberries—Cranberries are tart tiny red berries. You can buy them fresh or frozen. They are not very sweet on their own, so they should be added to smoothies with plenty of sweet ingredients.

Cranberries are rich in fiber, vitamin C, and manganese. They have also been known to aid in treating urinary infections, as they may act as a natural antibacterial agent.

Cucumbers—Cucumbers are a long green fruit (that acts like a vegetable) with a thick buttery skin and juicy, cool, tender flesh. The inside of a cucumber may actually be up to 20 degrees cooler than the outside. Cucumbers add much hydration to smoothies from their high water content. They are cooling and soothing and may aid the body in detoxification and purification. I like to freeze cucumbers for blending into smoothies for an extra frosty touch.

Cucumbers are rich in vitamin K and low in calories.

Dates—The date is a brown leathery fruit. Dates are highly concentrated in natural sugars, so they are often used as a sweetener for raw desserts and smoothies. You can soak your dates overnight so they will easily blend into your smoothies; remove the pits before blending. Feel free to add a few dates to your smoothies anytime you crave an extra hint of sweetness.

Flax—Flax seeds are small brown or golden seeds; they are shiny, smooth, and buttery. They can be ground or eaten whole; there is also flax oil, the oil made from flax seeds. The oil can easily be blended into smoothies. Note that ground flax seeds can go bad quickly, so if you are grinding seeds, do so right before consuming.

Flax seeds are rich in fiber and are one of the richest vegan sources of omega-3 fatty acids. Omega-3 fatty acids are helpful in many areas of wellness, including brain health, mood health, and heart health.

Flax seeds become gel-like when they come in contact with liquid, so they can be used to thicken smoothies and in batters for cookie dough and other baked goods, dressings, and veggie burgers.

Flax seeds can be beneficial in aiding digestive regularity, but they can cause constipation if not consumed with enough water since they absorb so much liquid by nature. Always drink enough liquid when adding flax seeds to your diet and ask your doctor about possible medication interactions.

Garlic—Pungent and spicy when eaten raw, garlic has been known to aid the immune system, metabolism, and detoxification. Garlic is also known as a natural antibacterial agent. Raw garlic can be added to smoothies, but it pairs best with savory flavors like those in green smoothies.

Ginger—Raw ginger root is spicy and stimulating; it can be added to smoothies for an invigorating flavor. It pairs well with everything from fruits to veggies. Ginger root is quite fibrous and may be a tricky ingredient for your blender to handle, so grate your ginger into fine strands or mince it before adding to your smoothie. You could also juice ginger as you're juicing other ingredients. As the skin of ginger can be quite thick and gritty, you may want to remove it before adding to your smoothies.

Goji berries—Sweet-tart pink goji berries are tiny and oval-shaped, and they have a super-perky flavor. They are chewy in texture and firmer than a raisin. Goji berries can become quite hard when chilled. They come in dried form and can easily be added directly to smoothies or—even better—soaked in water or fruit juice and then added to smoothies for easier blending. When soaked, goji berries become tender and velvety, and you will notice that the pink color turns a pinkish-orange. Some people enjoy goji berry tea, made by soaking the berries in warm water.

Goji berries are rich in antioxidants, including vitamins A and C, as well as fiber.

Grapefruit—Perky pink or white grapefruit is a sweet citrus with a slightly sour accent. It is juicy and acidic. Grapefruit is delicious juiced or added whole to smoothies. You may remove the seeds if you like, as they can be slightly bitter when juiced or blended. The thick white flesh is a nice addition to give your smoothies extra fiber; it has a mild flavor and blends up frothy and white. Remove the rind of your grapefruit before using, but you may want to use some of the zest for an aromatic citrus accent.

Grapefruit is rich in fiber, vitamin C, and potassium. Red or pink grapefruit also contains vitamin A and lycopene. Grapefruit, like most citrus, has been known to boost the immune system. Grapefruit is famous as an ideal slim-down food because of its low calorie count, rich flavor, and satisfying amounts of fiber. The uplifting color and citrus flavor of grapefruit are bound to put you in a sunny mood.

Grapes—Sweet grapes, juicy with a thin shiny skin, come in a variety of colors: green, red, purple, and black. Grapes are rich in natural sugars and are perfect for adding sweetness to a smoothie. Because grapes have a thin outer skin, it is suggested that you buy organic. If using non-organic grapes, wash them very well.

Grapes are rich in vitamins C and K and copper, and the skins are rich in the free-radical-fighting, anti-aging antioxidant resveratrol.

Green tea—Green tea is a mildly caffeinated antioxidant-rich type of tea. It can be brewed and chilled and used in tea-based smoothies. Green tea can also be added to smoothies in the form of matcha green tea powder, a pastel green–colored powder that will turn smoothies a rich green color. See page 69 for more information.

Hemp—Hemp is a variety of the cannabis plant, and velvety hemp seeds are tiny soft flakes with a mild nutty flavor. Hemp seeds are quite popular among vegans, as they are considered a complete protein food source. Hemp oil is very rich in essential fatty acids, including omega-3 fatty acids.

You can add hemp to smoothies in the form of hemp oil, seeds, powder, or milk. Adding hemp protein powder (or protein powder blends featuring some hemp) is an excellent way to boost the protein content of your smoothie. Store-bought hemp milk may not be the most nutritious option, as it is heated and the essential fatty acids are thus most likely destroyed. When choosing hemp products, go for raw and organic options. You can make your own raw hemp milk by blending water with raw shelled hemp seeds and sweetener and salt to taste, then straining the pulp through a nut bag.

Honeydew—Honeydew is a juicy, green-and-white-fleshed melon that is sweet and succulent when perfectly ripe. Honeydew can be added to smoothies fresh and raw (chilled is best for smoothies), or you can add it in the form of frozen cubes for a frosty blend. Honeydew is rich in potassium and is also a good source of vitamin B_6 and folate.

Kale—Kale is a fluffy, leafy dark green vegetable packed with oodles of nutrients. Kale is one of my favorite ingredients to add to green smoothies, as it has a very mild grassy yet slightly sweet flavor and blends well with other veggies and fruit. For ease of blending, be sure to remove the thick vein from each kale leaf.

Kale is rich in vitamins A, C, K, and B$_6$. It is a good source of fiber, iron, copper, manganese, and calcium, and even contains a fair amount of protein. Talk about a superfood!

Kiwis—The kiwi is an oval-shaped fruit with tender green—sometimes golden—flesh and edible black seeds. Kiwis have a very zesty sweet flavor. They are covered in a grassy brown skin, which is actually quite edible and flavorless, but it will turn your smoothies brownish in color and make them gritty in texture.

Kiwis are rich in vitamins C, E, and K, and in fiber, folate, copper, and potassium. They are also rich in digestive enzymes.

Lavender (culinary)—Lavender is a pastel purple flower with a soothing aroma that inspires a calm state. Lavender-infused juices and teas, such as lavender lemonade, can be blended into smoothies. You could even blend a few buds directly into your smoothie. Always use lavender that is for culinary use and make sure it's organic so that it is free of pesticides.

Lemons—Zesty, sour, acidic lemons are surprisingly alkalizing on the body. Their juice helps stimulate, cleanse, and purify while adding a bright, sunny flavor to smoothie recipes. Lemon is a wonderful accent to a wide variety of smoothie flavors, particularly green smoothies. However, you probably don't want to add lemon to any recipe including soy milk or other non-dairy milks, as it could have a curdling effect on the smoothie. Lemon zest is also a nice accent to smoothies.

Lemons are rich in vitamin C and contain a good amount of potassium and folate.

Limes—Limes offer the perky qualities of lemons, but with a slightly milder sourness. Lime juice pairs well with both fruit and veggie smoothies. Lime zest is also a fragrant accent to smoothies.

Limes are rich in vitamin C and contain a good amount of potassium.

Lychees—The lychee is a tropical fruit with a silky white flesh. The easiest way to buy lychees in the United States is canned. While canned ones are not gloriously beneficial in terms of nutrition, lychees provide a luxurious flavor when blended into smoothies. And if you can find fresh lychees, you will definitely want to give them a try!

Lychees contain copper and vitamins C and B_6.

Mangos—The mango is a sweet, succulent, golden yellow tropical fruit. Mangos have a silky, slightly fibrous flesh. They are firm enough to be cubed like an avocado or melon. Mangos are delicious blended up fresh or frozen in smoothies; frozen mango smoothies have a rich, creamy texture.

Mangos are rich in vitamins A, C, E, K, and B_6, and in fiber, potassium, and copper.

Maple syrup—Maple syrup is an excellent sweetener for smoothies. It has a thin liquid consistency similar to agave syrup, but maple syrup has a distinct flavor. Pure maple syrup is made from maple tree sap, which is boiled into a syrup. Maple syrup naturally contains a wide variety of vitamins and minerals. You will notice that I specify grade B maple syrup in a few recipes; I favor it because of its dark amber color.

Matcha green tea powder—Matcha green tea has been around for more than eight hundred years and is beloved for its wide range of wellness benefits. Pastel-green matcha green tea powder is made by grinding the whole leaf of matcha green tea. So instead of soaking the tea leaves and drinking an infusion, you are actually consuming the entire leaf.

One serving of matcha has about the same amount of caffeine as black tea. Matcha has a unique, smoky, slightly bitter flavor. Matcha varieties differ in flavor, so you will want to experiment with the amount you add to your smoothies. A good starting point for smoothies is

½ teaspoon matcha powder; I like about 1 teaspoon in my matcha shakes.

Matcha is an excellent alternative to coffee when you are looking for a gentle caffeine boost. Some studies show that the energy boost from matcha is released in a milder fashion so that the energy lasts throughout the day. Matcha has also been known to increase focus and clarity and induce a sense of calmness.

Nut milk—Nut milk is a non-dairy milk made from almonds, cashews, or other nuts that is both healthy and delicious. You can easily make your own nut milk at home using raw nuts, a high-speed blender, and a nut milk bag (see pages 43–44). See also the **Almond** entry (pages 52–53).

Oranges—Oranges are one of the most popular and diverse fruits around. They are sweet and vibrant with a distinct citrus flavor and aroma. Oranges can be added to smoothies in whole form or as juice. I love freezing peeled oranges and blending them in smoothies. Orange zest is a vibrant smoothie add-in.

Oranges are rich in fiber, folate, potassium, and vitamin C. They are well known for aiding immunity. The fiber and potassium make them quite heart-healthy as well, and their natural sugars provide energy.

Papaya—The papaya is a creamy pink fleshy tropical fruit that is sweet and soft. Papayas contain large sphere-shaped seeds that have a peppery flavor. Papayas are delicious blended into smoothies, as their high water content makes for a hydrating, silky sip.

Papayas are rich in the digestive enzyme papain; they are the only natural food source of this powerful enzyme. Papain may also aid in immunity and fighting allergies. Papayas are also rich in potassium, vitamins C and A, folate, and fiber.

Parsley—Parsley is a green herb with small deep green leaves and a bitter, grassy flavor. It is a wonderful add-in for green smoothies. It can be slightly fibrous, so you may want to chop it before adding to your blender. Remember that a little bit goes a long way in terms of adding flavor and color to your smoothies.

Parsley is rich in vitamins A, C, and K, and in fiber, folate, iron, and potassium.

Peaches—The peach is a velvet-skinned tree fruit. Peaches are low in calories and have a sweet and slightly tart flavor. They can be added to smoothies in frozen form—where the skin is removed—or in fresh form with the skin left on. You will get more nutrients and fiber by including the peach skins in your smoothie.

Peaches are rich in fiber, potassium, and vitamins A and C.

Peanuts—Peanuts are most often added to smoothies in the form of peanut butter. Fun fact: Peanuts are actually not nuts but rather legumes.

Peanuts are rich in protein, fiber, manganese, copper, pantothenic acid, and several B vitamins.

Pears—The pear is a juicy sweet tree fruit with a slightly gritty texture similar to the apple. Pears are very sweet, and their tender flesh easily blends into smoothies and acts as a natural sweetener.

Pears are rich in fiber and vitamin C.

Peppermint—Peppermint is a plant with soft green leaves and a cooling aroma and flavor. Fresh mint meshes well with a wide variety of smoothie flavors, including berry, citrus, green veggie, melon, and pineapple. Mint is soothing to the mind and body.

Pineapple—Zesty yellow pineapple is a tangy tropical fruit with a sweet flavor and almost meaty yet juicy texture. You must remove its tough skin before blending. Pineapple can be added frozen, fresh, or as juice to smoothies.

Pineapple is rich in fiber, vitamin C, manganese, and the powerful digestive enzyme bromelain, which not only aids in digestion but also may aid in immunity, reducing inflammation, and fighting allergies.

Pistachios—Pistachios are wrinkly green-grayish nuts with a buttery, relatively tender texture. Their softness makes them perfect for blending into smoothies. For best results, soak pistachios in water before adding to smoothies.

Pistachios are rich in vitamins E, B_6, and A, and in fiber, iron, thiamine, and folate. They are also rich in a variety of minerals, most notably copper, phosphorus, and manganese.

Plums—The plum is a juicy sweet tree fruit with a slightly tart, silky, thin skin. Plums range in color from deep purple to light red or even golden. Plums can be blended raw into smoothies after removing the pit. Because the skin is so thin, it is best to buy organic plums, or wash non-organic plums very well.

Plums are rich in vitamins C and K and fiber.

Pomegranates—The pomegranate is a unique fruit for sure! It has a thick, hard outer flesh and tiny juicy seeds inside. The seeds are where we get pomegranate juice and where all the nutrients lie. You can add fresh pomegranate seeds or juice to smoothies.

Pomegranate is rich in vitamins C and K, folate, copper, and potassium. Its deep red color means it is rich in red-pigment phytochemicals. Pomegranates help fight free radicals and may also contribute to heart health.

Protein powder—You can find vegan protein powders from a wide array of sources, including soy, hemp, and pea. Protein powder can be added to most any smoothie to boost protein content. Protein powder may change the taste, color, and texture of your beverage slightly and may thicken it a bit.

Pumpkin—Canned unsweetened pumpkin puree is a delicious ingredient to add to your smoothies, and it is low in calories. Be sure to add sweetener and salt your pumpkin smoothies, as pumpkin puree on its own can be quite bland.

Pumpkin is rich in vitamin A and fiber.

Pumpkin seeds—Pumpkin seeds, also called pepitas, are long, flat seeds with a shiny green skin. They are slightly chewy, mildly crunchy, and buttery in texture and have a nutty flavor. Pumpkin seeds can be added to smoothies whole and raw or soaked until slightly softened for easier blending. Pumpkin seed oil is another way to retrieve some of the nutrients of pumpkin seeds.

Pumpkin seeds are rich in iron, zinc, vitamins A and K, manganese, magnesium, tryptophan, and phosphorus. Pumpkin seeds and pumpkin seed oil are good sources of essential fatty acids.

Radishes—A radish is a spicy, peppery, firm, crisp root vegetable. In smoothie making, the texture of radishes is similar to that of carrots or beets: they are crunchy rather than soft and juicy, and can be grated for addition to a recipe. Radishes can easily be blended into veggie and green smoothies and provide a spicy, zesty accent.

Radishes are rich in fiber, vitamin C, and potassium. They may be helpful in aiding digestion and detoxification and may act as an anti-inflammatory.

Raspberries—The raspberry is a tender pink berry with bumpy flesh and plenty of tiny seeds. Raspberries are sweet yet tart, with a juicy, velvety texture. Both fresh and frozen raspberries are delicious blended into smoothies, and they lend a vibrant red-pink color.

Raspberries are rich in fiber, vitamins C and K, and manganese.

Rice milk—Rice milk is a light and milky white beverage that is probably the least creamy of the non-dairy milk options. Rice milk has a mild sweet flavor and can easily be used in place of any non-dairy milk. If you do not like soy or hemp milk because the flavors are too pronounced, give rice milk a try, as it is very simple and pure. However, rice milk does not have as much protein as bean- or nut-based non-dairy milks.

Try making your own rice milk by blending cooked brown or white rice with water in a high-speed blender, adding sweetener and salt to taste.

Rolled oats—Oats may not be the most obvious of smoothie ingredients, but they work wonders to create a creamy, rich texture and satisfying flavor. Oats can be soaked and then blended into smoothies or added dry and raw. Unsweetened whole rolled oats are what you should use.

Oats are rich in fiber, iron, protein, thiamine, magnesium, manganese, phosphorus, zinc, and selenium. The mixture of soluble and insoluble fiber makes oats a heart-healthy food that may help lower cholesterol.

Romaine lettuce—If you think that romaine lettuce is just like any other lettuce variety, think again. Romaine has a crisp, hydrating texture that blends well into green smoothies. It has a mild, refreshing flavor with very little grassiness.

Although romaine is not dark green in color like spinach or kale, it is actually quite nutritious. Romaine lettuce is rich in vitamins A, C, and K and folate. It is a good source of iron, potassium, and manganese.

Soy—Soy is a widely used ingredient in vegan smoothies and is probably the creamiest of non-dairy milk varieties. Soy products contribute complete protein nutrition in a wide variety of products, including soy milk, soy protein powder, silken tofu, and soy yogurt. Soy milk, as a basic dairy milk substitute, comes in vanilla or plain flavors, sweetened or unsweetened. You can also find chocolate and strawberry flavors. Around the holidays you can find seasonal soy nog and pumpkin spice–flavored soy milk. Soy yogurt comes in a wide variety of flavors. Try vanilla or plain for smoothies for their neutral flavor.

When purchasing soy milk, it is best to buy brands that are fortified with vitamins and minerals, particularly vitamins B_{12} and D. These two nutrients can be tricky to get adequate amounts of in a vegan diet.

Spinach—Popeye was right. This deep green–colored leafy vegetable is one of the most nutritious greens around. Spinach has a soft, silky texture, and when eaten raw, it has a desirable almost salty savory flavor. Spinach can easily be added directly to smoothies; a simple handful will boost your smoothie with a wide array of nutrients.

Spinach is rich in fiber, iron, calcium, vitamins A, E, C, and K, folate, manganese, potassium, magnesium, and riboflavin.

Spirulina—Spirulina is a blue-green algae that can be added to smoothies in powder form. Spirulina is often called a superfood because it is rich in a wide variety of vitamins and minerals and is made of up to 70 percent complete amino acid–containing protein. Spirulina is rich in plant pigments—also called phytochemicals—which help fight free radicals. Add about ¼ to ½ teaspoon powdered spirulina to your smoothies.

Stevia—Stevia is a calorie-free natural sweetener. You can use it in place of other sweeteners like agave syrup or maple syrup in your smoothies if you like.

Strawberries—The strawberry is a heart-shaped, juicy, bright red berry. Strawberries can be added to smoothies in fresh or frozen form. They provide a very appealing gentle sweet flavor. Strawberries have a creamy texture when frozen and blended—perfect for creating frosty, thick smoothies.

Strawberries are low in calories and rich in fiber, vitamin C, and manganese. Their fruity, flowery essence is said to be calming.

Sunflower seeds—Sunny indeed, these buttery tiny seeds come straight from those beautiful sunflowers. Nutty, slightly crunchy, and silky to touch, shelled sunflower seeds make an excellent smoothie addition. Also try sunflower butter; it has a peanut butter–like texture and actually makes a perfect peanut butter alternative.

Sunflower seeds are rich in healthy fats and also contain iron, protein, and minerals, including magnesium.

Vanilla bean—Vanilla is a soothing flavor to add to a smoothie and is also delicious in homemade nut milks. Vanilla bean seeds can be scraped from the pod, and some high-speed blenders can even handle pulverizing the whole bean. Pure vanilla extract can be used as a flavor substitute for the bean.

Walnuts—Walnuts are brain-shaped nuts that just happen to be very healthy for your brain! Raw walnuts have a buttery crisp texture, and they can be soaked in water to soften them. You can add whole raw walnuts or walnut oil to smoothies.

Walnuts are rich in iron, vitamin B_6, copper, magnesium, and manganese. They are also one of the richest sources of essential fatty acids.

Watercress—Watercress is a soft leafy green with tender leaves. It has a peppery, spicy flavor. It can easily be blended into most smoothies and is a welcome addition to green smoothies.

Watercress is rich in vitamins C, A, and K, and in manganese and calcium.

Watermelon—Watermelon is a juicy pinkish-red–fleshed melon. It is low in calories, about 50 calories per cup, with a simple sweet flavor. It can easily be blended raw into smoothies and coolers. Frozen watermelon cubes also create delicious frosty blends.

Watermelon is rich in vitamins A and C and potassium. It is also a source of lycopene from its red pigment.

PART 2
THE
RECIPES

Sassy Green Kick-Start

4

365 SMOOTHIE RECIPES

Modifications: Remember, you can always adjust ingredients—including ice, liquid, type of ingredient, frozen or fresh—slightly to suit your preferences. Tweaking recipes will change the nutritional information.

Nutritional information: This is to be used as a guided estimate, since specific brands and ingredients will vary greatly. Boost-it ingredients are not included in the nutritional information. Recommended daily allowance (RDA) percentages are based on a 2,000-calorie diet. A few important nutrients, such as calcium, iron, and vitamins A and C, are listed to give you further insight into the wellness value of your smoothie.

1 sassy green kick-start

1 cup chopped kale
  leaves

¼ cup green grapes

1 orange, peeled and
  segmented

1 banana

½ cup coconut water

2 tablespoons fresh
  lemon juice

2 to 3 pinches of
  cayenne

½ cup ice

BOOST IT: 1 teaspoon
aloe vera juice

Kick-start your day with this vibrant, spicy blend of nutrient-rich kale and fruit. Stimulating lemon and cayenne ease you into detox mode. This frothy green smoothie provides a sweet start to your day. Try using a frozen orange for a frostier sip!

DIRECTIONS: Combine all the ingredients in a blender and blend from low to high until frosty smooth.

CALORIES: 272, FAT: 1.5G, CARBS: 66G, PROTEIN: 6G, FIBER: 11G | VITAMIN A: 220%, CALCIUM: 21%, VITAMIN C: 345%, IRON: 12% | ALSO RICH IN MANGANESE, POTASSIUM, AND VITAMIN B$_6$.

2 fresh blackberry buzz

1 cup fresh or frozen
  blackberries

1 frozen banana

1 cup vanilla soy milk

½ cup coconut water
  ice cubes (see
  page 40)

2 to 3 pinches of
  cayenne

BOOST IT: 1 teaspoon
flax oil

You'll be buzzing with blackberry bliss all day long after drinking this creamy purple smoothie. Juicy antioxidant- and fiber-rich blackberries mingle with creamy soy milk, cayenne, and banana. Add some flax oil for a healthy boost of omega-3 fatty acids. Including some healthy fats in your smoothies may help you absorb certain nutrients like fat-soluble vitamins A, D, E, and K.

DIRECTIONS: Combine all the ingredients in a blender and blend from low to high until frosty smooth.

CALORIES: 290, FAT: 5G, CARBS: 53G, PROTEIN: 12G, FIBER: 13G | VITAMIN A: 18%, CALCIUM: 38%, VITAMIN C: 73%, IRON: 15%

3 c-green detox

1 kiwi, peeled

1 tablespoon fresh
   lemon juice

½ cup chopped parsley

1 cup chopped kale
   leaves

1 cup frozen
   strawberries

1 cup coconut water

½ cup ice cubes

BOOST IT: 1 teaspoon
chia seeds

We all overindulge. Caffeine, alcohol, sugar, chemicals. Pair that with clumsy sleep habits, not enough exercise, and dehydration and you will soon be feeling like you need a serious tune-up. Or detox. Pause and rethink your lifestyle habits. Then revive your stressed, tired, overindulged body with the help of vitamin C–rich kiwi, lemon, and strawberries, potassium-rich coconut water, and superfood greens. Do you finally "C" the light?

DIRECTIONS: Combine all the ingredients in a blender and blend from low to high speed until frosty smooth.

CALORIES: 175, FAT: 2G, CARBS: 38G, PROTEIN: 7G, FIBER: 10G | VITAMIN A: 258%, CALCIUM: 24%, VITAMIN C: 445%, IRON: 24% | ALSO RICH IN MAGNESIUM, MANGANESE, POTASSIUM, AND VITAMIN B_6.

4 strawberry-chia synergy

1 cup frozen
   strawberries

1 frozen banana

½ cup orange juice

½ cup soy milk

2 teaspoons chia seeds

Pinch of orange zest
   (optional)

1 teaspoon grated fresh
   ginger

A few pinches of
   cayenne

¼ cup ice cubes

Rich in fiber and omega-3 fatty acids, chia seeds blend with protein-rich soy milk and sweet strawberries to strengthen, renew, and energize your body and synergize your day.

DIRECTIONS: Combine all the ingredients in a blender and blend from low to high until smooth. For plumped chia seeds, soak them in the coconut water for at least ten minutes before blending.

BOOST IT: 1 teaspoon aloe vera juice

CALORIES: 310, FAT: 7G, CARBS: 60G, PROTEIN: 9G, FIBER: 11G | VITAMIN A: 12%, CALCIUM: 25%, VITAMIN C: 262%, IRON: 15% | ALSO RICH IN MANGANESE.

5 green aloe detox

1 cup chopped spinach

1 frozen banana

¼ cup mashed avocado

1 cup coconut water

1 tablespoon aloe vera
juice

2 tablespoons fresh
lemon juice

2 to 3 pinches of
cayenne

¼ cup coconut water
ice cubes

BOOST IT: ½ teaspoon
spirulina powder

This frothy, cool green smoothie will send you into superfood mode—lively, energized, and ready to take on the world. Healing aloe helps renew you from the inside out as superfood spinach mingles with perky lemon and cayenne, crushing free radicals as you sip. Electrolyte-rich coconut water helps you stay hydrated.

DIRECTIONS: Combine all the ingredients in a blender and blend from low to high until frosty smooth.

CALORIES: 243, FAT: 6G, CARBS: 46G, PROTEIN: 6G,
FIBER: 10G | VITAMIN A: 119%, CALCIUM: 14%, VITAMIN C: 87%,
IRON: 17% | ALSO RICH IN MAGNESIUM, MANGANESE,
POTASSIUM, AND VITAMIN B$_6$.

6 piña-vocado

1 cup orange juice

1 cup frozen pineapple
chunks

⅓ cup mashed avocado

1 frozen banana

½ cup coconut water
ice cubes

BOOST IT: 1 teaspoon
shredded unsweetened
coconut

Take a mini detox-motivating vacation with this swoon-worthy, sunny smoothie, which features tropical banana, bromelain-rich pineapple, and electrolyte-rich coconut water ice cubes to help you revive your body and satisfy your taste buds. A nice dose of fiber from the banana and pineapple helps you detox from the inside out.

DIRECTIONS: Combine all the ingredients in a blender and blend from low to high until frosty smooth.

CALORIES: 401, FAT: 9G, CARBS: 81G, PROTEIN: 6G,
FIBER: 11G | VITAMIN A: 15%, CALCIUM: 9%, VITAMIN C: 360%,
IRON: 11% | ALSO RICH IN MANGANESE AND POTASSIUM.

Piña-vocado

7 super blue recharge

2 teaspoons hemp
    seeds

1 cup vanilla soy milk

1¼ cups frozen
    blueberries

1 frozen banana

1 teaspoon açaí powder

½ cup ice

BOOST IT: **2 to 3
tablespoons non-dairy
yogurt**

Things that clear my mind: blue skies, blue ocean water, and a frosty blue smoothie like this one. This blueberry-filled blend is bursting with antioxidants and free-radical-fighting bliss. Fluffy hemp seeds add protein, and açaí powder adds even more blue-purple antioxidant power to help recharge your body.

DIRECTIONS: Combine the hemp seeds and soy milk in a blender and blend from low to high until smooth. Add the remaining ingredients and blend from low to high until frosty smooth.

CALORIES: 355, FAT: 9G, CARBS: 62G, PROTEIN: 12G, FIBER: 9G | VITAMIN A: 17%, CALCIUM: 35%, VITAMIN C: 61%, IRON: 16%

8 ginger-berry sunrise

½ cup frozen
    strawberries

¼ cup chopped frozen
    peaches

1 fresh or frozen banana

1 orange, peeled and
    segmented, plus a
    pinch of orange zest

½ cup coconut water

1 teaspoon grated fresh
    ginger

½ cup ice

BOOST IT: **1 teaspoon
chia seeds**

Spicy ginger, lively orange, and sweet banana perk up your taste buds as frosty strawberries and peaches blend with electrolyte-rich coconut water. Sip this frosty blend at sunrise for a berry sweet start to your day. Add some chia seeds for extra fiber and a boost of omega-3 fatty acids.

DIRECTIONS: Combine all the ingredients in a blender and blend from low to high until frosty smooth.

CALORIES: 260, FAT: 1G, CARBS: 63G, PROTEIN: 5G, FIBER: 11G | VITAMIN A: 13%, CALCIUM: 13%, VITAMIN C: 261%, IRON: 8% | ALSO RICH IN MANGANESE, POTASSIUM, AND VITAMIN B$_6$.

9 frozen cucumber cleanse

1½ cups frozen diced cucumber

2 tablespoons fresh lime juice, plus a pinch of lime zest

¾ cup coconut water

½ banana

1 kiwi, peeled

A few pinches of cayenne

Sweetener to taste (optional)

BOOST IT: 1 teaspoon aloe vera juice and/or chopped fresh mint

Cucumber is the ultimate cool-down ingredient—especially when frozen! Embrace a new level of chill from this frosty-sweet green smoothie. Add some healing aloe vera juice to further calm and renew your mind, body, and soul as you cleanse. Fresh mint is also a nice touch.

DIRECTIONS: Combine all the ingredients in a blender and blend from low to high until frosty smooth.

CALORIES: 164, FAT: 1G, CARBS: 40G, PROTEIN: 4G, FIBER: 7G | VITAMIN A: 6%, CALCIUM: 10%, VITAMIN C: 156%, IRON: 8% | ALSO RICH IN MAGNESIUM, MANGANESE, POTASSIUM, AND VITAMIN B$_6$.

10 papaya-citrus-pineapple colada

½ cup orange juice

½ cup coconut water

1 cup papaya chunks

1 cup frozen pineapple chunks

1 frozen banana

1 teaspoon unsweetened dried coconut flakes

Splash of coconut milk (optional)

BOOST IT: 1 teaspoon spirulina powder

This pink version of a piña colada smoothie is for all you papaya lovers out there. This detox-worthy drink helps you renew from the inside out, as it is rich in the digestive enzymes papain (found in papaya) and bromelain (found in pineapple). It's also rich in free-radical-fighting vitamin C.

DIRECTIONS: Combine all the ingredients in a blender and blend from low to high until frosty smooth.

CALORIES: 322, FAT: 2G, CARBS: 78G, PROTEIN: 5G, FIBER: 10G | VITAMIN A: 39%, CALCIUM: 10%, VITAMIN C: 393%, IRON: 9% | ALSO RICH IN POTASSIUM, MANGANESE, AND VITAMIN B$_6$.

11 get glowing! grapefruit cooler

1 grapefruit, peeled and segmented

½ banana

2 cups watermelon chunks

¼ cup coconut water

1 tablespoon fresh lemon juice

¼ cup ice

BOOST IT: **a few fresh mint leaves**

Grapefruit lovers—let's get glowing! Start your glow-agenda with this super-invigorating blend of cool watermelon, perky pink grapefruit, hydrating coconut water, and sassy lemon juice. This cooler will help you crush free radicals and hydrate your body to inspire detoxification. Blend in a few fresh mint leaves to further stimulate your senses.

DIRECTIONS: Combine all the ingredients in a blender and blend from low to high until frosty smooth.

CALORIES: 241, FAT: 1G, CARBS: 60G, PROTEIN: 5G, FIBER: 7G | VITAMIN A: 83%, CALCIUM: 7%, VITAMIN C: 210%, IRON: 8% | ALSO RICH IN POTASSIUM AND VITAMIN B$_6$.

12 spicy cantaloupe cooler

2 cups fresh or frozen cantaloupe chunks

1 fresh or frozen banana

1 teaspoon maple syrup

½ cup ice

2 to 4 pinches of cayenne

Coconut water, if needed

BOOST IT: **1 teaspoon aloe vera juice**

Juicy vitamin A–rich cantaloupe is a sweet treat when blended into this hydrating smoothie. Accented by sweet maple syrup and spicy cayenne, this golden blend will refresh your body and inspire your spirit. If you choose frozen cantaloupe for a frosty texture, use a fresh banana and add a few splashes of coconut water to ease blending.

DIRECTIONS: Combine all the ingredients in a blender and blend from low to high until frosty smooth.

CALORIES: 229, FAT: 1G, CARBS: 56G, PROTEIN: 4G, FIBER: 6G | VITAMIN A: 213%, CALCIUM: 4%, VITAMIN C: 208%, IRON: 6% | ALSO RICH IN POTASSIUM AND VITAMIN B$_6$.

13 green pepper purify

1½ cups chopped
    seeded green bell
    pepper
1 cup chopped spinach
1 cup orange juice
1 banana
2 to 3 pinches of
    cayenne
½ cup ice

BOOST IT: 1 teaspoon
apple cider vinegar

Crisp green bell peppers—rich in free-radical-fighting vitamin C—are a worthy purifying ingredient. Enjoy them with superfood spinach and sweet vibrant orange juice in this sweet green smoothie. Add more ice for a frostier blend.

DIRECTIONS: Combine all the ingredients in a blender and blend from low to high until frosty smooth.

CALORIES: 268, FAT: 1G, CARBS: 62G, PROTEIN: 5G, FIBER: 7G | VITAMIN A: 158%, CALCIUM: 8%, VITAMIN C: 532%, IRON: 13% | ALSO RICH IN POTASSIUM AND VITAMIN B$_6$.

14 bananas for almonds and greens

1 cup plain almond milk
1 tablespoon almond
    butter
1 orange, peeled and
    segmented
1 banana
2 cups chopped kale
    leaves
½ cup water
½ cup ice

BOOST IT: ½ teaspoon
spirulina powder

When you need to fuel up for a busy day, reach for the superfood power of two of nature's healthiest foods: kale and almonds. Toss in some citrus, banana, non-dairy milk, and frosty ice and blend! Try it with homemade raw almond milk.

DIRECTIONS: Combine the almond milk and almond butter in a blender and blend from low to high until smooth. Add the remaining ingredients and blend from low to high until frosty smooth.

CALORIES: 410, FAT: 14G, CARBS: 71G, PROTEIN: 11G, FIBER: 12G | VITAMIN A: 442%, CALCIUM: 61%, VITAMIN C: 448%, IRON: 21% | ALSO RICH IN POTASSIUM.

15 pink grapefruit–walnut

1¼ cups grapefruit juice
(or substitute
1 whole grapefruit,
peeled, plus ¼ cup
water)

¼ cup raw walnuts

1 frozen banana

1 teaspoon maple syrup

½ cup coconut water
ice cubes

BOOST IT: 1 teaspoon
chia seeds

Get a pink grapefruit glow with this sassy citrus, banana, and walnut smoothie. Walnuts add a dose of wellness-boosting omega-3 fatty acids.

DIRECTIONS: Combine all the ingredients in a blender and blend from low to high until frosty smooth.

CALORIES: 422, FAT: 19G, CARBS: 60G, PROTEIN: 12G, FIBER: 10G | VITAMIN A: 55%, CALCIUM: 9%, VITAMIN C: 188%, IRON: 11% | ALSO RICH IN MANGANESE AND POTASSIUM.

16 lemon-beet clarifying cooler

2 tablespoons grated
beet

2 tablespoons fresh
lemon juice

¾ cup chopped green
apple

¼ cup frozen
strawberries

1½ cups coconut water

2 to 3 pinches of
cayenne

1 teaspoon maple syrup
(optional)

½ cup ice

BOOST IT: 1 teaspoon
aloe vera juice

Detox your day with this vibrant pink blend of cleansing green apple, lively lemon, and perky beet.

DIRECTIONS: Combine all the ingredients in a blender and blend from low to high until frosty smooth.

CALORIES: 149, FAT: 1G, CARBS: 34G, PROTEIN: 4G, FIBER: 8G | VITAMIN A: 1%, CALCIUM: 11%, VITAMIN C: 82%, IRON: 9% | ALSO RICH IN POTASSIUM AND MANGANESE.

17 aloe-watermelon beachside sipper

2 cups fresh
   watermelon chunks

1 frozen banana

3 tablespoons fresh
   lemon juice, plus a
   pinch of zest

1 tablespoon aloe vera
   juice

½ cup ice

BOOST IT: **a few pinches
of cayenne**

Imagine this: You, on a tropical island. Sipping this beach-perfect pink drink. Detox your mind, body, and spirit with this cooling and hydrating blend of watermelon, banana, and lemon. Aloe nurtures and heals your digestive tract to promote detoxification from the inside out. Sip, hydrate, swoon. Sunshine not included. For a sweet side, add a drizzle of maple syrup along with the cayenne.

DIRECTIONS: Combine all the ingredients in a blender and blend from low to high until frosty smooth.

CALORIES: 208, FAT: 1G, CARBS: 53G, PROTEIN: 3G, FIBER: 5G | VITAMIN A: 37%, CALCIUM: 4%, VITAMIN C: 81%, IRON: 6% | ALSO RICH IN POTASSIUM AND VITAMIN B$_6$.

18 fresh-start strawberry-lime frosty

1½ cups frozen
   strawberries

3 tablespoons fresh
   lime juice, plus a
   pinch of zest

½ banana

1 cup coconut water

½ cup ice

BOOST IT: **a few pinches
of cayenne**

Enjoy this fresh start to your day. Strawberries, hydrating coconut water, banana, and lime juice swirl into this light, sweet, vibrant red frosty. Being well hydrated will help your body release toxins and promote a deeper state of wellness. So drink up! Tip: Keep a giant water bottle by your side during your detox phase to further inspire hydration. Coconut water is also excellent for hydration because of its electrolyte content.

DIRECTIONS: Combine all the ingredients in a blender and blend from low to high until frosty smooth.

CALORIES: 179, FAT: 1G, CARBS: 42G, PROTEIN: 4G, FIBER: 9G | VITAMIN A: 2%, CALCIUM: 10%, VITAMIN C: 253%, IRON: 10% | ALSO RICH IN MAGNESIUM, MANGANESE, POTASSIUM, AND VITAMIN B$_6$.

19 the cool pink cucumber

1½ cups frozen chopped cucumber

1 cup pink grapefruit juice

½ cup frozen peach chunks

1 banana

BOOST IT: **1 tablespoon chopped fresh mint leaves**

Cool meets pink in this frosty grapefruit-cucumber smoothie. Grapefruit is a cleansing ingredient for detox mode and contains plentiful amounts of the amazing antioxidant vitamin C. This blend is also rich in potassium to help you stay hydrated. Tip: Freshly squeezed citrus is best for flavor and nutrients!

DIRECTIONS: Combine the cucumber and grapefruit juice in a blender and blend from low to high until smooth. Add the remaining ingredients and blend from low to high until frosty smooth.

CALORIES: 226, FAT: 1G, CARBS: 58G, PROTEIN: 4G, FIBER: 4G | VITAMIN A: 24%, CALCIUM: 4%, VITAMIN C: 124%, IRON: 5% | ALSO RICH IN POTASSIUM AND VITAMIN B$_6$.

20 sweet carrot green shake

1 cup chopped kale leaves

1 banana

¾ cup coconut water (or try soy milk for creamy version)

½ teaspoon grated fresh ginger

1 cup carrot juice ice cubes

BOOST IT: **2 to 3 tablespoons mashed avocado**

This sweet carrot green shake has an accent of spicy ginger and plenty of free-radical-fighting nutrients. Frosty carrot juice ice cubes make this a unique cooling blend! Vitamin A fills your cells with each sip, crushing free radicals and helping you detox your way to a deeper state of wellness. Tip: If you are juicing carrots yourself, you can juice the ginger along with the carrots.

DIRECTIONS: In a blender, combine the kale, banana, coconut water, ginger, and avocado, if using, and blend from low to high until smooth. Add the carrot juice ice cubes and blend from low to high until frosty smooth.

CALORIES: 246, FAT: 1G, CARBS: 55G, PROTEIN: 7G, FIBER: 8G | VITAMIN A: 908%, CALCIUM: 18%, VITAMIN C: 183%, IRON: 14% | ALSO RICH IN MAGNESIUM, MANGANESE, POTASSIUM, AND VITAMIN B$_6$.

21 mojito grape frosty

2 tablespoons fresh lime juice, plus a pinch of zest

1 tablespoon chopped fresh mint leaves

½ cup coconut water

2 cups frozen green grapes

BOOST IT: **1 teaspoon aloe vera juice and/or cayenne**

Green grapes, cool mint leaves, and a sassy splash of lime juice give you that South Beach feel wherever you may be. This light and frosty drink will hydrate, energize, and calm to help you stay in (and enjoy) your detox mode. For a thicker texture, use less coconut water.

DIRECTIONS: Combine the lime juice, mint, and coconut water in a blender and blend from low to high until smooth. Add the grapes and blend from low to high until frosty smooth.

CALORIES: 213, FAT: 2.3G, CARBS: 7.5G, PROTEIN: 3G, FIBER: 2G | VITAMIN A: 9%, CALCIUM: 10%, VITAMIN C: 35%, IRON: 10% | ALSO RICH IN MANGANESE AND POTASSIUM.

22 sunny green apple cooler

1 cup chopped green apple

½ cup frozen diced cucumber

2 kiwis, peeled

2 tablespoons fresh lemon juice

¼ cup coconut water

¼ cup ice

BOOST IT: **1 tablespoon chopped fresh mint leaves**

Let in the sunshine with each sip of this frosty cooler filled with cleansing apple and lemon and soothing cucumber.

DIRECTIONS: Combine all the ingredients in a blender and blend from low to high until frosty smooth.

CALORIES: 178, FAT: 1G, CARBS: 44G, PROTEIN: 3G, FIBER: 9G | VITAMIN A: 7%, CALCIUM: 9%, VITAMIN C: 272%, IRON: 6% | ALSO RICH IN POTASSIUM.

23 green chia monster

2 cups chopped kale
  leaves

½ cup coconut water

½ cup soy milk

2 teaspoons chia seeds

1 tangerine or small
  orange, peeled and
  segmented

1 frozen banana

½ cup ice (optional)

BOOST IT: 1 teaspoon
aloe vera juice

Yikes, there is a green chia monster in your kitchen! Wait, no, that's just you. And that's a good thing, as chia seeds are rich in omega-3s, protein, and cleansing fiber. Grab this chia-kale green smoothie and power through your day—just like a chia monster.

DIRECTIONS: Combine all the ingredients in a blender and blend from low to high until frosty smooth.

CALORIES: 337, FAT: 7G, CARBS: 64G, PROTEIN: 13G, FIBER: 13G | VITAMIN A: 423%, CALCIUM: 46%, VITAMIN C: 375%, IRON: 24% | ALSO RICH IN MAGNESIUM, MANGANESE, POTASSIUM, AND VITAMIN B$_6$.

24 blueberry beginning

1 cup fresh or frozen
  blueberries

1 frozen banana

1 cup vanilla soy milk

2 tablespoons chopped
  fresh mint leaves

1 teaspoon chia seeds
  (optional)

½ cup ice

BOOST IT: 2 to 3
tablespoons non-dairy
vanilla yogurt

We know all about green smoothies by now. Well, I'm starting a new trend: the blue smoothie. This blue smoothie is filled with tender blueberries, refreshing mint, cleansing chia seeds, and creamy banana— simple and sweet for your new beginning. Add some non-dairy yogurt for a boost of probiotics.

DIRECTIONS: Combine all the ingredients in a blender and blend from low to high until frosty smooth.

CALORIES: 316, FAT: 7G, CARBS: 58G, PROTEIN: 11G, FIBER: 10G | VITAMIN A: 22%, CALCIUM: 37%, VITAMIN C: 43%, IRON: 20% | ALSO RICH IN RIBOFLAVIN.

Blueberry Beginning

25 vibrant kiwi-pineapple

1 cup frozen pineapple
   chunks

1 kiwi, peeled

1 frozen banana

1 cup orange juice

½ cup ice

BOOST IT: **1 to 2**
teaspoons aloe
vera juice

This bold blend of sassy citrus, exotic pineapple, soothing banana, and zesty kiwi is packed with vitamin C to get you glowing with vibrancy while crushing free radicals that can weigh you down as you detox and start anew.

DIRECTIONS: Combine all the ingredients in a blender and blend from low to high until frosty smooth.

CALORIES: 340, FAT: 2G, CARBS: 85G, PROTEIN: 5G, FIBER: 8G | VITAMIN A: 15%, CALCIUM: 8%, VITAMIN C: 465%, IRON: 8% | ALSO RICH IN POTASSIUM, MANGANESE, AND VITAMIN B$_6$.

26 sunburst watermelon

2 cups cubed
   watermelon

½ cup grapefruit juice
   or ½ grapefruit,
   peeled and
   segmented

½ cup frozen
   strawberries

½ cup coconut water
   ice cubes

2 teaspoons chamomile
   blossoms (optional)

Sweetener to taste
   (optional)

BOOST IT: **2 to 3 pinches**
of cayenne

Soothing chilled watermelon twirls with strawberries, grapefruit, and hydrating coconut water to leave you feeling refreshed and hydrated. Chamomile flowers add a boost of Zen. This light and frosty blend is the perfect sip for your detox phase.

DIRECTIONS: Combine all the ingredients in a blender and blend from low to high until frosty smooth.

CALORIES: 166, FAT: 1G, CARBS: 41G, PROTEIN: 3G, FIBER: 4G | VITAMIN A: 41%, CALCIUM: 7%, VITAMIN C: 153%, IRON: 9% | ALSO RICH IN POTASSIUM.

27 mango-carrot island

1 cup chopped fresh
 mango
½ cup grated carrot
¼ cup coconut water
½ cup frozen pineapple
 chunks
1 fresh or frozen banana
½ cup ice

BOOST IT: 1 teaspoon
unsweetened dried
coconut flakes

Sweet golden carrots and zingy pineapple swirl with juicy fresh mango and creamy banana in this antioxidant-rich smoothie to give you a golden, tropical glow. Vitamin A–rich carrots and mango are helpful in fighting free radicals so you feel and look your best during this detox phase.

DIRECTIONS: Combine all the ingredients in a blender and blend from low to high until frosty smooth.

CALORIES: 285, FAT: 1G, CARBS: 72G, PROTEIN: 4G, FIBER: 10G | VITAMIN A: 211%, CALCIUM: 7%, VITAMIN C: 163%, IRON: 6% | ALSO RICH IN MANGANESE, POTASSIUM, AND VITAMIN B$_6$.

28 purple power-up green smoothie

1 to 2 cups chopped
 purple kale leaves
½ cup plain soy milk
½ cup coconut water
½ cup frozen
 blueberries
½ cup frozen
 strawberries
1 banana
1 teaspoon açaí powder

BOOST IT: 1 teaspoon
chia seeds

Want to feel like a superhero? Flash into superpower mode with this purple blend of greens and berries, superhero fuel to nurture your body in this detox phase. If you can't find purple kale, it's fine to use green kale.

DIRECTIONS: Combine all the ingredients in a blender and blend from low to high until frosty smooth.

CALORIES: 328, FAT: 6G, CARBS: 65G, PROTEIN: 11G, FIBER: 11G | VITAMIN A: 424%, CALCIUM: 39%, VITAMIN C: 387%, IRON: 23% | ALSO RICH IN MAGNESIUM, MANGANESE, POTASSIUM, AND VITAMIN B$_6$.

29 carrot cake antioxidant

½ cup carrot juice

¼ cup vanilla soy milk

1 cup frozen peach
    chunks

1 frozen banana

1 tablespoon rolled oats

2 to 3 pinches of
    ground cinnamon

BOOST IT: 1 to 2
tablespoons soy yogurt

A hint of spice and nutty oats combine with bright carrot juice, peaches, and a frozen banana. Carrot juice, rich in the antioxidant vitamin A, is easier on the digestive system than eating a big pile of carrots, so carrot juice smoothies are perfect for your detox phase! Vitamin A infuses your body with each sip of this sweet carrot cake–flavored blend.

DIRECTIONS: Combine all the ingredients in a blender and blend from low to high until frosty smooth.

CALORIES: 238, FAT: 2G, CARBS: 5G, PROTEIN: 6G, FIBER: 8G | VITAMIN A: 199%, CALCIUM: 11%, VITAMIN C: 41%, IRON: 8% | ALSO RICH IN POTASSIUM AND VITAMIN B_6.

30 kale sunshine refresh

½ cup soy milk

½ cup orange juice

1½ cups chopped kale
    leaves

1 cup frozen mango
    chunks

1 fresh or frozen banana

½ cup ice

BOOST IT: 1 teaspoon
chia seeds

This sunny sweet green smoothie will brighten your day and refresh your body as you detox. Those antioxidant-rich kale greens twirl with tropical mango, banana, orange juice, and a bit of silky non-dairy milk. Use a frozen banana for a thicker blend.

DIRECTIONS: Combine all the ingredients in a blender and blend from low to high until frosty smooth.

CALORIES: 394, FAT: 3.3G, CARBS: 86G, PROTEIN: 10G, FIBER: 10G | VITAMIN A: 347%, CALCIUM: 33%, VITAMIN C: 401%, IRON: 16% | ALSO RICH IN MANGANESE, POTASSIUM, AND VITAMIN B_6.

31 green with energy

1 cup chopped kale
    leaves

1 cup chopped spinach

1 kiwi, peeled

½ cup green grapes

½ cup soy milk

1 banana

½ cup coconut water
    ice cubes

BOOST IT: 1 tablespoon
nut butter

"Don't be jealous of my super-charged energy."
That's what you'll be telling everyone as you roar
through your busy day fueled by sweet fruit and
vibrant greens. *Grrr.*

DIRECTIONS: Combine all the ingredients in a blender and
blend from low to high until frosty smooth.

CALORIES: 295, FAT: 4G, CARBS: 61G, PROTEIN: 10G,
FIBER: 10G | VITAMIN A: 271%, CALCIUM: 34%, VITAMIN C: 290%,
IRON: 20% | ALSO RICH IN MANGANESE, POTASSIUM, VITAMIN B$_6$,
AND RIBOFLAVIN.

32 citrus blitz

1 cup freshly squeezed
    orange juice, plus a
    pinch of orange zest

1 frozen banana

¾ cup frozen peach
    chunks or
    strawberries

½ cup ice

BOOST IT: a few pinches
of cayenne

This smoothie is an orange juice lover's dream.
Switch out your usual glass of OJ for this frosty,
zingy sip that will leave you buzzing with vitamin
C–powered pizzazz.

DIRECTIONS: Combine all the ingredients in a blender and
blend from low to high until frosty smooth.

CALORIES: 266, FAT: 1G, CARBS: 64G, PROTEIN: 4G, FIBER: 6G
| VITAMIN A: 20%, CALCIUM: 4%, VITAMIN C: 238%, IRON: 6%
| ALSO RICH IN POTASSIUM AND VITAMIN B$_6$.

33 g's chocolate espresso frosty

1 shot espresso, or ¼ cup strong brewed and cooled coffee, or 2 teaspoons instant coffee granules

1 cup vanilla soy milk

1 tablespoon raw cacao powder

2 teaspoons raw cacao nibs (optional)

1 cup ice

Sweetener to taste

Ground cinnamon to taste

BOOST IT: 1 banana

This blend is for all you espresso lovers out there—like my cappuccino-craving husband. This is your vegan answer to a frosty espresso-infused blended beverage. Go ahead, enjoy your mocha-flavored espresso buzz—luckily, cacao and coffee contain antioxidants!

DIRECTIONS: Combine all the ingredients in a blender and blend from low to high until frosty smooth.

CALORIES: 193, FAT: 5G, CARBS: 27G, PROTEIN: 9G, FIBER: 4G | VITAMIN A: 10%, CALCIUM: 33%, VITAMIN C: 0%, IRON: 13% | ALSO RICH IN RIBOFLAVIN.

34 green glow energizer slush

2 cups frozen green grapes

½ banana

1 teaspoon freshly squeezed lime or lemon juice

½ cup ice

½ cup coconut water

BOOST IT: ½ teaspoon spirulina powder

Forget those fluorescent-colored icy drinks—this frosty green grape slush is brimming with sweet fruity flavors and energy-boosting carbohydrates.

DIRECTIONS: Combine the grapes, banana, citrus juice, and ice in a blender and blend, starting on low. Slowly add the coconut water, increasing the speed to high until a slushy texture is created.

CALORIES: 277, FAT: 1G, CARBS: 78G, PROTEIN: 6G, FIBER: 7G | VITAMIN A: 4%, CALCIUM: 3%, VITAMIN C: 41%, IRON: 3% | ALSO RICH IN POTASSIUM.

35 pistachio power-up shake

¼ cup raw shelled
   pistachios, soaked if
   you like

1 frozen banana

2 tablespoons mashed
   avocado

1 cup vanilla soy milk

2 teaspoons agave
   syrup, or to taste

Pinch of salt

½ cup ice

BOOST IT: 1 to 2
teaspoons matcha
powder

Pistachios, banana, and creamy avocado blend into this energizing shake that tastes like dessert! This combination of healthy fats, protein, and carbs means you will prolong your pistachio-powered energy boost.

DIRECTIONS: Combine all the ingredients in a blender and blend from low to high until frosty smooth.

CALORIES: 425, FAT: 19G, CARBS: 56G, PROTEIN: 14G, FIBER: 9G | VITAMIN A: 16%, CALCIUM: 35%, VITAMIN C: 23%, IRON: 16% | ALSO RICH IN VITAMIN B$_6$.

36 "c" you before sunrise

1 orange, peeled and
   segmented, plus
   ½ cup water, or
   ¾ cup orange juice

1 kiwi, peeled

½ cup frozen peach
   chunks

½ cup frozen mango
   chunks

1 banana

½ cup coconut water
   ice cubes

BOOST IT: 1 teaspoon
chia seeds

I like to think of myself as a morning person—but sometimes even early risers need help energizing their a.m. This frosty citrus, kiwi, banana, mango, peach smoothie makes it easy to rise and shine. Plus, its golden color mirrors the rising sun. Cheers to a new day—fueled by fruit!

DIRECTIONS: Combine all the ingredients in a blender and blend from low to high until frosty smooth.

CALORIES: 347, FAT: 2G, CARBS: 86G, PROTEIN: 6G, FIBER: 14G | VITAMIN A: 29%, CALCIUM: 15%, VITAMIN C: 350%, IRON: 8% | ALSO RICH IN POTASSIUM AND VITAMIN B$_6$.

37 triple-berry boost

1 cup vanilla soy milk

⅓ cup frozen or fresh
blueberries

⅓ cup frozen or fresh
raspberries

⅓ cup frozen or fresh
strawberries

½ fresh or frozen
banana

¼ cup coconut water
ice cubes

Drizzle of agave syrup
or maple syrup
(optional)

Boost your day with a triple shot of one of nature's
most prized, most energy-building superfoods:
colorful, sweet berries! This creamy pink smoothie
is for the berry lover in all of us.

DIRECTIONS: Combine all the ingredients in a blender and
blend from low to high until frosty smooth.

BOOST IT: ½ **teaspoon spirulina**

CALORIES: 287, FAT: 4G, CARBS: 58G, PROTEIN: 9G,
FIBER: 9G | VITAMIN A: 12%, CALCIUM: 34%, VITAMIN C: 72%,
IRON: 7%

38 açaí awakener shake

¾ cup açaí juice (or
substitute plain
soy milk with
2 tablespoons açaí
powder or an açaí
smoothie pack)

½ cup vanilla soy milk

1 frozen banana

½ cup frozen
blueberries

½ cup frozen
raspberries (or
substitute additional
blueberries)

¼ cup ice

It took me a while to figure out how to pronounce
the name of the deep purple berry açaí: AH-sigh-ee.
But it didn't take me long to learn that I loved it! One
sip of this berry, banana, soy smoothie and I was
hooked. Açaí smoothie craving: satisfied! Each
antioxidant-rich sip helps you fight free radicals that
can make you feel worn down.

DIRECTIONS: Combine all the ingredients in a blender and
blend from low to high until frosty smooth.

BOOST IT: **2 pinches of cayenne**

CALORIES: 384, FAT: 7G, CARBS: 80G, PROTEIN: 7G,
FIBER: 8G | VITAMIN A: 20%, CALCIUM: 19%,
VITAMIN C: 73%, IRON: 6%

39 get up and "goji"

1 tablespoon goji
   berries
¾ cup orange juice
½ cup frozen
   strawberries
¼ cup frozen pineapple
   chunks
1 banana
½ cup coconut water
   ice cubes

BOOST IT: **1 to 2
teaspoons shredded
coconut**

Island daydreams, how I love you. Thank goodness for tropical ingredient smoothies that have the magical ability to transport my mind to a less stressful place—sip by sip. Pink goji berries help energize your spirit when blended with sunny orange juice, island coconut, pineapple, and strawberries. Where's my beach towel? Take a sun snooze and then get up and goji!

DIRECTIONS: Combine the goji berries and orange juice in a blender and soak for at least 5 minutes to hydrate and soften the berries. Add the remaining ingredients to the blender and blend until frosty smooth.

CALORIES: 296, FAT: 3G, CARBS: 67G, PROTEIN: 4G, FIBER: 8G | VITAMIN A: 43%, CALCIUM: 9%, VITAMIN C: 257%, IRON: 12% | ALSO RICH IN MANGANESE, POTASSIUM, AND VITAMIN B$_6$.

40 mocha motivation

1 tablespoon raw cacao
   powder
1½ frozen bananas
1¼ cups vanilla soy milk
2 to 3 pinches of
   ground cinnamon
Sweetener to taste
½ cup coffee ice cubes

BOOST IT: **1 teaspoon
maca powder**

This energizing blend of cacao, banana, coffee ice cubes, and soy milk is filled with mocha flavor. Optional maca is a superfood known for inspiring energy; it has a malt-like flavor to give a chocolate-malt accent to each sip. You can substitute plain ice plus 1 teaspoon instant coffee granules for the coffee ice cubes if you don't have them on hand.

DIRECTIONS: Combine all the ingredients in a blender and blend from low to high until frosty smooth.

CALORIES: 302, FAT: 7G, CARBS: 54G, PROTEIN: 12G, FIBER: 8G | VITAMIN A: 15%, CALCIUM: 41%, VITAMIN C: 26%, IRON: 13%

41 raspberry runner's high

1 cup frozen raspberries

1 frozen banana

1 cup vanilla soy milk

¼ cup coconut water ice cubes

2 teaspoons agave syrup, or to taste

BOOST IT: **2 tablespoons vanilla soy yogurt**

Don't you love how food tastes better after a workout? Especially smoothies! This creamy sweet blend of protein-rich soy milk, fiber-rich raspberries, and potassium-rich banana and coconut water makes for a refreshing post-run sip. Refuel after you work out so that your energy doesn't crash later on in the day.

DIRECTIONS: Combine all the ingredients in a blender and blend from low to high until frosty smooth.

CALORIES: 313, FAT: 5G, CARBS: 64G, PROTEIN: 11G, FIBER: 13G | VITAMIN A: 12%, CALCIUM: 35%, VITAMIN C: 73%, IRON: 8%

42 hazelnut mocha shake

¼ cup raw hazelnuts

1 cup vanilla soy milk

1 tablespoon raw cacao powder

1 to 2 teaspoons instant coffee granules or 1 shot espresso

1 tablespoon agave syrup, or to taste

3 to 5 pinches of ground cinnamon

½ frozen banana

1 cup ice

BOOST IT: **1 tablespoon raw cacao nibs**

This nutty blend of crunchy hazelnuts, rich cacao, and creamy soy milk is a tempting way to energize your day. Hazelnuts contain iron, which nurtures your natural energy. Add a teaspoon of cacao nibs for a mocha-chip accent.

DIRECTIONS: Combine all the ingredients in a blender and blend from low to high until frosty smooth.

CALORIES: 352, FAT: 16G, CARBS: 50G, PROTEIN: 12G, FIBER: 7G | VITAMIN A: 11%, CALCIUM: 34%, VITAMIN C: 13%, IRON: 10%

43 super-c kiwi kick-start smoothie

3 kiwis, peeled
½ frozen banana
½ cup orange juice
½ cup frozen
  strawberries
½ cup coconut water
  ice cubes

BOOST IT: 1 teaspoon
unsweetened dried
coconut flakes

Super-C your busy day with this vibrant blend of vitamin C–rich kiwis, sunny orange juice, sweet strawberries, and energizing banana. Vitamin C is a powerful free-radical-fighting antioxidant, which is a good thing, as free radicals can zap your precious natural energy. Load up on "C" to kick-start your day.

DIRECTIONS: Combine all the ingredients in a blender and blend from low to high until frosty smooth.

CALORIES: 293, FAT: 2G, CARBS: 69G, PROTEIN: 6G, FIBER: 12G | VITAMIN A: 10%, CALCIUM: 13%, VITAMIN C: 540%, IRON: 10% | ALSO RICH IN POTASSIUM.

44 fresh strawberry-matcha morning

1 cup frozen
  strawberries
½ frozen banana
¾ cup vanilla soy milk
½ cup ice
½ cup fresh
  strawberries
½ to 1 teaspoon matcha
  powder
1 teaspoon agave syrup
  (optional)

BOOST IT: ⅛ teaspoon
grated fresh ginger or a
few pinches of cayenne

Green tea is well known for infusing us with energy and antioxidants. This matcha shake has a craveable tea-meets-berry flavor with a base of creamy soy milk and energizing banana.

DIRECTIONS: Combine the frozen strawberries, banana, soy milk, and ice in a blender and blend from low to high until smooth. Add the fresh strawberries, matcha powder, and agave and lightly blend until frosty smooth.

CALORIES: 228, FAT: 4G, CARBS: 46G, PROTEIN: 9G, FIBER: 8G | VITAMIN A: 9%, CALCIUM: 27%, VITAMIN C: 224%, IRON: 7%

45 dancing blackberry

1¼ cups fresh or frozen blackberries

1¼ cups vanilla soy milk

1 fresh or frozen banana

2 tablespoons raw walnuts

½ cup ice

BOOST IT: **1 tablespoon chopped fresh mint**

You'll be in a dancing mood after drinking this simple, sweet blackberry shake, swirled with creamy banana and nutty walnuts. Why, you ask? Well, blackberries are rich in vibrant antioxidants to help reduce inflammation, fight energy-zapping free radicals, and fill you with fiber to make you feel good. And feeling good usually means having more energy. And anyone feeling a burst of energy should really just get up and dance! Use frozen blackberries for a frostier blend.

DIRECTIONS: Combine all the ingredients in a blender and blend from low to high until frosty smooth.

CALORIES: 425, FAT: 15G, CARBS: 61G, PROTEIN: 16G, FIBER: 15G | VITAMIN A: 22%, CALCIUM: 45%, VITAMIN C: 81%, IRON: 18%

46 jazzy ginger grape

1½ cups fresh or frozen green grapes

1 cup chopped spinach

¾ cup coconut water

½ teaspoon grated fresh ginger

½ cup ice

BOOST IT: **a few pinches of cayenne**

Energizing green grapes and spicy ginger blend with cool coconut water and superfood spinach for a frosty sip that is yours to crave. If you're using fresh rather than frozen grapes, add some extra ice.

DIRECTIONS: Combine all the ingredients in a blender and blend from low to high until frosty smooth.

CALORIES: 167, FAT: 1G, CARBS: 39G, PROTEIN: 4G, FIBER: 15G | VITAMIN A: 60%, CALCIUM: 12%, VITAMIN C: 35%, IRON: 12% | ALSO RICH IN MAGNESIUM, MANGANESE, AND THIAMINE.

47 green kiwi glow

½ cup coconut water

2 kiwis, peeled

1 banana

1 to 2 cups chopped spinach

2 tablespoons fresh lemon juice

½ cup ice

Maple syrup to taste (optional)

BOOST IT: 1 teaspoon flax oil

Vitamin C–rich kiwi, lemon, spinach, and banana blend into this silky green sip that will have everyone asking, "What gave you that energized glow today?" Your energy smoothie of course! Add some flax oil for a boost of healthy omega-3 fatty acids.

DIRECTIONS: Combine all the ingredients in a blender and blend from low to high until frosty smooth.

CALORIES: 242, FAT: 2G, CARBS: 58G, PROTEIN: 6G, FIBER: 10G | VITAMIN A: 117%, CALCIUM: 15%, VITAMIN C: 308%, IRON: 15% | ALSO RICH IN MANGANESE AND POTASSIUM.

48 secret-ingredient matcha shake

1 cup vanilla soy milk

1 frozen banana

1½ cups frozen watermelon chunks, or more for a frostier shake

1 to 2 teaspoons matcha powder

BOOST IT: 1 teaspoon chia seeds

I discovered this shake by accident when I was blending a matcha soy shake and realized I was out of ice. I subbed some frozen watermelon and realized my shake tasted better than ever! The pastel green color tricks you because the flavor is deliciously pure pink.

DIRECTIONS: Combine all the ingredients in a blender and blend from low to high until frosty smooth.

CALORIES: 273, FAT: 5G, CARBS: 52G, PROTEIN: 10G, FIBER: 5G | VITAMIN A: 37%, CALCIUM: 32%, VITAMIN C: 48%, IRON: 11% | ALSO RICH IN RIBOFLAVIN AND POTASSIUM.

Secret-Ingredient Matcha Shake

49 pomegranate power-up

1 cup pomegranate
  juice
¼ cup plain soy yogurt
1 cup frozen blueberries
1 fresh or frozen banana
½ cup ice

BOOST IT: **splash of
soy milk**

Pomegranate juice is rich in antioxidants in the form of phytochemicals called polyphenols. It is also rich in energizing carbohydrates. This purple smoothie blended with frosty berries, creamy soy yogurt, and potassium-rich banana is a pom-tastic way to power up your day.

DIRECTIONS: Combine all the ingredients in a blender and blend from low to high until frosty smooth.

CALORIES: 382, FAT: 2G, CARBS: 92G, PROTEIN: 4G, FIBER: 7G | VITAMIN A: 3%, CALCIUM: 13%, VITAMIN C: 41%, IRON: 6%

50 mango-citrus-chard charger

1 cup chopped Swiss
  chard leaves
½ cup coconut water
1 frozen peeled and
  segmented orange
½ cup fresh mango
  chunks
1 banana
½ cup soy milk
½ cup ice

BOOST IT: **1 teaspoon
maple syrup**

Charge forward with this chard, mango, citrus green smoothie. Superfood greens like chard help you fight free radicals that can zap your energy.

DIRECTIONS: Combine the chard and coconut water in a blender and blend from low to high until smooth. Add the remaining ingredients and blend until frosty smooth.

CALORIES: 325, FAT: 3G, CARBS: 72G, PROTEIN: 9G, FIBER: 12G | VITAMIN A: 71%, CALCIUM: 28%, VITAMIN C: 241%, IRON: 12% | ALSO RICH IN MAGNESIUM, POTASSIUM, AND VITAMINS K AND B$_6$.

Almond Butter Morning Shake

51 almond butter morning shake

1 cup vanilla soy milk

1 tablespoon rolled oats

1½ frozen bananas

1½ tablespoons almond butter

2 teaspoons maple syrup

A few pinches of ground cinnamon, nutmeg, and cayenne

¼ cup ice

BOOST IT: **1 teaspoon chia seeds**

This creamy and frosty banana–almond butter shake with accents of maple syrup, cinnamon, and oats is the chilled-out way to energize your day. A balanced blend of protein, fat, and complex carbohydrates will help you prolong your energy burst.

DIRECTIONS: Combine the soy milk and oats in a blender and soak until softened, about five minutes. Add the remaining ingredients and blend from low to high until frosty smooth.

CALORIES: 464, FAT: 19G, CARBS: 65G, PROTEIN: 13G, FIBER: 7G | VITAMIN A: 12%, CALCIUM: 39%, VITAMIN C: 26%, IRON: 16% | ALSO RICH IN MANGANESE.

52 pineapple pizzazz

1 cup fresh pineapple chunks

1 cup frozen cantaloupe chunks

1 fresh or frozen banana

½ cup orange juice

½ cup coconut water ice cubes

BOOST IT: **splash of coconut milk or one tablespoon of unsweetened dried coconut flakes**

For a boost of bromelain and potassium, try this frothy-fresh pineapple, melon, citrus smoothie. It's a taste of the tropics in every sweet sunshine sip, and rich in antioxidants to fight free radicals and reduce body inflammation that can zap your natural energy!

DIRECTIONS: Combine all the ingredients in a blender and blend from low to high until frosty smooth.

CALORIES: 314, FAT: 1G, CARBS: 77G, PROTEIN: 5G, FIBER: 8G | VITAMIN A: 114%, CALCIUM: 8%, VITAMIN C: 344%, IRON: 9% | ALSO RICH IN MANGANESE, POTASSIUM, AND VITAMIN B_6.

53 citrus-aloe thirst quencher

1½ cups coconut water

1 teaspoon aloe vera juice

1 tablespoon fresh lime juice, plus a pinch of zest

1 tablespoon fresh lemon juice, plus a pinch of zest

1 tablespoon agave syrup, or to taste

¾ cup coconut water ice cubes

BOOST IT: **1 teaspoon chopped fresh mint leaves**

It's hot. You're parched. Your energy is dipping and you need something cool and invigorating to gulp down—fast! Guzzle this ultra-hydrating lemon-lime coconut water–based frosty with a nice dose of aloe.

DIRECTIONS: Combine all the ingredients in a blender and blend from low to high until frosty smooth.

CALORIES: 175, FAT: 1G, CARBS: 39G, PROTEIN: 4G, FIBER: 6G | VITAMIN A: 2%, CALCIUM: 14%, VITAMIN C: 41%, IRON: 11% | ALSO RICH IN POTASSIUM.

54 mango-matcha mixer

1 cup soy milk

¾ cup frozen mango chunks

1 teaspoon matcha powder

1 banana

½ cup frozen orange slices

½ cup ice

BOOST IT: **Substitute coconut water for half of the soy milk**

If you crave a hint of caffeine, mix it up with matcha! Citrus and mango accent this creamy sweet green tea shake. Matcha not only provides a slow release of green tea–fueled Zen-ergy but also helps neutralize free radicals that can make you feel tired and worn down.

DIRECTIONS: Combine all the ingredients in a blender and blend from low to high until frosty smooth.

CALORIES: 328, FAT: 5G, CARBS: 67G, PROTEIN: 10G, FIBER: 9G | VITAMIN A: 34%, CALCIUM: 36%, VITAMIN C: 154%, IRON: 9%

Coffee-Banana Freeze

55 coffee-banana freeze

1 cup vanilla soy milk

1 scoop instant coffee granules (or shot of espresso or strong coffee)

1 or 2 frozen bananas

Agave syrup to taste

4 to 5 pinches of ground cinnamon

½ to ¾ cup ice

BOOST IT: 1 to 3 teaspoons raw cacao nibs or cacao powder for topping

This frosty coffee-banana blend is perfect for a caffeinated energy boost. Top with some rich cacao nibs or cacao powder to make it a mocha. Use chilled espresso for a cooler sip, and use the two bananas and the lesser amount of ice for a creamier blend.

DIRECTIONS: Combine all the ingredients in a blender and blend from low to high until frosty smooth.

CALORIES: 259, FAT: 5G, CARBS: 48G, PROTEIN: 9G, FIBER: 5G | VITAMIN A: 12%, CALCIUM: 33%, VITAMIN C: 17%, IRON: 9%

56 mega mango morning shake

1 cup vanilla soy milk

2 tablespoons rolled oats

1 cup fresh or frozen mango chunks

1 frozen banana

1 tablespoon raw walnuts

2 to 4 pinches of ground cinnamon

Pinch of salt

½ cup ice

BOOST IT: maple syrup or agave syrup to taste

Sweet mango blends with creamy soy milk, buttery walnuts, and tender rolled oats here. Blend this shake when you are craving oatmeal but can't stand the heat. The complex carbohydrates in rolled oats help you stay energized all through your morning. Adding monounsaturated fats, like those found in walnuts, further prolongs your smoothie energy buzz by slowing down the release of energy. Slow and steady wins the race.

DIRECTIONS: Combine the soy milk and oats in a blender and soak until the oats are softened, about five minutes. Add the remaining ingredients and blend until frosty smooth.

CALORIES: 423, FAT: 10G, CARBS: 75G, PROTEIN: 13G, FIBER: 10G | VITAMIN A: 37%, CALCIUM: 37%, VITAMIN C: 98%, IRON: 15%

57 sweet green kale glow

1½ cups chopped kale leaves

1 banana

½ cup chopped fresh pear

½ cup frozen peeled and segmented orange

½ cup soy milk

1 teaspoon grated fresh ginger

½ cup ice

BOOST IT: **1 tablespoon sunflower seeds**

Frosty frozen citrus boosts your spirit, superfood kale revs up your body, and spicy ginger puts some bounce in your step. Sip this spirited combo for an energized glow, and add some sunflower seeds for an extra boost of energy-helping iron and minerals.

DIRECTIONS: Combine all the ingredients in a blender and blend from low to high until frosty smooth.

CALORIES: 294, FAT: 3G, CARBS: 64G, PROTEIN: 9G, FIBER: 10G | VITAMIN A: 320%, CALCIUM: 34%, VITAMIN C: 304%, IRON: 16% | ALSO RICH IN POTASSIUM, MANGANESE, AND VITAMIN B$_6$.

58 cashew-hemp energy shake

¼ cup raw cashews, soaked and drained

1 tablespoon hemp seeds

1 teaspoon rolled oats

1¼ cups water

2 teaspoons maple syrup

1½ frozen bananas

A few pinches of ground cinnamon

¼ cup ice

Pinch of salt

Get energized with this cool, creamy, frothy energy milk made from sweet bananas, cashews, protein-rich hemp seeds, and cozy cinnamon. Cashews contain iron, which can help you stay energized.

DIRECTIONS: In a blender, combine the cashews, hemp seeds, oats, and water and blend from low to high until creamy and opaque. Add the remaining ingredients and blend from low to high until frosty smooth.

BOOST IT: **a few pinches of cayenne and/or ginger powder**

CALORIES: 404, FAT: 16G, CARBS: 59G, PROTEIN: 10G, FIBER: 6G | VITAMIN A: 2%, CALCIUM: 3%, VITAMIN C: 26%, IRON: 9%

59 green zen-ergy matcha shake

1 tablespoon matcha powder

1 cup vanilla rice milk

1 to 2 cups chopped spinach

2 frozen bananas

¼ cup ice

Sweetener of choice to taste (optional)

BOOST IT: **Substitute ½ cup frozen watermelon chunks for ½ banana**

Light and creamy rice milk blends with Zen-ergizing matcha and superfood spinach. Add a couple of frozen bananas and your frosty, creamy, feel-good shake is served!

DIRECTIONS: Combine the matcha, rice milk, and spinach in a blender and blend until smooth. Add the bananas, ice, and sweetener, if using, and blend until thick and creamy.

CALORIES: 346, FAT: 3G, CARBS: 80G, PROTEIN: 6G, FIBER: 9G | VITAMIN A: 92%, CALCIUM: 9%, VITAMIN C: 60%, IRON: 16% | ALSO RICH IN MANGANESE AND VITAMIN B$_6$.

60 the green-ergizer

1 kiwi, peeled

1 fresh or frozen banana

1 cup chopped kale leaves

1 cup chopped spinach

1 small orange or tangerine, peeled (frozen for a frostier blend)

½ cup plain soy milk

½ cup cold water or coconut water, or more if needed

½ cup ice (optional)

BOOST IT: **½ teaspoon spirulina powder**

Running on empty? Refuel with the power of this nutrient-dense superfood green cooler. Get green-ergized!

DIRECTIONS: Combine all the ingredients in a blender and blend from low to high until frosty smooth.

CALORIES: 290, FAT: 4G, CARBS: 61G, PROTEIN: 10G, FIBER: 11G | VITAMIN A: 303%, CALCIUM: 36%, VITAMIN C: 375%, IRON: 20% | ALSO RICH IN RIBOFLAVIN, POTASSIUM, VITAMIN B$_6$, MAGNESIUM, AND MANGANESE.

61 pineapple-berry bounce

½ **avocado**

½ **cup frozen blueberries**

1 **banana**

¾ **cup fresh pineapple chunks**

½ **to 1 cup coconut water**

½ **cup ice (optional)**

BOOST IT: 1 **handful of spinach or kale to green things up**

Poor digestion can easily zap your energy. Bromelain-rich pineapple to the rescue! We'll toss in some sweet blueberries, banana, and avocado too. This smoothie blends up frothy and inviting. You will be glowing with energy after just one sip!

DIRECTIONS: Combine all the ingredients in a blender and blend from low to high until frosty smooth.

CALORIES: 388, FAT: 15G, CARBS: 65G, PROTEIN: 6G, FIBER: 15G | VITAMIN A: 7%, CALCIUM: 7%, VITAMIN C: 143%, IRON: 10% | ALSO RICH IN MANGANESE, POTASSIUM, AND VITAMIN B$_6$.

Watermelon Frosty

Note: If some of these smoothies seem a bit rich in calories to be a "snack" or side-dish smoothie, you are right. The smoothies that range in calories above 300 per smoothie are meant to be meal replacements. These nutrient-rich blends will fill you up and keep you energized through your busy day.

62 watermelon frosty

2 cups frozen watermelon chunks

2 tablespoons fresh lime juice

½ banana

1 teaspoon maple syrup or agave syrup

½ to 1 cup coconut water

BOOST IT: **2 to 4 pinches of cayenne**

Stay in a skinny mood by sipping on this frosty pink blend of watermelon, lime, banana, and coconut water. Add some cayenne to heat things up; spicy foods like cayenne may even boost your metabolism.

DIRECTIONS: Combine the watermelon, lime juice, banana, maple or agave syrup, and ½ cup coconut water in a blender. Turn the blender to low and get things moving, using a blender plunger (like a Vitamix tamper) if needed. Slowly add more coconut water and blend, increasing the speed to high, until the mixture blends into thick, frosty bliss.

CALORIES: 201, FAT: 1G, CARBS: 49G, PROTEIN: 5G, FIBER: 6G | VITAMIN A: 44%, CALCIUM: 10%, VITAMIN C: 76%, IRON: 13% | ALSO RICH IN POTASSIUM AND VITAMIN B$_6$.

63 skinny purple berry

¾ cup silken tofu

½ cup vanilla soy milk

1 frozen banana

½ cup fresh
blackberries

1 teaspoon maple syrup

Pinch of salt, or to taste

¼ cup ice

BOOST IT: **1 teaspoon
açaí powder**

This satisfying, protein-rich, silken tofu and deep purple berry blend is the skinny way to fuel your day. It makes an excellent meal replacement smoothie. The salt is there to counter the blandness of the tofu.

DIRECTIONS: Combine all the ingredients in a blender and blend from low to high until frosty smooth.

CALORIES: 357, FAT: 10G, CARBS: 48G, PROTEIN: 22G, FIBER: 8G | VITAMIN A: 12%, CALCIUM: 26%, VITAMIN C: 52%, IRON: 21%

64 frozen orange bliss

1½ cups frozen orange
slices

½ cup soy milk

1 banana

BOOST IT: **2 to 3
tablespoons freshly
squeezed orange juice,
plus a pinch of grated
zest**

I tried to get all creative on this smoothie name, but the only thing that came to me when sipping this frosty, creamy orange-banana smoothie is exactly what it is: frozen orange bliss. A bit of soy milk makes things creamy. This simple smoothie is rich in fruit fiber, using whole oranges instead of juice to help curb your appetite.

DIRECTIONS: Combine all the ingredients in a blender and blend from low to high until frosty smooth.

CALORIES: 276, FAT: 3G, CARBS: 62G, PROTEIN: 7G, FIBER: 9G | VITAMIN A: 19%, CALCIUM: 26%, VITAMIN C: 261%, IRON: 8%

Frozen Orange Bliss

65 grapefruit-berry-lime twirl

1 cup pink grapefruit
  juice

1 cup frozen
  strawberries

½ frozen banana

1 tablespoon fresh lime
  juice, plus a pinch of
  grated zest

1 tablespoon chopped
  fresh mint leaves
  (optional)

½ cup ice (optional)

BOOST IT: 2 to 3
tablespoons soy yogurt

Pink grapefruit juice, rich in the free-radical-fighting antioxidant vitamins A and C, twirls with frosty strawberries and sunny lime juice for a drink that is a pure delight. Grapefruit is a classic slim-down food, so embrace your fondness for it by sipping this perky sweet blend.

DIRECTIONS: Combine all the ingredients in a blender and blend from low to high until frosty smooth.

CALORIES: 222, FAT: 1G, CARBS: 57G, PROTEIN: 4G, FIBER: 17G
| VITAMIN A: 31%, CALCIUM: 7%, VITAMIN C: 377%, IRON: 4%
| ALSO RICH IN POTASSIUM AND MANGANESE.

66 peanut butter–banana swirl shake

2 frozen bananas

2 heaping tablespoons
  peanut butter

½ cup vanilla soy milk

1 tablespoon maple
  syrup

Dash of ground
  cinnamon

BOOST IT: 1 teaspoon raw
cacao nibs

Don't do a double take. Yes, this peanut butter–banana smoothie (that tastes like a peanut butter milkshake) is here to help you slim down. How? Blend this shake when you crave a decadent dessert treat. Indulge your craving and feel good about it. Tip: Using room-temperature or slightly warmed peanut butter will help facilitate blending.

DIRECTIONS: Combine all the ingredients in a blender and blend from low to high until frosty smooth.

CALORIES: 512, FAT: 19G, CARBS: 77G, PROTEIN: 16G, FIBER: 9G
| VITAMIN A: 3%, CALCIUM: 18%, VITAMIN C: 34%, IRON: 12%
| ALSO RICH IN MANGANESE AND POTASSIUM.

67 green island cooler

½ to 1 cup coconut water

1 cup chopped fresh or frozen cucumber

½ cup frozen pineapple chunks

1 tablespoon fresh lime juice, plus a pinch of grated zest

1 tablespoon chopped fresh mint leaves

2 teaspoons maple syrup or agave syrup (optional)

½ cup ice

BOOST IT: ½ frozen banana

For some people, stress contributes to unwanted weight gain. So learning how to chill out is a smart way to maintain or reach your body weight goals. This tropical green drink can help. One sip of this low-calorie cucumber, pineapple, lime, and mint cooler and you will be swept away. Not even a sweltering glow of sunshine could interrupt your chilled-out mood from sipping this lime green blend. Hydrate, refresh, chill, and easily reach your slim-down goals.

DIRECTIONS: Combine all the ingredients in a blender and blend from low to high until frosty smooth. Start with ½ cup coconut water and add more for a thinner blend.

CALORIES: 124, FAT: 0G, CARBS: 29G, PROTEIN: 3G, FIBER: 5G | VITAMIN A: 8%, CALCIUM: 10%, VITAMIN C: 85%, IRON: 11% | ALSO RICH IN MAGNESIUM, MANGANESE, AND POTASSIUM.

68 minted melon citrus frosty

1 cup coconut water (use less for a frostier blend)

1 cup frozen watermelon chunks

1 frozen banana

1 small orange, peeled and segmented

1 tablespoon fresh lime juice

1 tablespoon chopped fresh mint leaves

½ cup ice

Mint, frozen melon, and citrus craft a chilled-out glow of frosty green bliss. Watermelon (and melon in general) is hydrating, rich in potassium, and low in calories for slim-sipping.

DIRECTIONS: Combine all the ingredients in a blender and blend from low to high until frosty smooth.

BOOST IT: 1 teaspoon aloe vera juice

CALORIES: 289, FAT: 1G, CARBS: 70G, PROTEIN: 6G, FIBER: 11G | VITAMIN A: 32%, CALCIUM: 16%, VITAMIN C: 219%, IRON: 12% | ALSO RICH IN POTASSIUM.

69 skinny vanilla retreat

½ cup vanilla soy milk

1 heaping scoop vanilla vegan protein powder

1 cup frozen watermelon chunks

1 frozen banana

¼ teaspoon ground cinnamon

BOOST IT: **2 to 3 tablespoons vanilla soy milk**

Escape the day with this protein-rich vanilla smoothie with an accent of warming cinnamon—it tastes as thick and creamy as a cool milkshake. But this version is low in fat and calories. Frozen mildly sweet melon gives a super-frosty texture.

DIRECTIONS: Combine the soy milk and protein powder in a blender and blend from low to high until smooth. Add the remaining ingredients and blend from low to high until frosty smooth.

CALORIES: 282, FAT: 2G, CARBS: 42G, PROTEIN: 27G, FIBER: 5G
| VITAMIN A: 22%, CALCIUM: 17%, VITAMIN C: 30%, IRON: 7%

70 spicy lime-mango motivation

1½ cups fresh mango chunks

½ frozen banana

2 to 3 tablespoons fresh lime juice

½ cup coconut water

A few pinches of cayenne

½ cup ice

BOOST IT: **splash of coconut milk**

You are on a mission to improve your body, and this juicy, spicy, citrus mango shake is here to help. Vibrant mango twirls with cool coconut water, frozen banana, and ice, and cayenne may help speed up metabolism.

DIRECTIONS: Combine all the ingredients except the ice in a blender and blend from low to high until smooth and thick. Add the ice and blend until you reach a consistency you like.

CALORIES: 244, FAT: 1G, CARBS: 62G, PROTEIN: 3G, FIBER: 7G
| VITAMIN A: 39%, CALCIUM: 6%, VITAMIN C: 143%, IRON: 5%
| ALSO RICH IN POTASSIUM.

71 lean green tangerine

1 cup frozen peeled
   tangerine segments
1½ cups chopped kale
   leaves
1 fresh or frozen banana
1 cup coconut water

BOOST IT: **a few pinches
of cayenne**

Superfood kale leads the way in this lean, mean, tangerine green smoothie. Kale and tangerine segments are rich in fiber to help fill you up, with nutrients like vitamin A and potassium to nurture your body. If you are cutting back on calories, you still want to make sure your body is getting the nutrients it needs: Superfoods like kale can help boost your nutrition goals as you slim down.

DIRECTIONS: Combine all the ingredients in a blender and blend from low to high until frosty smooth.

CALORIES: 293, FAT: 2G, CARBS: 69G, PROTEIN: 8G, FIBER: 10G | VITAMIN A: 353%, CALCIUM: 23%, VITAMIN C: 370%, IRON: 19% | ALSO RICH IN MAGNESIUM, MANGANESE, AND POTASSIUM.

72 peach-raspberry rice shimmy shake

1 cup sliced fresh
   peaches
½ cup frozen
   raspberries
1 frozen banana
½ cup vanilla rice milk
½ cup ice

BOOST IT: **2 to 3
tablespoons non-dairy
yogurt**

Fresh seasonal peaches, fuzzy and sweet, swirl with rice milk and frozen raspberries here. This uplifting, light fruity blend will make you want to shimmy and shake your awesome self to help you burn a few extra calories.

DIRECTIONS: Combine all the ingredients in a blender and blend from low to high until frosty smooth.

CALORIES: 263, FAT: 2G, CARBS: 62G, PROTEIN: 4G, FIBER: 10G | VITAMIN A: 13%, CALCIUM: 4%, VITAMIN C: 64%, IRON: 8% | ALSO RICH IN MANGANESE.

73 sweet peach sunshine

1 cup frozen peach
chunks

¼ cup frozen
strawberries

1 banana

½ cup orange juice

½ cup water

½ cup ice

BOOST IT: **1 teaspoon
chia seeds**

Cool, low-calorie peaches swirl with frosty ruby strawberries and creamy banana in this zingy oasis of fruit. Low in fat and calories, vibrant with flavor: smoothie heaven.

DIRECTIONS: Combine all the ingredients in a blender and blend from low to high until frosty smooth.

CALORIES: 240, FAT: 1G, CARBS: 59G, PROTEIN: 4G, FIBER: 7G | VITAMIN A: 18%, CALCIUM: 4%, VITAMIN C: 162%, IRON: 7% | ALSO RICH IN POTASSIUM AND VITAMIN B$_6$.

74 frozen raspberry lemonade

¾ cup water

3 tablespoons fresh
lemon juice

2 tablespoons agave
syrup or maple syrup

1 cup frozen raspberries

½ cup ice (optional)

BOOST IT: **½ fresh or
frozen banana**

This raspberry lemonade blends into a frosty, frozen, low-calorie treat. Raspberries are rich in fiber and vitamin C to both fill you up and fight free radicals. If you don't have time to make your own lemonade, substitute 1 cup store-bought lemonade; you can also substitute calorie-free stevia to taste in the recipe here for a no-sugar-added lemonade.

DIRECTIONS: To make the lemonade, combine the water, lemon juice, and agave (you can combine them directly in the blender if you're using it right away). Add the raspberries and ice and blend until smooth and frosty.

CALORIES: 163, FAT: 1G, CARBS: 40G, PROTEIN: 2G, FIBER: 8G | VITAMIN A: 1%, CALCIUM: 4%, VITAMIN C: 70%, IRON: 7%

75 skinny glow matcha shake

½ cup coconut water

½ cup vanilla soy milk

1½ frozen bananas

2 teaspoons matcha powder

½ cup frozen cantaloupe chunks

½ cup ice

BOOST IT: **1 scoop vanilla vegan protein powder**

Golden-glow cantaloupe combines with banana and soy for this totally craveable matcha shake. Matcha green tea, rich in free-radical-fighting antioxidants, can give you a slow release of Zen-ergy to fuel your weight loss goals and calm your mind at the same time. Coconut water and cantaloupe both contain potassium to help keep you hydrated too! Add vanilla protein powder to thicken the blend and add nutrients.

DIRECTIONS: Combine all the ingredients in a blender and blend from low to high until frosty smooth.

CALORIES: 263, FAT: 3G, CARBS: 55G, PROTEIN: 9G, FIBER: 9G | VITAMIN A: 60%, CALCIUM: 20%, VITAMIN C: 80%, IRON: 10% | ALSO RICH IN POTASSIUM AND MAGNESIUM.

76 peach-aloe watermelon

1½ cups fresh watermelon chunks

½ cup frozen peach chunks

2 teaspoons aloe vera juice

½ fresh or frozen banana

½ cup coconut water ice cubes

BOOST IT: **1 tablespoon chopped fresh mint**

Whimsical watermelon and sunny peaches mingle with soothing aloe vera juice and creamy banana for a super-cool summertime sip that's light in calories and frosty-fabulous in flavor. Add some mint to boost the calming effects of this cool drink. It is much easier to stick to your weight-loss goals when you are in a chilled-out, stress-free mood!

DIRECTIONS: Combine all the ingredients in a blender and blend from low to high until frosty smooth.

CALORIES: 177, FAT: 1G, CARBS: 43G, PROTEIN: 4G, FIBER: 5G | VITAMIN A: 32%, CALCIUM: 5%, VITAMIN C: 53%, IRON: 7% | ALSO RICH IN POTASSIUM, MAGNESIUM, AND VITAMIN B$_6$.

77 "beet" the scale

¼ cup grated beets

1 to 2 teaspoons grated
  fresh ginger

1 cup coconut water

1 cup banana

1 cup chopped kale
  leaves

1 cup chopped spinach

¼ cup chopped
  watercress

½ cup ice

BOOST IT: a few pinches
of cayenne

This sweet sip is light in calories but rich in antioxidants and fiber from superfoods spinach, watercress, and raw beets. Add some stimulating ginger, cayenne, and hydrating coconut water for a diet-friendly way to fuel your day.

DIRECTIONS: Combine the grated beets, ginger, and coconut water in a blender and blend from low to high until smooth. Strain out the pulp if you like and return the mixture to the blender. Add the remaining ingredients and blend from low to high until frosty smooth.

CALORIES: 239, FAT: 2G, CARBS: 55G, PROTEIN: 7G, FIBER: 9G
| VITAMIN A: 270%, CALCIUM: 21%, VITAMIN C: 188%, IRON: 19%
| ALSO RICH IN MAGNESIUM, MANGANESE, POTASSIUM,
AND VITAMIN B$_6$.

78 goji soy sunrise

½ cup coconut water

2 tablespoons goji
  berries

1 cup frozen pineapple
  chunks

1 orange, peeled and
  segmented

1 banana

2 tablespoons soy milk

½ cup ice

BOOST IT: scoop of
vegan protein powder

Pair sweet goji berries with tropical pineapple, vibrant orange, and a splash of coconut water and you've got a lovely start to your day. Goji berries are rich in fiber to help you stay full longer.

DIRECTIONS: Combine the coconut water and goji berries in a blender and soak until softened, about fifteen minutes. Add the remaining ingredients and blend from low to high until frosty smooth.

CALORIES: 349, FAT: 2G, CARBS: 84G, PROTEIN: 6G, FIBER: 12G
| VITAMIN A: 81%, CALCIUM: 20%, VITAMIN C: 317%, IRON: 13%
| ALSO RICH IN POTASSIUM, MANGANESE, AND VITAMIN B$_6$.

79 green mango breeze

¾ cup soy milk

1 cup frozen mango chunks

1 cup chopped kale leaves

2 tablespoons chopped parsley

1 orange, peeled and segmented (fresh or frozen)

¼ cup ice

BOOST IT: ½ banana and/ or ⅛ teaspoon grated fresh ginger

Tropical mango and silky soy milk blend with kale and citrus—satisfying fuel for a skinny glow day. Antioxidants may help your body stay in fat-burning mode by reducing overall oxidative stress caused by free radicals.

DIRECTIONS: Combine all the ingredients in a blender and blend from low to high until frosty smooth.

CALORIES: 305, FAT: 4G, CARBS: 62G, PROTEIN: 10G, FIBER: 10G | VITAMIN A: 260%, CALCIUM: 42%, VITAMIN C: 390%, IRON: 16% | ALSO RICH IN POTASSIUM AND VITAMIN B$_6$.

80 banilla skinny shake

1 cup vanilla soy milk ice cubes

½ cup vanilla soy milk

2 to 3 tablespoons vanilla soy yogurt

1 fresh or frozen banana

½ teaspoon ground cinnamon

¼ teaspoon vanilla extract or vanilla bean pod seeds

BOOST IT: 1 teaspoon chia seeds

This guilt-free vanilla soy blend is oozing with "dessert shake" appeal. Frosty vanilla soy milk ice cubes, creamy banana, and cinnamon make this a recipe to enjoy, even when you are in slim-down mode! Add some chia seeds for a boost of fiber and omega-3 fatty acids.

DIRECTIONS: Combine all the ingredients in a blender and blend from low to high until frosty smooth.

CALORIES: 277, FAT: 7G, CARBS: 42G, PROTEIN: 13G, FIBER: 5G | VITAMIN A: 17%, CALCIUM: 50%, VITAMIN C: 17%, IRON: 12% | ALSO RICH IN RIBOFLAVIN.

81 skinny avocado-peach

½ cup mashed avocado

1¼ cups frozen peach chunks

1 cup orange juice (freshly squeezed is best)

½ cup ice

BOOST IT: **a few pinches of cayenne**

Keep it simple with this smoothie: rich and creamy avocado, blended with sweet peaches, skinny citrus, and ice. Monounsaturated fats found in avocado are beneficial in stabilizing blood sugar, reducing those nasty energy highs and lows that can lead to unwanted food cravings. Don't fear fat when watching your weight; instead focus on total calories in and your body's total energy output! And add spicy cayenne to help boost your metabolism.

DIRECTIONS: Combine all the ingredients in a blender and blend from low to high until frosty smooth.

CALORIES: 311, FAT: 11G, CARBS: 52G, PROTEIN: 5G, FIBER: 9G | VITAMIN A: 26%, CALCIUM: 5%, VITAMIN C: 242%, IRON: 8% | ALSO RICH IN POTASSIUM.

82 heavenly honeydew

2 cups frozen honeydew chunks

½ banana

½ cup water or coconut water

Squeeze of lime juice (optional)

BOOST IT: **1 tablespoon chopped fresh mint**

This simple honeydew frosty is incredibly refreshing, like diving into a cool swimming pool on a hot summer day. One tall glass is low in calories and sugar-free, sweetened by potassium-rich banana. Tip: Make sure you freeze your honeydew when it is super-ripe, sweet, and juicy. The better the melon tastes when you freeze it, the better it will taste when you blend it.

DIRECTIONS: Combine all the ingredients in a blender and blend from low to high until the smoothie has the consistency of a thick, icy slush or very soft sorbet.

CALORIES: 175, FAT: 1G, CARBS: 44G, PROTEIN: 3G, FIBER: 4G | VITAMIN A: 4%, CALCIUM: 2%, VITAMIN C: 111%, IRON: 4% | ALSO RICH IN POTASSIUM AND VITAMIN B$_6$.

Heavenly Honeydew

83 perfect peach shake

1 cup frozen
  watermelon chunks

½ cup frozen peach
  chunks

1 frozen banana

1 cup vanilla soy milk

BOOST IT: **2 to 3
tablespoons soy yogurt**

This is my perfect blend of low-calorie frozen peaches and watermelon, paired with creamy banana and soy milk. It looks like a pink-glow milkshake. Guilt-free. Bliss-infused.

DIRECTIONS: Combine all the ingredients in a blender and blend from low to high until frosty smooth.

CALORIES: 284, FAT: 4G, CARBS: 54G, PROTEIN: 10G, FIBER: 6G | VITAMIN A: 34%, CALCIUM: 32%, VITAMIN C: 47%, IRON: 11% | ALSO RICH IN POTASSIUM AND RIBOFLAVIN.

84 berry blender oatmeal

2 tablespoons rolled
  oats

½ cup vanilla soy milk,
  plus more if needed

1 cup vanilla or plain
  soy yogurt

½ cup frozen
  strawberries or other
  berries

1 frozen banana

Pinch of salt

½ cup ice (optional)

BOOST IT: **1 tablespoon
raw walnuts**

Berry oatmeal lovers will find what they crave in this oat-infused breakfast smoothie swirled into frosty silk with soy yogurt, banana, and berries. Fiber-rich oats may help slow digestion, which can help prevent blood sugar spikes and crashes that contribute to cravings and mood swings and sabotage your diet. This recipe is a perfect meal replacement, or you can share it with a friend for a lighter option.

DIRECTIONS: Combine the oats and soy milk in a blender and soak until the oats are softened, about five minutes. Add the remaining ingredients and blend from low to high until frosty smooth.

CALORIES: 369, FAT: 6.6G, CARBS: 72G, PROTEIN: 12G, FIBER: 8G | VITAMIN A: 7%, CALCIUM: 47%, VITAMIN C: 62%, IRON: 16%

85 hot pink frosty

1½ cups frozen watermelon chunks

1 fresh or frozen banana

½ cup pink grapefruit juice

½ cup coconut water

BOOST IT: **2 to 3 pinches of cayenne**

Glow hot pink from the inside out with this sassy-sweet watermelon-grapefruit smoothie. Add some cayenne for more heat. Spicy foods like cayenne may boost your metabolism to help you burn fat. Watermelon is a perfect diet food, as it contains only 50 calories per delicious cup! If you'd like a creamier texture, substitute soy milk for the coconut water.

DIRECTIONS: Combine all the ingredients in a blender and blend from low to high until frosty smooth.

CALORIES: 236, FAT: 1G, CARBS: 58G, PROTEIN: 5G, FIBER: 7G | VITAMIN A: 53%, CALCIUM: 8%, VITAMIN C: 120%, IRON: 11% | ALSO RICH IN POTASSIUM AND MANGANESE.

86 green banana jungle shake

2 cups chopped kale leaves

½ cup plain soy milk

½ cup coconut water

½ cup frozen mango chunks (or substitute pineapple)

1 frozen banana

1 tablespoon unsweetened dried coconut flakes

½ cup ice

BOOST IT: **2 teaspoons soaked and drained goji berries and/or 2 raw Brazil nuts**

Sip on some green goodness via this exotic smoothie infused with jungle-green kale, mango, banana, and a sprinkle of coconut flakes. This fiber-rich green smoothie makes a delicious, skinny meal replacement. Add goji berries and Brazil nuts for even more healthy nutrients like vitamin A, selenium, and fiber.

DIRECTIONS: Combine the kale, soy milk, and coconut water and blend from low to high until smooth. Add the remaining ingredients and blend from low to high until frosty smooth.

CALORIES: 316, FAT: 6G, CARBS: 63G, PROTEIN: 11G, FIBER: 10G | VITAMIN A: 431%, CALCIUM: 37%, VITAMIN C: 328%, IRON: 21% | ALSO RICH IN MAGNESIUM, MANGANESE, POTASSIUM, VITAMIN B$_6$, AND RIBOFLAVIN.

87 pineapple sunbeam

1 cup frozen pineapple
  chunks

1 small orange, peeled
  and segmented

1 frozen banana

½ cup vanilla soy milk

½ cup coconut water

½ cup ice

BOOST IT: **Substitute
guava juice for the soy
milk for a Hawaiian
twist**

Pineapple island, here you come. Soak in
the sunshine—via your straw—with this vibrant
pineapple-banana-citrus smoothie. This bromelain-
rich smoothie helps reduce inflammation to keep
your body feeling strong and in an energized, fat-
burning mode. If you like, you can substitute ½ cup
orange juice for the fresh orange and omit the
coconut water.

DIRECTIONS: Combine all the ingredients in a blender and
blend from low to high until frosty smooth.

**CALORIES: 300, FAT: 3G, CARBS: 67G, PROTEIN: 8G, FIBER: 10G
| VITAMIN A: 13%, CALCIUM: 25%, VITAMIN C: 231%, IRON: 10%
| ALSO RICH IN MANGANESE AND POTASSIUM.**

88 strawberry-cucumber cool-down

1 cup frozen
  strawberries

1 cup frozen cucumber

1 cup orange juice

½ cup coconut water
  ice cubes

Splash of coconut
  water, if needed to
  thin

BOOST IT: **chopped fresh
mint or whole mint
leaves for garnish**

You'll be saying *"Ahhhh"* when you gulp down this
frosty blend of vibrant orange, sweet strawberries,
and frosty chilled cucumber. Light in calories but big
on flavor.

DIRECTIONS: Combine all the ingredients in a blender and
blend from low to high until frosty smooth.

**CALORIES: 196, FAT: 1G, CARBS: 45G, PROTEIN: 4G, FIBER: 5G
| VITAMIN A: 12%, CALCIUM: 0%, VITAMIN C: 357%, IRON: 10%
| ALSO RICH IN MAGNESIUM, MANGANESE, POTASSIUM,
AND THIAMINE.**

89 skinny "caramel" apple cider

1 cup apple cider

½ frozen banana

3 to 4 tablespoons soy milk

1¼ cups ice or coconut water ice cubes

2 to 3 pinches of ground cinnamon

BOOST IT: **a few soy yogurt ice cubes for added creaminess**

TOPPING: **½ teaspoon agave syrup and a dollop of soy whipped topping (optional)**

Hot caramel apple cider doesn't have anything on this cool, frosty, frozen version. Top with soy whipped topping for an extra-special treat! Sip and smile. This frosty looks like a decadent dessert treat, but it is in fact low in fat and calories.

DIRECTIONS: Combine all the ingredients in a blender and blend from low to high until frosty smooth. Drizzle the agave over the top and finish with the soy whipped topping if you like.

CALORIES: 215, FAT: 2G, CARBS: 50G, PROTEIN: 3G, FIBER: 2G | VITAMIN A: 3%, CALCIUM: 11%, VITAMIN C: 12%, IRON: 8%

90 green pineapple island

½ cup chopped frozen cucumber

1 cup frozen pineapple chunks

1¼ cups coconut water

½ banana

½ cup ice

BOOST IT: **½ teaspoon chopped fresh mint**

Blend up this first-class ticket to frosty cool paradise. Just grab a straw and prepare for landing. Cool cucumber and sweet enzyme-rich pineapple make for an uplifting sip. This tall frosty glass is low in calories to keep you feeling skinny.

DIRECTIONS: Combine all the ingredients in a blender and blend from low to high until frosty smooth.

CALORIES: 195, FAT: 1G, CARBS: 46G, PROTEIN: 4G, FIBER: 8G | VITAMIN A: 4%, CALCIUM: 10%, VITAMIN C: 146%, IRON: 9% | ALSO RICH IN POTASSIUM, MANGANESE, AND VITAMIN B$_6$.

Skinny "Caramel" Apple Cider

91 summer strawberries and "cream" shake

1 cup vanilla soy milk

1 cup frozen strawberries

¼ cup fresh or frozen strawberries

1 frozen sliced banana

3 tablespoons plain soy yogurt

1 teaspoon agave syrup

½ cup ice

BOOST IT: **a few drops of pure vanilla extract**

GARNISHES: **sprig of mint and sliced fresh strawberries**

Sweet strawberries swirl with creamy banana and soy in this skinny dessert shake. Satisfy your craving for something sweet while getting a healthy dose of fiber, antioxidants, and protein.

DIRECTIONS: Combine all the ingredients in a blender and blend from low to high until frosty smooth. Top with the garnishes.

CALORIES: 328, FAT: 6G, CARBS: 62G, PROTEIN: 11G, FIBER: 8G | VITAMIN A: 12%, CALCIUM: 42%, VITAMIN C: 194%, IRON: 14% | ALSO RICH IN MANGANESE AND RIBOFLAVIN.

92 blueberry-banana builder

1 cup frozen blueberries

1 frozen banana

1¼ cups vanilla soy milk

1 teaspoon agave syrup

1 tablespoon almond butter

½ cup ice

BOOST IT: 1 scoop vanilla vegan protein powder

Fuel up and build strength from the inside out with the help of sweet blueberries, creamy banana, protein-rich vanilla soy milk, and an accent of almond butter! Antioxidants found in blueberries help fight inflammation, which can weaken your body. Almond butter and fortified soy milk (remember to choose fortified non-dairy milks when possible) contain iron, calcium, and protein to nurture strength.

DIRECTIONS: Combine all the ingredients in a blender and blend from low to high until frosty smooth.

CALORIES: 435, FAT: 15G, CARBS: 67G, PROTEIN: 14G, FIBER: 8G | VITAMIN A: 16%, CALCIUM: 44%, VITAMIN C: 41%, IRON: 15%

93 sunny strawberry protein

1 small orange, peeled and segmented

1 frozen banana

1 cup frozen strawberries

1 cup plain soy milk

1 to 2 teaspoons agave syrup

1 scoop vanilla or plain vegan protein powder

¼ cup ice

BOOST IT: 1 tablespoon sunflower seeds

Sunny strawberry and orange fill this protein-rich sip. Creamy soy milk and banana smooth and balance the flavor. Strawberries and oranges are rich in vitamin C, which helps your body produce collagen, and collagen may support bone health and strength in your body. Boost your smoothie by adding iron- and vitamin E–containing sunflower seeds.

DIRECTIONS: Combine all the ingredients in a blender and blend from low to high until frosty smooth.

CALORIES: 413, FAT: 5G, CARBS: 79G, PROTEIN: 18G, FIBER: 15G | VITAMIN A: 22%, CALCIUM: 42%, VITAMIN C: 270%, IRON: 23%

94 watercress weight lifter

1½ cups watercress

¼ cup mashed avocado

1 banana

1 orange, peeled and segmented

½ cup green grapes

½ cup ice

BOOST IT: 2 to 3 tablespoons hemp seeds

Show up at the gym with this whole food green smoothie in hand and you will have everyone swooning. Spicy watercress leads the pack in this powerhouse blend of antioxidant-rich foods. Antioxidants help fight free radicals and reduce inflammation, which can weaken the body. Watercress is also rich in vitamins A, C, and K; vitamin K is essential to building and maintaining healthy, strong bones.

DIRECTIONS: Combine all the ingredients in a blender and blend from low to high until frosty smooth, adding a few splashes of liquid if needed.

CALORIES: 328, FAT: 9G, CARBS: 61G, PROTEIN: 8G, FIBER: 11G | VITAMIN A: 44%, CALCIUM: 16%, VITAMIN C: 226%, IRON: 10% | RICH IN POTASSIUM AND VITAMIN B$_6$.

95 peach protein power-up

3 tablespoons raw walnuts

1¼ cups vanilla soy milk

1 cup frozen peach chunks

1 frozen banana

1 teaspoon maple syrup (optional)

3 pinches of ground cinnamon

½ cup ice

BOOST IT: 2 to 3 tablespoons soy yogurt

This creamy powerhouse peach smoothie is a delicious way to fuel up for a busy day. Walnut, cinnamon, and maple flavors accent soy, bananas, and peaches. It's protein-rich to help your body repair and build lean muscle mass.

DIRECTIONS: In a blender, combine the walnuts and soy milk and blend from low to high until smooth. Add the remaining ingredients and blend from low to high until frosty smooth.

CALORIES: 471, FAT: 20G, CARBS: 60G, PROTEIN: 16G, FIBER: 9G | VITAMIN A: 25%, CALCIUM: 41%, VITAMIN C: 36%, IRON: 17%

96 "seed" you at the gym!

1 cup plain soy milk

1 teaspoon chia seeds

1 teaspoon hemp seeds

½ cup frozen mango

1 frozen banana

1 cup chopped kale
  leaves

½ cup chopped pear

½ cup ice

BOOST IT: 1 to 2
tablespoons pumpkin
seeds

This sweet mango green smoothie will seed-uce you at first swanky sip. Boosted with chia and hemp seeds, this blend is the perfect post-workout refresher or breakfast-hour sip. Boost it by adding iron- and mineral-rich pumpkin seeds.

DIRECTIONS: Combine the soy milk, chia seeds, and hemp seeds in a blender and blend from low to high until smooth. Wait a few minutes for chia seeds to plump, then add the remaining ingredients and blend until frosty smooth.

CALORIES: 376, FAT: 8G, CARBS: 70G, PROTEIN: 13G, FIBER: 11G | VITAMIN A: 231%, CALCIUM: 44%, VITAMIN C: 195%, IRON: 19% | ALSO RICH IN MANGANESE AND VITAMIN B$_6$.

97 pink hummingbird

1 cup fresh strawberries

1 frozen banana

½ cup vanilla soy milk

½ cup silken tofu

½ cup coconut water
  ice cubes

Pinch of salt

Drizzle of agave syrup,
  or to taste

BOOST IT: 1 tablespoon
raw walnuts

Sing and flutter as you sip this silky strawberry-tofu smoothie accented with creamy banana. It's rich in protein from the tofu, soy milk, and walnuts.

DIRECTIONS: Combine all the ingredients in a blender and blend from low to high until frosty smooth.

CALORIES: 265, FAT: 5G, CARBS: 47G, PROTEIN: 10G, FIBER: 8G | VITAMIN A: 7%, CALCIUM: 26%, VITAMIN C: 163%, IRON: 14% | ALSO RICH IN MANGANESE AND POTASSIUM.

98 spiced brazil nut shake

6 roughly chopped raw Brazil nuts

1 tablespoon almond butter

1¼ cups vanilla soy milk

1½ frozen bananas

A few pinches of ground cinnamon, nutmeg, and ginger

½ cup coconut water ice cubes

BOOST IT: 1 teaspoon unsweetened dried coconut flakes

This warmly spiced shake contains antioxidant-rich almond butter and Brazil nuts. Brazil nuts are famously rich in the mineral selenium, and like almonds they contain iron to boost strength. Creamy banana, soy, and spices deliver a cozy, craveable flavor. Spices may help reduce inflammation, which can weaken the body.

DIRECTIONS: Combine the Brazil nuts, almond butter, and soy milk in a blender and blend from low to high until smooth. Add the bananas, spices, and coconut water ice cubes and blend until frosty smooth.

CALORIES: 544, FAT: 28G, CARBS: 58G, PROTEIN: 17G, FIBER: 9G | VITAMIN A: 15%, CALCIUM: 46%, VITAMIN C: 31%, IRON: 15% | ALSO RICH IN SELENIUM.

99 raspberry-cashew cheesecake shake

1¼ cups vanilla soy milk

¼ cup raw cashews, soaked and drained

¾ cup frozen raspberries

1 frozen banana

1 tablespoon agave syrup, or to taste

Pinch of salt

BOOST IT: 1 scoop vanilla vegan protein powder

TOPPING: crushed vegan graham crackers (optional)

Satisfy your sweet tooth with this creamy cheesecake-inspired blend. Zingy berries swirl with soy, cashews, and banana for a surprisingly healthy dessert–approved treat. Cashews contain iron and copper to nurture strength, and adding a scoop of protein powder gives the shake a boost.

DIRECTIONS: Combine the soy milk and cashews in a blender and blend from low to high until smooth. Add the remaining ingredients and blend until frosty smooth. Top with crushed graham crackers if you like.

CALORIES: 538, FAT: 22G, CARBS: 75G, PROTEIN: 16G, FIBER: 11G | VITAMIN A: 15%, CALCIUM: 43%, VITAMIN C: 57%, IRON: 25%

100 pb&j shake

1¼ cups vanilla soy milk

2 tablespoons peanut butter

1 cup frozen strawberries or raspberries

1 frozen banana

½ cup ice

BOOST IT: **1 to 2 tablespoons rolled oats**

All the flavor of your favorite classic sandwich: the PB&J, swirled into a sweet and nutty shake. Peanuts are known as the most protein-rich nut, although they are technically a legume. They also contain vitamin E, niacin, magnesium, and iron to nurture your body's natural strength. Berries, rich in antioxidants, can help reduce strength-inhibiting inflammation. Add some oats for a boost of fiber and energizing complex carbohydrates!

DIRECTIONS: Combine all the ingredients in a blender and blend from low to high until frosty smooth.

CALORIES: 464, FAT: 22G, CARBS: 54G, PROTEIN: 19G, FIBER: 9G | VITAMIN A: 14%, CALCIUM: 42%, VITAMIN C: 158%, IRON: 16%

101 green gusto

2 cups chopped kale leaves

½ cup frozen or fresh diced avocado

1 frozen banana

1¼ cups soy milk (or substitute citrus juice)

1 teaspoon agave syrup

Cayenne to taste (optional)

½ cup ice

BOOST IT: **1 to 2 tablespoons pumpkin seeds and/or ¼ cup raw broccoli florets**

This avocado-banana-and-kale-infused green shake will inspire gusto! The blend is rich in vitamin A, a powerful antioxidant that may help you build healthy bones. Add some calcium-rich broccoli and/or iron-rich pumpkin seeds to further boost the strengthening power of this sweet green sip. Tip: Too many ripe avocados in your fruit bowl? Peel, dice, and freeze them so you can use them later in your smoothies. Frozen avocado smoothies blend up creamy and chilled.

DIRECTIONS: Combine all the ingredients in a blender and blend from low to high until frosty smooth.

CALORIES: 435, FAT: 17G, CARBS: 62G, PROTEIN: 16G, FIBER: 12G | VITAMIN A: 428%, CALCIUM: 58%, VITAMIN C: 297%, IRON: 24% | ALSO RICH IN POTASSIUM, MANGANESE, AND VITAMIN B$_6$.

102 cacao-coconut joy shake

1 cup vanilla soy milk

1 tablespoon raw cacao powder

1 tablespoon almond butter

1½ frozen bananas

½ cup soy yogurt

1 teaspoon unsweetened shredded coconut

½ cup coconut water ice cubes

BOOST IT: 1 to 2 teaspoons raw cacao nibs

You will be sipping on some joy with this blissful, frosty, nutrient-filled swirl of flavors: almond butter, coconut, banana, and chocolate. This healthy treat is rich in calcium and protein. Almonds are a good source of iron and protein, which help your body stay strong. Antioxidant-rich cacao fights free radicals, which can weaken your body.

DIRECTIONS: Combine all the ingredients in a blender and blend from low to high until frosty smooth.

CALORIES: 486, FAT: 19G, CARBS: 73G, PROTEIN: 16G, FIBER: 10G | VITAMIN A: 12%, CALCIUM: 54%, VITAMIN C: 31%, IRON: 20% | ALSO RICH IN POTASSIUM, MANGANESE, AND VITAMIN B$_6$.

103 sweet green pistachio shake

⅓ cup raw pistachios (soak them for a silkier shake)

1 cup plain soy milk

1 frozen banana

1 cup chopped kale leaves

½ cup fresh or frozen green grapes

½ cup ice

BOOST IT: 1 to 2 teaspoons matcha powder

Pistachios, rich in minerals, protein, and healthy fats, add flavor and strength to this green smoothie swirled with superfood kale, soy milk, and sweet grapes. Add some matcha powder for a boost of antioxidant-rich green tea Zen-ergy.

DIRECTIONS: In a blender, combine the pistachios and soy milk and blend on low until relatively smooth. Add the remaining ingredients and blend from low to high until frosty smooth.

CALORIES: 510, FAT: 24G, CARBS: 60G, PROTEIN: 21G, FIBER: 12G | VITAMIN A: 223%, CALCIUM: 48%, VITAMIN C: 163%, IRON: 27% | ALSO RICH IN MANGANESE AND VITAMIN B$_6$.

104 golden blueberry burst

1 cup fresh blueberries

1 cup chopped spinach

1¼ cups vanilla soy milk

1½ frozen bananas

⅛ teaspoon ground turmeric

Sweetener of choice to taste (optional)

½ cup ice

BOOST IT: 1 tablespoon hemp seeds

This blueberry-filled green and gold smoothie is bursting with fresh blueberry flavor. Superfood spinach adds nutrients galore, and banana adds potassium and fiber. Turmeric helps reduce inflammation, which can weaken your muscles and lessen strength.

DIRECTIONS: Combine all the ingredients in a blender and blend from low to high until frosty smooth.

CALORIES: 414, FAT: 15G, CARBS: 73G, PROTEIN: 15G, FIBER: 11G | VITAMIN A: 73%, CALCIUM: 43%, VITAMIN C: 63%, IRON: 22% | ALSO RICH IN POTASSIUM, MANGANESE, MAGNESIUM, AND RIBOFLAVIN.

105 "flax" those muscles for açaí

1¼ cups vanilla soy milk

1 frozen banana

½ cup frozen blackberries

2 teaspoons açaí powder

1 tablespoon flax seeds

½ cup ice

BOOST IT: 1 teaspoon flax oil

Show off, it's OK. You've worked hard for that buff bod, and a little pride is a good thing. So flex, or should I say "flax" those muscles after enjoying this frosty açaí berry blend. Flax contains omega-3 fatty acids, which may help reduce joint inflammation and pain. Blackberries and açaí are rich in free-radical-fighting antioxidants to further reduce inflammation.

CALORIES: 312, FAT: 9G, CARBS: 47G, PROTEIN: 12G, FIBER: 10G | VITAMIN A: 44%, CALCIUM: 42%, VITAMIN C: 48%, IRON: 15% | ALSO RICH IN MANGANESE, MAGNESIUM, AND RIBOFLAVIN.

106 crazy cookie bar shake

1¼ cups vanilla soy milk

2 tablespoons raw walnuts

1 frozen banana

2 teaspoons unsweetened dried coconut flakes

2 teaspoons agave syrup

2 teaspoons raw cacao powder

Dash of ground cinnamon

½ cup coconut water ice cubes

This fun blend of coconut, walnuts, banana, cinnamon, and cacao reminds me of a chunky vegan cookie bar. Cinnamon and antioxidant-rich cacao can help calm inflammation, which can weaken your body. Walnuts contain iron and copper to keep you feeling strong.

DIRECTIONS: Combine all the ingredients in a blender and blend from low to high until frosty smooth.

BOOST IT: 1 teaspoon raw cacao nibs or vegan chocolate chips

CALORIES: 413, FAT: 16G, CARBS: 56G, PROTEIN: 16G, FIBER: 8G | VITAMIN A: 14%, CALCIUM: 43%, VITAMIN C: 23%, IRON: 17%

107 pecan-maple pie shake

1 cup water

¼ cup raw pecans

1 frozen banana

1 tablespoon maple syrup

3 pinches of ground cinnamon

Drop of pure vanilla extract

Pinch of salt

¼ cup ice

TOPPING: Drizzle of maple syrup and 1 pecan half

This strengthening pecan pie–flavored shake combines cozy maple syrup, buttery pecans, cinnamon, and sweet banana. Pecans are rich in iron to help nurture your strength and cinnamon has anti-inflammatory benefits to help ease muscle and joint pain. For an extra-creamy shake, substitute non-dairy milk for some of the water.

DIRECTIONS: Combine the water and pecans in a blender and blend from low to high until creamy. Add the remaining ingredients and blend from low to high until smooth. Finish with the toppings.

BOOST IT: 1 tablespoon raw cacao powder

CALORIES: 389, FAT: 23G, CARBS: 44G, PROTEIN: 7G, FIBER: 9G | VITAMIN A: 4%, CALCIUM: 8%, VITAMIN C: 18%, IRON: 13%

Pecan-Maple Pie Shake

108 watermelon "milk" shake

1½ cups frozen
   watermelon chunks

1½ frozen bananas

¾ to 1 cup vanilla
   soy milk

**BOOST IT: 1 scoop vanilla
vegan protein powder**

Love a pink strawberry milkshake? Well, try this frosty frozen non-dairy watermelon version—the pastel pink blend will leave you swooning. Add a scoop of vanilla protein powder for a strengthening boost.

DIRECTIONS: Combine all the ingredients in a blender and blend from low to high until frosty smooth.

CALORIES: 326, FAT: 5G, CARBS: 65G, PROTEIN: 11G, FIBER: 7G | VITAMIN A: 38%, CALCIUM: 32%, VITAMIN C: 56%, IRON: 12% | ALSO RICH IN POTASSIUM, RIBOFLAVIN, AND VITAMIN B$_6$.

109 mighty mint chip

1 tablespoon chopped
   fresh peppermint
   leaves

1 cup plain soy milk

½ cup plain soy yogurt

2 to 3 tablespoons raw
   cacao nibs

1 frozen banana

1 to 2 tablespoons
   agave syrup

½ cup ice

**BOOST IT: 1 tablespoon
raw cacao powder for
a double chocolate
mint shake!**

Mint chip lovers, this creamy cool shake is for you. I've replaced standard chocolate chips and fake mint flavor with rich raw cacao nibs and fresh mint. Cacao nibs are rich in antioxidants that help fight free radicals and reduce inflammation, which can weaken your body. Peppermint also has anti-inflammatory effects.

DIRECTIONS: Combine the mint and soy milk in a blender and blend from low to high until smooth. Add the remaining ingredients and blend from low to high until frosty smooth.

CALORIES: 411, FAT: 12G, CARBS: 71G, PROTEIN: 14G, FIBER: 10G | VITAMIN A: 16%, CALCIUM: 49%, VITAMIN C: 18%, IRON: 19%

Watermelon "Milk" Shake

110 chocolate-covered cherry

1 cup vanilla soy milk

½ cup cherries, pitted

1 tablespoon raw cacao powder and/or 1 teaspoon raw cacao nibs

1½ frozen bananas

2 teaspoons vanilla vegan protein powder

½ cup ice

BOOST IT: **2 to 3 tablespoons soy yogurt**

Rich cacao meets juicy, sweet fresh cherries in this protein-infused blend. Protein helps repair and grow lean muscle mass, while cherries fight joint inflammation with their powerful antioxidant vibrancy.

DIRECTIONS: Combine all the ingredients in a blender and blend from low to high until frosty smooth.

CALORIES: 335, FAT: 5G, CARBS: 61G, PROTEIN: 16G, FIBER: 9G | VITAMIN A: 13%, CALCIUM: 33%, VITAMIN C: 33%, IRON: 16%

111 coconut shimmy shake shake shake

3 tablespoons coconut milk

2 frozen bananas

¾ cup vanilla soy milk

3 tablespoons unsweetened dried coconut flakes

2 to 3 pinches of ground cinnamon

A few drops of vanilla extract

½ cup ice

BOOST IT: **scoop of vegan protein powder**

This creamy, tropical coconut-banana shake tastes like a vanilla coconut ice cream shake. It is delicious with a strengthening scoop of protein powder added to it. Shimmy-shake all the way to a beachside hula party.

DIRECTIONS: Combine all the ingredients in a blender and blend from low to high until frosty smooth.

CALORIES: 442, FAT: 19G, CARBS: 64G, PROTEIN: 10G, FIBER: 9G | VITAMIN A: 11%, CALCIUM: 25%, VITAMIN C: 37%, IRON: 14% | ALSO RICH IN MANGANESE.

112 cozy cinna-bun

2 tablespoons raw
    walnuts

¼ cup rolled oats

1 cup vanilla soy milk

1½ frozen bananas

½ teaspoon ground
    cinnamon

2 teaspoons maple
    syrup (or substitute
    1 tablespoon raisins)

A few drops pure
    vanilla extract or a
    few vanilla bean
    seeds

Pinch of fresh orange
    zest

Pinch of salt

Creamy and comfy, this cinnamon-flavored shake is
rich in strengthening nutrients like protein, calcium,
and iron. For added protein, blend in some protein
powder. You can also try this recipe using soaked
buckwheat groats in place of the oats.

DIRECTIONS: In a blender, combine the walnuts, oats, and
soy milk and blend from low to high until smooth. Add
the remaining ingredients and blend from low to high
until frosty smooth.

BOOST IT: 1 scoop vanilla vegan protein powder

CALORIES: 478, FAT: 16G, CARBS: 73G, PROTEIN: 15G,
FIBER: 10G | VITAMIN A: 12%, CALCIUM: 35%, VITAMIN C: 26%,
IRON: 18%

113 chocolate-pecan pie shake

1 cup vanilla soy milk

1 tablespoon raw cacao
    powder

1½ frozen bananas

¼ cup raw pecans

1 to 3 teaspoons agave
    syrup or maple syrup

2 to 3 pinches of
    ground cinnamon

½ cup ice

BOOST IT: 1 to 2
teaspoons hemp seeds

Rich cacao swirls with nutty pecans and spices
in this creamy banana-pecan shake. It tastes like
biting into a slice of chocolate pecan pie. Pecans
contain protein, copper, manganese, and iron; iron
is important for muscle strength. Add hemp seeds
for an extra boost of complete protein.

DIRECTIONS: Combine all the ingredients in a blender and
blend from low to high until frosty smooth.

CALORIES: 480, FAT: 25G, CARBS: 61G, PROTEIN: 13G,
FIBER: 10G | VITAMIN A: 13%, CALCIUM: 35%, VITAMIN C: 26%,
IRON: 16% | ALSO RICH IN MANGANESE.

Maple-Spice Buckwheat Shake

114 maple-spice buckwheat shake

½ cup dry buckwheat groats

Salt

1 frozen banana

1 cup plain soy milk

1 teaspoon maple syrup

¼ cup ice

BOOST IT: **a few pinches of cayenne**

Buckwheat is for more than just your weekend morning pancakes. Sweet maple blends perfectly with creamy, nutty, detoxifying buckwheat groats, and this grain shake will fill you with lasting energy and a nice boost of protein and iron for strength. Give buckwheat a try!

DIRECTIONS: Soak the buckwheat groats in a bowl with about 1 cup water and a pinch of salt for at least 5 minutes, until softened. Drain the water and add the soaked groats to a blender. Add the remaining ingredients, including another pinch of salt, and blend until smooth.

CALORIES: 525, FAT: 7G, CARBS: 102G, PROTEIN: 18G, FIBER: 13G | VITAMIN A: 15%, CALCIUM: 32%, VITAMIN C: 18%, IRON: 21% | ALSO RICH IN MAGNESIUM, MANGANESE, AND VITAMIN B$_6$.

115 peanut butter dreams

2½ tablespoons salted peanut butter

2 fresh or frozen bananas

1 cup vanilla soy milk

Maple syrup or agave syrup to taste (optional)

Pinch of ground cinnamon

BOOST IT: **1 to 2 tablespoons soy yogurt or a scoop of vegan protein powder**

I dream of . . . peanut butter. And I like *a lot* of it swirled into my peanut butter–banana shakes. But you can start with one spoonful and then add more if you dare. Peanuts contain more protein than any other nut (though they are actually a legume). And protein helps you repair and grow muscle mass.

DIRECTIONS: Combine all the ingredients in a blender and blend from low to high until frosty smooth.

CALORIES: 545, FAT: 25G, CARBS: 70G, PROTEIN: 20G, FIBER: 10G | VITAMIN A: 13%, CALCIUM: 33%, VITAMIN C: 34%, IRON: 14%

Peanut Butter Dreams

116 coco-açaí protein shake

1 cup açaí juice

½ cup vanilla soy milk

1½ frozen bananas

2 teaspoons
unsweetened dried
coconut flakes

1 scoop vegan protein
powder

¼ cup ice

BOOST IT: 1 tablespoon
chilled coconut milk

This banana-açaí shake is delicious as an after-workout protein boost. Purple açaí juice blends with soy, bananas, and coconut flakes. The protein helps your body repair and build muscle mass after a workout session.

DIRECTIONS: Combine all the ingredients in a blender and blend from low to high until frosty smooth.

CALORIES: 513, FAT: 12G, CARBS: 76G, PROTEIN: 31G, FIBER: 7G | VITAMIN A: 17%, CALCIUM: 18%, VITAMIN C: 62%, IRON: 7%

117 blue pumpkin seed power-up

1 cup frozen blueberries

1½ tablespoons raw
pumpkin seeds

1 cup soy milk

1 banana

1 cup chopped spinach

1 teaspoon agave syrup

½ cup coconut water
ice cubes

BOOST IT: 2 tablespoons
soy yogurt

Pumpkin seeds are rich in a variety of nutrients to keep your body feeling strong, including zinc, magnesium, copper, and iron. (Soak them for a smoother blend.) Antioxidant-rich blueberries help fight inflammation, which can lead to joint and muscle stress. And a dose of superfood spinach further boosts this smoothie into a super-strengthening blend.

DIRECTIONS: Combine all the ingredients in a blender and blend from low to high until frosty smooth.

CALORIES: 441, FAT: 12G, CARBS: 75G, PROTEIN: 16G, FIBER: 13G | VITAMIN A: 14%, CALCIUM: 41%, VITAMIN C: 55%, IRON: 27% | ALSO RICH IN POTASSIUM, MANGANESE, MAGNESIUM, AND RIBOFLAVIN.

118 cookies and cream double-chocolate shake

1½ frozen bananas

½ cup frozen watermelon chunks (or substitute additional frozen banana)

2 teaspoons raw cacao powder

1 cup vanilla soy milk

¼ cup crushed vegan chocolate sandwich cookies

BOOST IT: 1 scoop of vanilla or chocolate vegan protein powder

Cacao is rich in antioxidants! And that is all I need to hear to send me swooning for this healthy-delicious cookies and cream–style double-chocolate shake. And don't let the secret ingredient, watermelon, confuse you—it "frosts" things up quite nicely. Boost this shake by adding a scoop of vanilla or chocolate vegan protein powder.

DIRECTIONS: Combine the first four ingredients in a blender and blend from low to high until frosty smooth. Add the cookies and blend lightly just until swirled in; alternatively, fold the cookies into the shake.

CALORIES: 449, FAT: 11G, CARBS: 80G, PROTEIN: 13G, FIBER: 9G | VITAMIN A: 21%, CALCIUM: 32%, VITAMIN C: 36%, IRON: 21% | ALSO RICH IN POTASSIUM.

119 blue-nana builder

1 cup fresh or frozen blueberries

1 frozen banana

1 cup vanilla soy milk

2 teaspoons agave syrup

2 tablespoons vegan protein powder

½ cup coconut water ice cubes

BOOST IT: ½ teaspoon spirulina powder

This creamy, purple blueberry-banana shake is boosted with soy protein to keep you fueled up and ready for anything. It's blended with berries, which are rich in antioxidants to help fight free radicals that can weaken your body by causing inflammation.

DIRECTIONS: In a blender, combine all the ingredients except the ice cubes and blend from low to high until smooth. Add the ice cubes and blend from low to high until frosty smooth.

CALORIES: 408, FAT: 6G, CARBS: 71G, PROTEIN: 23G, FIBER: 9G | VITAMIN A: 13%, CALCIUM: 35%, VITAMIN C: 45%, IRON: 13%

120 cherry yogurt shake

1 cup fresh pitted
   cherries

1 cup vanilla soy yogurt

1½ frozen bananas

A few splashes of soy
milk or soy creamer,
as needed

BOOST IT: **1 scoop vegan
protein powder**

Fresh cherries and creamy vanilla soy yogurt blend into a frosty, frozen mixture reminiscent of creamy (dairy-free!) cherry frozen yogurt. This drink is soothing and summer-sweet. It's rich in calcium and protein; add protein powder for an extra nutrition boost and an even thicker texture.

DIRECTIONS: In a blender, combine the cherries and soy yogurt and blend from low to high until smooth. Add the bananas and blend from low to high until frosty smooth, adding a few splashes of soy milk to loosen if needed.

CALORIES: 424, FAT: 4G, CARBS: 94G, PROTEIN: 11G, FIBER: 10G | VITAMIN A: 4%, CALCIUM: 39%, VITAMIN C: 41%, IRON: 11%

121 hazelnut haze

⅓ cup raw hazelnuts

1½ cups vanilla soy milk

2 frozen bananas

Ground cinnamon and
   ginger powder to
   taste

Pinch of salt

½ cup ice

BOOST IT: **1 tablespoon
raw cacao powder**

Gladly melt into a calm cinnamon-hazelnut haze with this cooling banana shake. Hazelnuts are rich in iron, magnesium, copper, B vitamins, vitamin E, and healthy fats to nurture your body; add some cacao powder for a chocolate twist and an extra boost of antioxidants.

DIRECTIONS: In a blender, combine the hazelnuts and soy milk and blend from low to high until smooth. Add the remaining ingredients and blend from low to high until frosty smooth.

CALORIES: 480, FAT: 18G, CARBS: 69G, PROTEIN: 18G, FIBER: 10G | VITAMIN A: 18%, CALCIUM: 50%, VITAMIN C: 36%, IRON: 18% | ALSO RICH IN POTASSIUM AND MANGANESE.

122 green kiss

½ cup orange juice

2 cups chopped spinach

1 cup frozen diced cucumber

½ cup fresh or frozen green grapes

1 fresh or frozen banana

½ cup ice

Coconut water as needed

BOOST IT: **2 to 3 tablespoons fresh lemon juice**

Kiss me, I'm a smoothie drinker! Build strength from the inside out with superfood greens. Popeye knew what he was talking about with that can of spinach! This green citrus blend is rich in antioxidants to fight free radicals that could inhibit your body from performing at its best. For an even greener kiss, add an extra handful of leafy greens.

DIRECTIONS: Combine all the ingredients in a blender and blend from low to high until frosty smooth.

CALORIES: 221, FAT: 1G, CARBS: 53G, PROTEIN: 5G, FIBER: 6G | VITAMIN A: 122%, CALCIUM: 10%, VITAMIN C: 156%, IRON: 15% | ALSO RICH IN MAGNESIUM, MANGANESE, AND POTASSIUM.

123 watermelon-citrus stress melter

½ cup coconut water

1 teaspoon fresh chamomile flower blossoms

1½ cups watermelon chunks

1 orange, peeled and segmented

2 tablespoons fresh lime juice

1 banana

½ cup ice

BOOST IT: **drizzle of maple syrup**

This is my go-to blend for instant calm. This pink sip is a light and frosty mixture of hydrating watermelon, lively orange, and soothing chamomile flowers. Whirl this mixture in your blender and get ready to feel your stress melt away. Add a drizzle of maple syrup for added sweetness.

DIRECTIONS: In a blender, combine the coconut water and chamomile flowers and blend from low to high until smooth. Add the remaining ingredients and blend from low to high until frosty smooth.

CALORIES: 290, FAT: 1G, CARBS: 72G, PROTEIN: 6G, FIBER: 10G | VITAMIN A: 36%, CALCIUM: 13%, VITAMIN C: 231%, IRON: 8% | ALSO RICH IN POTASSIUM AND VITAMIN B$_6$.

124 quiet bluebird

1 cup fresh blueberries

¾ cup vanilla or plain soy yogurt

1 banana

½ cup ice

Drizzle of maple syrup (optional)

BOOST IT: **1 teaspoon flax oil or 1 tablespoon raw walnuts**

Simple. Sweet. Blue. Quiet. Calming. This fresh blueberry and banana blend is rich in probiotics from the soy yogurt to keep your tummy feeling calm. Savor the sweet blueberry flavor with a side of peace and quiet. Boost this sip by adding healthy omega-3 fatty acids via flax oil or walnuts.

DIRECTIONS: Combine all the ingredients in a blender and blend from low to high until frosty smooth.

CALORIES: 338, FAT: 4G, CARBS: 75G, PROTEIN: 9G, FIBER: 9G | VITAMIN A: 3%, CALCIUM: 32%, VITAMIN C: 41%, IRON: 10%

Quiet Bluebird

125 peaches and calm

¾ cup vanilla soy milk

¼ cup strong brewed
chamomile tea,
chilled

1 frozen sliced banana

1 large peach, pitted

1 teaspoon maple syrup

Ground cinnamon to
taste

½ cup ice

BOOST IT: **2 tablespoons
soy yogurt**

This peachy-keen chamomile herb tea smoothie will
mellow you out with every sip.

DIRECTIONS: Combine all the ingredients in a blender and
blend from low to high until frosty smooth.

**CALORIES: 259, FAT: 4G, CARBS: 52G, PROTEIN: 8G, FIBER: 6G
| VITAMIN A: 19%, CALCIUM: 24%, VITAMIN C: 34%, IRON: 9%
| ALSO RICH IN POTASSIUM AND RIBOFLAVIN.**

126 easy breezy

1 banana

½ cup frozen
blueberries

½ cup frozen
strawberries

½ cup vanilla soy
yogurt

1 cup vanilla soy milk

Pinch of grated fresh
orange zest

½ cup ice

BOOST IT: **2 to 3
tablespoons mashed
avocado**

This easy breezy smoothie has simple, creamy
flavors from banana, berries, and soy. A hint of
orange zest gives it a "sunny day" feel. Sip, sigh,
and feel oh-so-easy-breezy. Boost this blend by
adding monounsaturated fat–rich avocado. Healthy
fats help slow digestion and the release of energy
to stabilize your blood sugar and keep you calm.

DIRECTIONS: Combine all the ingredients in a blender and
blend from low to high until frosty smooth.

**CALORIES: 306, FAT: 6G, CARBS: 57G, PROTEIN: 11G, FIBER: 8G
| VITAMIN A: 13%, CALCIUM: 40%, VITAMIN C: 102%, IRON: 12%
| ALSO RICH IN RIBOFLAVIN.**

127 lime-cantaloupe frosty

3 cups frozen
    cantaloupe chunks

½ cup coconut water

2 tablespoons fresh
    lime juice

½ banana

BOOST IT: **drizzle of
agave syrup or maple
syrup**

This frosty cantaloupe blend is soothing and cool,
rich in vitamins A and C to help your body manage
stress. I like to eat this frosty with a spoon, as it
blends up thick and chilled—almost like a sorbet.

DIRECTIONS: Combine all the ingredients in a blender and
blend from low to high until frosty smooth.

CALORIES: 238, FAT: 2G, CARBS: 57G, PROTEIN: 6G, FIBER: 7G
| VITAMIN A: 317%, CALCIUM: 8%, VITAMIN C: 307%, IRON: 8%
| ALSO RICH IN POTASSIUM, MAGNESIUM, AND VITAMIN B$_6$.

128 cool carrot-coconut

1 fresh young coconut

½ cup grated carrots or
    a splash of carrot
    juice

1 cup ice

BOOST IT: **a few pinches
of cinnamon**

This cool, dreamy smoothie requires finding and
opening a fresh young coconut. That's the hard part.
Blending and enjoying this carrot-coconut shake:
super-easy. Carrots are rich in vitamin A, which helps
improve nerve function. Add more ice or a frozen
banana for a frostier blend.

DIRECTIONS: If possible, find a whole coconut with the top
already sliced off. Many natural food stores like Whole
Foods carry them. If you cannot find a preopened
coconut, open one by slicing through the top of the
coconut with a sharp knife. This can be a tricky process,
so exercise extreme caution. There are several how-to
videos online for how to do this. Just google "how to
open a young coconut." Once you have opened it, pour
the coconut water and scrape the meat into the blender.
Add the carrots and ice and blend from low to high until
frosty smooth.

CALORIES: 209, FAT: 4G, CARBS: 41G, PROTEIN: 5G, FIBER: 6G
| VITAMIN A: 184% | ALSO RICH IN POTASSIUM.

129 chamomile calmer

1 cup strong brewed
   chamomile tea,
   chilled

½ cup frozen mango
   chunks

1 frozen banana

2 to 3 pinches of
   ground cinnamon

2 to 3 teaspoons maple
   syrup or agave syrup

¾ cup coconut water
   ice cubes

BOOST IT: **1 to 2
tablespoons vanilla
soy yogurt**

This tea-infused smoothie will chill you out via the power of calming chamomile tea, swirled with cozy cinnamon, mango, and creamy banana.

DIRECTIONS: Combine all the ingredients in a blender and blend from low to high until frosty smooth.

CALORIES: 246, FAT: 1G, CARBS: 61G, PROTEIN: 3G, FIBER: 7G | VITAMIN A: 14%, CALCIUM: 8%, VITAMIN C: 62%, IRON: 7% | ALSO RICH IN POTASSIUM, MANGANESE, AND VITAMIN B$_6$.

130 cozy cinnamon-cashew

¼ cup raw cashews,
   soaked and drained

½ cup water or soy milk

1½ frozen bananas

1 tablespoon rolled oats

½ teaspoon ground
   cinnamon

2 teaspoons maple
   syrup

¼ cup ice

BOOST IT: **ground
nutmeg or ginger
powder to taste**

Rich and creamy cashews swirl with oats, banana, cinnamon, and maple syrup here. This is a cozy cuddle of a shake. Cashews are a good source of magnesium and copper, nutrients that may calm your mood and help ease stress. The complex carbs in oats can help boost serotonin in the brain.

DIRECTIONS: Combine the cashews and water in a blender and blend from low to high until smooth. Add the remaining ingredients and blend until frosty smooth.

CALORIES (USING WATER AS LIQUID): 420, FAT: 16G, CARBS: 65G, PROTEIN: 9G, FIBER: 7G | VITAMIN A: 2%, CALCIUM: 6%, VITAMIN C: 26%, IRON: 18%

131 pumpkin-cider swoon

½ cup vanilla soy milk

1 cup apple cider (or substitute additional soy milk)

⅔ cup canned 100% pumpkin puree

1 frozen banana

Maple syrup to taste

1 teaspoon pumpkin pie spice (ginger, cinnamon, and nutmeg)

Pinch of salt

This golden-colored pumpkin and apple cider sweet shake will leave you feeling calm and cozy. Treat yourself as you cuddle up to this seasonal sip. Vitamin A may help improve nerve function to keep you feeling calm.

DIRECTIONS: Combine all the ingredients in a blender and blend from low to high until frosty smooth. Top with whipped topping and crumbled cookie, if using.

BOOST IT: **soy or coconut whipped topping and crumbled ginger cookie for topping**

CALORIES: 362, FAT: 3G, CARBS: 82G, PROTEIN: 7G, FIBER: 9G | VITAMIN A: 515%, CALCIUM: 22%, VITAMIN C: 32%, IRON: 23% | ALSO RICH IN MANGANESE.

132 cashew dreamin'

⅓ cup raw cashews, soaked and drained

1 cup vanilla soy milk

1 frozen banana

1 teaspoon maple syrup or agave syrup

1 tablespoon raw cacao powder or nibs (optional)

2 to 3 pinches ground cinnamon

½ cup ice

Pinch of salt

Cool creamy cashews, banana, and maple lift your stress as you sink back into a cozy spot to enjoy this calming shake. Add cacao powder or cacao nibs for a cocoa spin on this sip.

DIRECTIONS: Combine all the ingredients in a blender and blend from low to high until frosty smooth.

BOOST IT: **1 to 2 tablespoons raw cacao powder or cacao nibs**

CALORIES: 386, FAT: 16G, CARBS: 47G, PROTEIN: 14G, FIBER: 5G | VITAMIN A: 12%, CALCIUM: 32%, VITAMIN C: 17%, IRON: 8%

Minted Cucumber-Kiwi Cooler

133 minted cucumber-kiwi cooler

1 cup frozen diced
   cucumber
½ cup chopped spinach
1 to 2 kiwis, peeled
1 cup coconut water
¼ cup ice
1 tablespoon chopped
   fresh mint

BOOST IT: **2 tablespoons
mashed avocado**

Don't get all hot and bothered—get cool and calm—with this frosty green cooler. Sweet kiwis and frozen cucumbers merge to make a perfect cool-me-down sip. Boost this blend with some creamy, monounsaturated fat-rich avocado; adding healthy fats to smoothies helps slow digestion and release of energy to prevent blood sugar spikes and crashes that can stress you out.

DIRECTIONS: Combine all the ingredients in a blender and blend from low to high until frosty smooth.

CALORIES: 160, FAT: 2G, CARBS: 36G, PROTEIN: 5G, FIBER: 9G | VITAMIN A: 38%, CALCIUM: 15%, VITAMIN C: 258%, IRON: 14% | ALSO RICH IN POTASSIUM, MANGANESE, AND MAGNESIUM.

134 avo-calmer green shake

1 cup cubed avocado
½ cup frozen pineapple
   chunks
½ frozen banana
1 cup chopped spinach
1 cup plain soy milk
½ cup ice

BOOST IT: **1 teaspoon
chia seeds**

This silky avocado and pineapple green shake is full of healthy fats and antioxidants for a rich and soothing way to slow down. An avocado lover's delight.

DIRECTIONS: Combine all the ingredients in a blender and blend from low to high until frosty smooth.

CALORIES: 432, FAT: 25G, CARBS: 45G, PROTEIN: 12G, FIBER: 14G | VITAMIN A: 72%, CALCIUM: 36%, VITAMIN C: 109%, IRON: 17% | ALSO RICH IN MANGANESE AND RIBOFLAVIN.

Pure Pistachio

135 pure pistachio

1 cup vanilla soy milk

⅓ cup raw pistachios, soaked and drained

1 frozen banana

Salt to taste

Sweetener to taste

BOOST IT: **1 teaspoon matcha powder**

This pastel green blend salutes the pure perfection of a plump pistachio. Pistachios are rich in copper, manganese, phosphorus, and B vitamins; B vitamins may help calm your mood and allow you to manage stress more effectively.

DIRECTIONS: Combine the soy milk and pistachios and blend from low to high until smooth. Add the remaining ingredients and blend from low to high until frosty smooth.

CALORIES: 443, FAT: 23G, CARBS: 46G, PROTEIN: 17G, FIBER: 9G | VITAMIN A: 16%, CALCIUM: 35%, VITAMIN C: 21%, IRON: 18%

136 basil strawberries-and-cream stress-crusher shake

½ cup vanilla soy milk

1 tablespoon chopped fresh basil leaves

1 cup frozen strawberries

1 frozen banana

½ cup soy yogurt

BOOST IT: **1 teaspoon flax oil or 1 tablespoon mashed avocado**

TOPPING: **a curl or pinch of grated lemon zest**

This strawberries-and-cream shake is accented with sweet basil and lemon zest. Rose-colored berries and elegant sweet basil leaves will melt you into strawberry serendipity, crushing all stress as you sip. Add some healthy fat via flax oil or avocado to help slow digestion and balance blood sugar to further stabilize your calm mood.

DIRECTIONS: In a blender, combine the soy milk and basil and blend from low to high until smooth. Add the remaining ingredients and blend from low to high until frosty smooth.

CALORIES: 290, FAT: 5G, CARBS: 58G, PROTEIN: 10G, FIBER: 8G | VITAMIN A: 10%, CALCIUM: 36%, VITAMIN C: 159%, IRON: 13% | ALSO RICH IN MANGANESE.

137 minty melon cool-down

3 tablespoons fresh
  lemon or lime juice

½ cup water or coconut
  water

2 tablespoons chopped
  fresh mint leaves

1 banana

Drizzle of sweetener
  (optional)

3 cups frozen
  honeydew melon
  chunks

BOOST IT: **1 teaspoon
aloe vera juice**

Remember back when people would tell you to go "take a chill pill" if you were worked up, stressed out, or had a twisted unhappy look on your face? Well, this is my version of a chill pill, in a smoothie. Sweet melon swirls with cheerful citrus, cooling mint, and soothing aloe for a boost. Instant cool-down. Chill-pill-free.

DIRECTIONS: In a blender, combine the citrus juice, water, mint, banana, and sweetener, if using, and blend from low to high until smooth. Add the melon and aloe vera juice, if using, and blend from low to high until frosty smooth.

CALORIES: 305, FAT: 1G, CARBS: 78G, PROTEIN: 5G, FIBER: 9G | VITAMIN A: 16%, CALCIUM: 7%, VITAMIN C: 208%, IRON: 15%

138 creamy vanilla daydream

¾ to 1 cup vanilla soy
  milk

¼ cup plain soy yogurt

1 tablespoon raw
  walnuts or Brazil nuts

1 frozen banana

1 tablespoon rolled oats

2 teaspoons maple
  syrup

3 to 4 pinches of
  ground cinnamon

Pinch of salt

A few drops of pure
  vanilla extract

This soothing blend of vanilla, walnuts, oats, and cinnamon will ease you into a calm state of vanilla daydream bliss. Omega-3 fatty acids, like those found in walnuts, may help regulate stress hormones. Add protein powder for a more balanced nutrient profile to keep you feeling centered and well nourished.

DIRECTIONS: Combine all the ingredients in a blender and blend from low to high until frosty smooth.

BOOST IT: **a scoop of vanilla vegan protein powder**

CALORIES: 346, FAT: 10G, CARBS: 55G, PROTEIN: 13G, FIBER: 6G | VITAMIN A: 12%, CALCIUM: 41%, VITAMIN C: 17%, IRON: 13% | ALSO RICH IN MANGANESE.

Coolheaded Flower

139 frozen aloe-kiwi lemonade

¼ cup fresh lemon juice

½ cup coconut water

2 kiwis, peeled

1 tablespoon agave syrup, or to taste

1 teaspoon aloe vera juice

1 cup ice

BOOST IT: 1 tablespoon chopped fresh mint

Step inside a dreamy, green, frosted lemonade wonderland with this frozen aloe-kiwi sip. It's perfect on a sizzling hot summer day or after a workout, as it cools and calms from the inside out.

DIRECTIONS: Combine all the ingredients in a blender and blend from low to high until frosty smooth.

CALORIES: 195, FAT: 1G, CARBS: 48G, PROTEIN: 3G, FIBER: 6G | VITAMIN A: 3%, CALCIUM: 10%, VITAMIN C: 286%, IRON: 16% | ALSO RICH IN POTASSIUM.

140 coolheaded flower

1 cup coconut water

1 tablespoon fresh chamomile flowers

¼ cup grapefruit juice

1½ cups frozen watermelon chunks

½ cup frozen peach chunks or 1 fresh peach, pitted and sliced

BOOST IT: 1 tablespoon chopped fresh mint leaves

Don't lose your cool. Mellow your mood with this pinky-peach slow-down sip. This blend features lazy, calm chamomile flowers with their drowsy buds and ruffled white petals.

DIRECTIONS: In a blender, combine the coconut water and chamomile flowers and blend until the buds smooth out. Add the remaining ingredients and blend from low to high until frosty smooth.

CALORIES: 171, FAT: 2G, CARBS: 36G, PROTEIN: 6G, FIBER: 9G | VITAMIN A: 17%, CALCIUM: 16%, VITAMIN C: 68%, IRON: 11% | ALSO RICH IN POTASSIUM, MANGANESE, MAGNESIUM, AND RIBOFLAVIN.

141 raspberry de-frazzler

1 cup vanilla soy yogurt

¼ cup vanilla soy milk

1 cup fresh or frozen raspberries

1 banana

2 teaspoons agave syrup

½ cup ice

BOOST IT: 1 teaspoon aloe vera and/or 1 teaspoon chamomile flower buds

Feeling frazzled, stressed, not yourself? Antioxidant-rich raspberries, perky and sweet in flavor, will put you back in a cheery state when blended with creamy banana and soy yogurt. Antioxidants like vitamin C help your body combat stress.

DIRECTIONS: Combine all the ingredients in a blender and blend from low to high until frosty smooth.

CALORIES: 413, FAT: 6G, CARBS: 86G, PROTEIN: 12G, FIBER: 14G | VITAMIN A: 5%, CALCIUM: 47%, VITAMIN C: 71%, IRON: 15%

142 sunset island frosty

1 cup coconut water

1 cup frozen mango chunks

¼ cup frozen pineapple chunks

1 orange, peeled and segmented (fresh or frozen)

1 frozen banana

Unsweetened dried coconut flakes (optional)

½ cup ice

BOOST IT: ¼ cup vanilla soy yogurt

Slink away to your favorite spot in the sun. Waves crashing. Sea breeze. Grab this pineapple-orange-mango coconut water frosty, find a palm tree hammock, and watch a cotton-candy–colored sunset. Stress be gone.

DIRECTIONS: Combine all the ingredients in a blender and blend from low to high until frosty smooth.

CALORIES: 364, FAT: 1G, CARBS: 90G, PROTEIN: 6G, FIBER: 14G | VITAMIN A: 35%, CALCIUM: 17%, VITAMIN C: 297%, IRON: 8% | ALSO RICH IN POTASSIUM AND VITAMIN B$_6$.

143 strawberry coconut-water frosty

1¼ cups coconut water

¾ cup frozen
  strawberries

2 tablespoons freshly
  squeezed lemon juice

2 teaspoons agave
  syrup

½ cup ice

BOOST IT: **1 frozen sliced
banana**

This light and frosty sip blends cool potassium-rich coconut water, frozen strawberries, perky lemon juice, and sweet agave syrup. Feel calm, light, and flirty with this pink frosty in hand. Electrolytes like potassium help you stay hydrated, which is key to maintaining a calm and de-stressed mood.

DIRECTIONS: Combine all the ingredients in a blender and blend from low to high until frosty smooth.

CALORIES: 145, FAT: 1G, CARBS: 35G, PROTEIN: 2G, FIBER: 6G | VITAMIN A: 2%, CALCIUM: 9%, VITAMIN C: 103%, IRON: 9% | ALSO RICH IN POTASSIUM AND MAGNESIUM.

144 peachy-ginger matcha shake

1 cup vanilla soy milk

1 small peach, pitted
  and sliced

2 frozen bananas

1 teaspoon matcha
  powder

¼ teaspoon ginger
  powder

¼ cup ice

BOOST IT: **1 teaspoon
chia seeds**

Tummy-soothing ginger, sweet mellow peach, and creamy banana blend with cool soy milk and matcha for this Zen-ergy–style sip. Matcha powder, with its pastel, powdery green color and mellow tea aroma, will give you your caffeine fix without the jitters you'd get from coffee. Matcha is also loaded with free-radical-fighting antioxidants to help your body fight stress.

DIRECTIONS: Combine all the ingredients in a blender and blend from low to high until frosty smooth.

CALORIES: 354, FAT: 5G, CARBS: 71G, PROTEIN: 12G, FIBER: 10G | VITAMIN A: 19%, CALCIUM: 32%, VITAMIN C: 46%, IRON: 12% | ALSO RICH IN POTASSIUM, RIBOFLAVIN, AND VITAMIN B$_6$.

145 stress-free sunrise shake

1 cup frozen cantaloupe
chunks

1 cup frozen
strawberries

1 banana

1 cup vanilla soy milk

BOOST IT: **1 teaspoon
chia seeds**

My secret ingredient swirled into this strawberry-banana sunrise smoothie is frozen cantaloupe. This cool blend of protein-rich soy milk and antioxidant-rich fruit is all you need to feel stress-free for your day ahead. Antioxidants like vitamin C help you combat stress.

DIRECTIONS: Combine all the ingredients in a blender and blend from low to high until frosty smooth.

CALORIES: 303, FAT: 5G, CARBS: 59G, PROTEIN: 10G, FIBER: 8G | VITAMIN A: 117%, CALCIUM: 34%, VITAMIN C: 254%, IRON: 13% | ALSO RICH IN POTASSIUM, RIBOFLAVIN, AND MANGANESE.

146 lovely lavender blackberry

1 cup frozen
blackberries

1 tablespoon fresh
culinary lavender
buds

1 frozen banana

1 cup vanilla rice milk

½ cup ice

BOOST IT: **pinch of
grated fresh ginger**

The intoxicating aroma of fresh lavender buds will whoosh you into a calm, gentle hum of relaxation. Breathe in the aroma as you sip on this blackberry-banana rice milk smoothie. Blackberries contain vitamin C, which may help your body manage the effects of stress.

DIRECTIONS: Combine all the ingredients in a blender and blend from low to high until frosty smooth.

CALORIES: 297, FAT: 3G, CARBS: 68G, PROTEIN: 4G, FIBER: 11G | VITAMIN A: 18%, CALCIUM: 35%, VITAMIN C: 68%, IRON: 7% | ALSO RICH IN MANGANESE.

Lovely Lavender Blackberry

147 strawberry-lemon cream

¾ cup vanilla soy yogurt

½ cup vanilla soy milk

½ cup frozen strawberries

1 frozen banana

½ cup ice

1 tablespoon fresh lemon juice, plus a pinch of grated lemon zest

BOOST IT: **1 tablespoon raw walnuts**

Sweet red strawberries and fresh lemon flavors swirl into this sunny sip that is sure to brighten your day. Fiber-rich bananas and soothing soy yogurt help nurture a calm body.

DIRECTIONS: Combine all the ingredients except the lemon juice and zest in a blender and blend from low to high until smooth. Reduce the blender speed to low; slowly add the lemon juice and zest and blend to incorporate.

CALORIES: 294, FAT: 4G, CARBS: 63G, PROTEIN: 8G, FIBER: 7G | VITAMIN A: 2%, CALCIUM: 34%, VITAMIN C: 111%, IRON: 9%

148 mango-cado kale kiss

½ cup orange juice

¼ cup soy milk

3 tablespoons mashed avocado

¾ cup frozen mango chunks

2 cups chopped kale leaves

1 frozen banana

½ cup ice

BOOST IT: **1 teaspoon chia seeds**

Soothing avocado and soy milk pair with creamy mango and banana for an antioxidant-rich way to infuse your day with wellness. Check out all the nutrients in this blend—that should make you feel well and calm!

DIRECTIONS: Combine all the ingredients in a blender and blend from low to high until frosty smooth.

CALORIES: 377, FAT: 7G, CARBS: 72G, PROTEIN: 10G, FIBER: 10G | VITAMIN A: 441%, CALCIUM: 29%, VITAMIN C: 450%, IRON: 19% | ALSO RICH IN POTASSIUM, VITAMIN B$_6$, AND MANGANESE.

149 raspberry-peach rise and shine

¾ cup frozen peach
   chunks

¾ cup fresh raspberries

½ cup plain soy yogurt

1 cup orange juice

1 banana

1 tablespoon rolled oats
   (optional)

½ cup ice

BOOST IT: **1 teaspoon
chia seeds**

Start your day off on a smooth, sweet note with the help of antioxidant- and fiber-rich raspberries. The mellow flavors of peaches and soy yogurt help calm, while the orange juice sweetens.

DIRECTIONS: Combine all the ingredients in a blender and blend from low to high until frosty smooth.

**CALORIES: 403, FAT: 4G, CARBS: 91G, PROTEIN: 9G, FIBER: 13G
| VITAMIN A: 20%, CALCIUM: 24%, VITAMIN C: 278%, IRON: 13%**

150 creamy kale coconut

2 cups chopped kale
   leaves

½ cup mashed avocado

Juice and meat of 1
   fresh young coconut
   (see page 160 for
   instructions on
   opening a coconut)

½ cup ice

BOOST IT: **½ frozen
banana**

Grab a fresh young coconut and blend up this electrolyte-rich green smoothie. Creamy avocado and coconut are perfect for calming your mood, and superfood kale's nutrients feed your spirit from the inside out. If you cannot find a fresh coconut, substitute 1 cup coconut water and 1 banana. Add a splash of coconut milk or soy yogurt to add extra creaminess.

DIRECTIONS: Combine all the ingredients in a blender and blend from low to high until frosty smooth.

**CALORIES: 454, FAT: 21G, CARBS: 62G, PROTEIN: 9G, FIBER: 9G
| VITAMIN A: 414%, CALCIUM: 29%, VITAMIN C: 280%, IRON: 23%
| ALSO RICH IN POTASSIUM, MANGANESE, AND MAGNESIUM.**

151 peachy melon mellower

½ cup frozen peach
  chunks

1½ cups frozen
  cantaloupe chunks

1 banana

1 cup vanilla soy milk

2 to 3 pinches of
  ground cinnamon or
  ginger powder

BOOST IT: **1 teaspoon
chia seeds**

This peaches and cantaloupe shake is sweet and
mellow, swirled with silky soy milk, sweet banana,
and a hint of cinnamon or ginger. Soothing flavors
inspire a calm mood.

DIRECTIONS: Combine all the ingredients in a blender and
blend from low to high until frosty smooth.

**CALORIES: 319, FAT: 5G, CARBS: 63G, PROTEIN: 11G, FIBER: 8G
| VITAMIN A: 179%, CALCIUM: 33%, VITAMIN C: 170%, IRON: 12%
| ALSO RICH IN POTASSIUM AND RIBOFLAVIN.**

152 walnut-carrot cake

½ cup finely grated
  carrot

1¼ cups vanilla soy milk

2 tablespoons raw
  walnuts

½ cup frozen pineapple
  chunks

½ frozen banana

1 teaspoon maple syrup

2 to 3 pinches of
  ground cinnamon

¼ cup ice

BOOST IT: **1 to 2
tablespoons soy yogurt**

This creamy smoothie tastes like carrot cake,
speckled with walnuts, sweet pineapple,
and perky cinnamon. Cool and cozy flavors. You
can also use carrot juice in place of the carrots
and reduce the soy milk a bit.

DIRECTIONS: Combine the carrots and soy milk in a
blender and blend from low to high until smooth. Add
the remaining ingredients and blend from low to high
until frosty smooth.

**CALORIES: 357, FAT: 15G, CARBS: 46G, PROTEIN: 14G, FIBER: 7G
| VITAMIN A: 198%, CALCIUM: 42%, VITAMIN C: 78%, IRON: 14%
| ALSO RICH IN MANGANESE AND RIBOFLAVIN.**

Mint-Kiwi Green Genius

153 mint-kiwi green genius

½ cup water or coconut water

2 kiwis, peeled

2 cups chopped kale leaves

1 orange, peeled and segmented

¼ cup green grapes

½ banana

1 tablespoon chopped fresh mint

¼ cup ice

BOOST IT: **1 to 2 teaspoons chia seeds**

You'll feel like a genius after sipping this minty cool kiwi and sweet greens whole food smoothie. It's rich in antioxidants to help combat oxidative stress to the brain. Add some chia seeds for a dose of brain-boosting omega-3 fatty acids.

DIRECTIONS: Combine all the ingredients in a blender and blend from low to high until frosty smooth.

CALORIES: 317, FAT: 2G, CARBS: 75G, PROTEIN: 9G, FIBER: 14G | VITAMIN A: 429%, CALCIUM: 33%, VITAMIN C: 429%, IRON: 21% | RICH IN POTASSIUM, MANGANESE, AND VITAMIN B$_6$.

154 tangerine thinker

½ cup soy milk

2 frozen peeled tangerines

½ cup frozen blueberries

1 banana

2 tablespoons raw walnuts

1 teaspoon flax seeds

½ cup ice

BOOST IT: **1 to 2 tablespoons soy yogurt**

Sweet blueberries, sassy tangerines, and omega-3–rich walnuts and flax seeds blend into this chill smoothie that will leave you feeling satisfied, smart, and ready for a study session.

DIRECTIONS: Combine all the ingredients in a blender and blend from low to high until frosty smooth.

CALORIES: 370, FAT: 14G, CARBS: 60G, PROTEIN: 9G, FIBER: 10G | VITAMIN A: 132%, CALCIUM: 19%, VITAMIN C: 99%, IRON: 9%

155 walnut banana-bread shake

1 cup vanilla soy milk

2 to 3 tablespoons raw walnuts

1½ frozen bananas

½ fresh banana

1 tablespoon rolled oats

2 to 3 pinches of ground cinnamon

Sweetener to taste

BOOST IT: **1 teaspoon flax seeds**

GARNISHES: **fresh banana slices and a pinch of crushed walnuts**

Get your cozy on as you sip in the comfort food flavors of banana bread: walnuts, oats, vanilla, and plenty of banana. Walnuts are rich in omega-3 fatty acids.

DIRECTIONS: Combine the soy milk and walnuts in a blender and blend from low to high until smooth. Add the remaining ingredients and blend from low to high until smooth. Top with the garnishes.

CALORIES: 421, FAT: 14G, CARBS: 67G, PROTEIN: 12G, FIBER: 9G | VITAMIN A: 13%, CALCIUM: 33%, VITAMIN C: 34%, IRON: 13%

156 tropical berry daydream

1 cup soy milk

½ cup fresh blueberries

¼ cup pineapple chunks

1 frozen banana

2 tablespoons raw walnuts

1 teaspoon unsweetened dried coconut flakes

½ cup ice

BOOST IT: **1 teaspoon flax seed oil**

Fresh berries and pineapple blend with creamy soy milk, coconut, and banana in this island-inspired, daydream-worthy sip—mental vacation in a glass.

DIRECTIONS: Combine all the ingredients in a blender and blend from low to high until frosty smooth.

CALORIES: 412, FAT: 20G, CARBS: 52G, PROTEIN: 12G, FIBER: 8G | VITAMIN A: 13%, CALCIUM: 34%, VITAMIN C: 60%, IRON: 12%

Walnut Banana-Bread Shake

157 smart mango freeze

½ cup mashed avocado

1 cup frozen mango chunks

1 cup grapefruit juice

½ cup coconut water ice cubes

BOOST IT: **1 teaspoon chia seeds**

Sweet, simple, satisfying. This smarty-pants blend of antioxidant-rich mango, grapefruit juice, and creamy avocado is the easy way to blend, sip, and stay focused on your day. Antioxidants may boost brain function by reducing oxidative stress and inflammation on the brain.

DIRECTIONS: Combine all the ingredients in a blender and blend from low to high until frosty smooth.

CALORIES: 340, FAT: 13G, CARBS: 59G, PROTEIN: 6G, FIBER: 14G | VITAMIN A: 70%, CALCIUM: 11%, VITAMIN C: 225%, IRON: 9% | ALSO RICH IN POTASSIUM.

158 chocolate-almond brain boost

1 teaspoon chia seeds

1 cup vanilla soy milk

1 tablespoon raw cacao powder

1 to 1½ frozen bananas

2 tablespoons almond butter

¼ cup ice

BOOST IT: **1 teaspoon flax seed oil**

Creamy almond butter swirls with rich cacao, banana, vanilla soy milk, and a sprinkle of omega-3 fatty acid–rich chia seeds. This frosty treat is perfect for a study snack or to satisfy a chocolate craving during a busy workday.

DIRECTIONS: Combine the chia seeds and soy milk in a blender and leave for 10 minutes to plump. Add the remaining ingredients and blend from low to high until frosty smooth.

CALORIES: 480, FAT: 28G, CARBS: 48G, PROTEIN: 17G, FIBER: 11G | VITAMIN A: 12%, CALCIUM: 48%, VITAMIN C: 118%, IRON: 22%

159 blueberry mind bender

2 tablespoons raw
   walnuts
1¼ cups vanilla soy milk
1 cup frozen blueberries
1 frozen banana
2 teaspoons chia seeds
½ cup ice

BOOST IT: **drizzle of
flax oil**

You don't have to think too hard about this one.
Blueberries, chia seeds, creamy banana, walnuts,
and vanilla soy milk are easy to understand—one
sip and your taste buds will get it.

DIRECTIONS: Combine the walnuts and soy milk in a
blender and blend from low to high until smooth. Add
the remaining ingredients and blend from low to high
until frosty smooth.

**CALORIES: 446, FAT: 18G, CARBS: 62G, PROTEIN: 15G, FIBER: 11G
| VITAMIN A: 16%, CALCIUM: 44%, VITAMIN C: 41%, IRON: 16%**

160 chia-mango memory

1 cup fresh mango
   chunks
1 teaspoon chia seeds
¼ cup vanilla soy milk
1 frozen banana
1 tablespoon fresh lime
   juice
½ cup ice

BOOST IT: **1 tablespoon
flax or algal oil**

Savor each sip of this velvety, fresh mango smoothie
infused with a bit of soy milk and a squeeze of lime.
Plump, omega-3–rich chia seeds dance in the golden
waves of this antioxidant-rich blend. Boost with flax
or algal oil for even more memory-boosting omega-3
essential fatty acids.

DIRECTIONS: Combine all the ingredients in a blender and
blend from low to high until frosty smooth.

**CALORIES: 247, FAT: 3G, CARBS: 56G, PROTEIN: 4G, FIBER: 8G
| VITAMIN A: 24%, CALCIUM: 11%, VITAMIN C: 85%, IRON: 5%
| ALSO RICH IN VITAMIN B$_6$.**

161 peanut flax-ination

1 tablespoon salted peanut butter

1¼ cups vanilla soy milk

1 frozen banana

2 teaspoons maple syrup

1 to 2 teaspoons flax oil or 1 teaspoon flax seeds

2 to 3 pinches of ground cinnamon

½ cup ice

BOOST IT: **1 to 2 teaspoons raw cacao nibs or cacao powder**

This shake will fascinate, er, flax-inate your taste buds. Flax is one of the richest sources of vegan omega-3 fatty acids, so don't be shy when adding this healthy ingredient. This shake is peanut butter bliss with a brain boost! Add antioxidant-rich cacao for a chocolate spin.

DIRECTIONS: Combine all the ingredients in a blender and blend from low to high until frosty smooth.

CALORIES: 445, FAT: 22G, CARBS: 52G, PROTEIN: 16G, FIBER: 9G | VITAMIN A: 14%, CALCIUM: 41%, VITAMIN C: 17%, IRON: 14%

162 orange-walnut cream shake

1½ frozen bananas

1 orange, peeled and segmented

½ cup vanilla soy milk

3 tablespoons raw walnuts

Pinch of ground cinnamon

¼ cup ice

BOOST IT: **1 teaspoon flax oil and/or 1 teaspoon maple syrup**

Frosty orange and creamy soy milk swirl together in this delightful golden sip with walnuts and a banana accent. I'm in love with this citrus-meets-walnut blend!

DIRECTIONS: Combine all the ingredients in a blender and blend from low to high until frosty smooth.

CALORIES: 444, FAT: 18G, CARBS: 70G, PROTEIN: 11G, FIBER: 11G | VITAMIN A: 16%, CALCIUM: 28%, VITAMIN C: 189%, IRON: 11%

163 mango mastermind shake

1 cup frozen mango
   chunks

1 cup vanilla soy milk

1 frozen banana

Pinch of ground
   cinnamon or cayenne
   (optional)

BOOST IT: **1 teaspoon flax
oil or 1 teaspoon flax
seeds**

Tropical mango and creamy banana blend with simple soy milk in this mind-soothing smoothie. Flax adds omega-3 fatty acids to boost brain health.

DIRECTIONS: Combine all the ingredients in a blender and blend from low to high until frosty smooth.

CALORIES: 352, FAT: 10G, CARBS: 63G, PROTEIN: 9G, FIBER: 7G | VITAMIN A: 37%, CALCIUM: 33%, VITAMIN C: 93%, IRON: 9% | ALSO RICH IN RIBOFLAVIN.

164 clever citrus cooler

1 cup frozen diced
   cucumber

1 cup chopped spinach

1 large orange, peeled
   and segmented, plus
   a pinch of grated zest

½ cup mashed avocado

½ cup coconut water

½ cup ice

BOOST IT: **1 teaspoon
flax oil**

This frosty green cooler—combining citrus, cucumber, and superfood spinach—will help you cool, calm, and collect your oh-so-clever thoughts.

DIRECTIONS: Combine all the ingredients in a blender and blend from low to high until frosty smooth.

CALORIES: 249, FAT: 11G, CARBS: 37G, PROTEIN: 6G, FIBER: 12G | VITAMIN A: 69%, CALCIUM: 16%, VITAMIN C: 199%, IRON: 11% | ALSO RICH IN POTASSIUM, THIAMINE, AND MAGNESIUM.

165 blueberry brainiac

1 cup fresh or frozen blueberries

1 frozen banana

¾ cup vanilla soy milk

¼ cup vanilla soy yogurt

1 teaspoon agave syrup (optional)

½ cup ice

BOOST IT: **1 tablespoon raw walnuts or a scoop of avocado**

OK, really, who doesn't love fresh blueberries? Anyone? Anyone? So grab a bowl of this favorite fruit and blend them into a creamy, dreamy smoothie. Add avocado for a boost of healthy fats or walnuts for brain-boosting omega-3 fatty acids.

DIRECTIONS: Combine all the ingredients in a blender and blend from low to high until frosty smooth.

CALORIES: 331, FAT: 5G, CARBS: 68G, PROTEIN: 10G, FIBER: 8G | VITAMIN A: 15%, CALCIUM: 34%, VITAMIN C: 42%, IRON: 14%

166 pumpkin seed superfood swirl

1 cup vanilla soy milk

½ cup frozen blueberries

1 cup chopped spinach

2 to 3 tablespoons pumpkin seeds, soaked and drained

1 frozen banana

½ cup ice

BOOST IT: **1 to 2 tablespoons mashed avocado**

Pumpkin seeds are rich in a variety of minerals, including zinc and magnesium—nutrients that may boost cognitive function. Sip this blueberry-sweet pumpkin seed smoothie when you want to feel creative and focused.

DIRECTIONS: Combine all the ingredients in a blender and blend from low to high until frosty smooth.

CALORIES: 347, FAT: 13G, CARBS: 50G, PROTEIN: 14G, FIBER: 7G | VITAMIN A: 70%, CALCIUM: 35%, VITAMIN C: 43%, IRON: 28% | ALSO RICH IN RIBOFLAVIN, MANGANESE, AND MAGNESIUM.

167 purple productivity

1½ cups chopped kale leaves

1¼ cups soy milk

1 tablespoon açaí powder

3 tablespoons mashed avocado

1 frozen banana

Sweetener to taste (optional)

½ cup ice

BOOST IT: ¼ cup frozen blueberries

Smoothies that consist of a blend of healthy fats, carbohydrates, and protein (as opposed to a mostly carbs energy jolt) can help sustain your energy. So this well-rounded, creamy açaí green smoothie is perfect for long study sessions, work projects, or anytime you need to get a lot done with minimal interruptions from a growling tummy.

DIRECTIONS: Combine the kale and soy milk in a blender and blend from low to high until smooth. Add the remaining ingredients and blend from low to high until frosty smooth.

CALORIES: 360, FAT: 12G, CARBS: 53G, PROTEIN: 15G, FIBER: 9G | VITAMIN A: 43%, CALCIUM: 58%, VITAMIN C: 305%, IRON: 24% | ALSO RICH IN MANGANESE, RIBOFLAVIN, AND VITAMIN B$_6$.

168 challenger chip cookie

1 tablespoon raw walnuts

1 teaspoon rolled oats

1 cup vanilla soy milk

¼ cup soy milk ice cubes

1½ frozen bananas

1 tablespoon raw cacao nibs or cacao powder

2 teaspoons agave syrup, or to taste

4 to 5 pinches of ground cinnamon

¼ cup ice

This rustic cookie-inspired blend of walnuts, cinnamon, banana, oats, cacao nibs, and soy milk is a worthy brain-boosting treat to prepare you for a challenging day. Toss in some flax seeds for extra omega-3 fatty acids.

DIRECTIONS: Combine the walnuts, oats, and soy milk in a blender and blend from low to high until smooth. Add the remaining ingredients and blend from low to high until frosty smooth.

BOOST IT: 1 teaspoon flax seeds

CALORIES: 337, FAT: 15G, CARBS: 65G, PROTEIN: 12G, FIBER: 9G | VITAMIN A: 15%, CALCIUM: 40%, VITAMIN C: 26%, IRON: 12%

169 orange-flax focus frosty

1¼ cups freshly squeezed orange juice

½ cup frozen pineapple chunks

1 frozen banana

¾ cup ice

1 teaspoon flax oil

BOOST IT: **a few pinches of cayenne**

Sweet orange and pineapple flavors blend with a hint of flax oil in this light and frosty sip. The omega-3 fatty acids found in flax oil may improve brain function to help you focus.

DIRECTIONS: Combine all the ingredients in a blender and blend from low to high until frosty smooth.

CALORIES: 323, FAT: 6G, CARBS: 69G, PROTEIN: 4G, FIBER: 5G | VITAMIN A: 15%, CALCIUM: 6%, VITAMIN C: 337%, IRON: 6% | ALSO RICH IN MANGANESE.

170 pop-quiz green smoothie

1 cup chopped kale leaves

1 cup chopped spinach

1 cup soy milk

1 frozen banana

½ cup diced apple

1 to 2 teaspoons salted almond or peanut butter

½ cup ice

BOOST IT: ¼ **cup fresh or frozen green grapes**

Pop quiz! What is green and leafy and packed with nutrients? Trick question! There are plenty of leafy greens that could answer this question—kale and spinach certainly qualify. Add some sweet apple and salty nut butter for an A+ smoothie.

DIRECTIONS: Combine the kale, spinach, and soy milk in a blender and blend from low to high until smooth. Add the remaining ingredients and blend from low to high until frosty smooth.

CALORIES: 285, FAT: 6G, CARBS: 51G, PROTEIN: 12G, FIBER: 8G | VITAMIN A: 274%, CALCIUM: 44%, VITAMIN C: 169%, IRON: 19% | ALSO RICH IN MAGNESIUM, MANGANESE, POTASSIUM, RIBOFLAVIN, AND VITAMIN B$_6$.

171 creativity shake

1 cup vanilla soy milk

1 frozen banana

1 cup frozen orange
segments

¼ cup ice

BOOST IT: **1 teaspoon
chia seeds**

Paint a blue sky pink, fill a flower vase with colored
pencils, make raspberry muffins instead of blueberry.
Let life's little inspirations lead the way and embrace
your creative side. And try my creative spin on a
banana-berry soy shake by swapping out
strawberries for frozen orange!

DIRECTIONS: Combine all the ingredients in a blender and
blend from low to high until frosty smooth.

**CALORIES: 290, FAT: 5G, CARBS: 56G, PROTEIN: 10G, FIBER: 8G
| VITAMIN A: 20%, CALCIUM: 38%, VITAMIN C: 177%, IRON: 9%
| ALSO RICH IN RIBOFLAVIN AND POTASSIUM.**

172 apple-almond analysis

1¼ cups diced apple

1 cup vanilla soy milk

1 to 2 tablespoons
almond butter

1 frozen banana

1 to 2 teaspoons maple
syrup

Pinch of ground
cinnamon

½ cup ice

BOOST IT: **1 teaspoon
flax seeds**

Don't overanalyze this sweet blend of fresh
apple, creamy almond butter, banana, and soy.
This soothing shake is easy to understand—just
take a sip! Almond butter is rich in brain-boosting
minerals like copper and magnesium.

DIRECTIONS: Combine all the ingredients in a blender and
blend from low to high until frosty smooth.

**CALORIES: 398, FAT: 14G, CARBS: 70G, PROTEIN: 11G, FIBER: 9G
| VITAMIN A: 13%, CALCIUM: 37%, VITAMIN C: 30%, IRON: 13%**

Flavor Swirl Shake

173 flavor swirl shake

PINK SMOOTHIE
1 cup frozen
 watermelon chunks
½ cup soy milk

BOOST IT: 1 teaspoon
flax oil

YELLOW SMOOTHIE
1 cup frozen pineapple
 chunks
½ banana
½ cup soy milk

Pink and golden smoothies swirl together in this sunny two-flavor blend of frosty, fruity bliss. Add some flax oil for a boost of omega-3 fatty acids.

DIRECTIONS: Combine all the ingredients for the pink smoothie in a blender and blend from low to high until frosty smooth. Pour into 2 glasses. Rinse the blender and add all the ingredients for the yellow smoothie; blend from low to high until frosty smooth. Tilt the glasses a little when pouring the yellow smoothie, allowing the two colors to swirl.

CALORIES: 276, FAT: 5G, CARBS: 53G, PROTEIN: 9G, FIBER: 5G | VITAMIN A: 30%, CALCIUM: 33%, VITAMIN C: 153%, IRON: 11% | ALSO RICH IN MANGANESE.

174 purple perception açaí shake

1½ cups frozen
 watermelon chunks
1 frozen banana
1 cup soy milk
1 tablespoon açaí
 powder

BOOST IT: 1 teaspoon
chia seeds

This frosty, creamy purple açaí shake isn't what it appears to be. It looks like açaí—and has a hint of it too—but the actual flavor is an alluring combination of watermelon, soy milk, and creamy banana. I love when food flavors are not what you might perceive them to be.

DIRECTIONS: Combine all the ingredients in a blender and blend from low to high until frosty smooth.

CALORIES: 300, FAT: 7G, CARBS: 54G, PROTEIN: 10G, FIBER: 5G | VITAMIN A: 47%, CALCIUM: 34%, VITAMIN C: 68%, IRON: 12% | ALSO RICH IN RIBOFLAVIN.

175 strawberry-pineapple inspiration

1 cup frozen
   strawberries

½ cup frozen pineapple
   chunks

1¼ cups vanilla rice milk

1 frozen banana

1 tablespoon raw
   walnuts

1 teaspoon maple syrup

½ cup ice

BOOST IT: **1 to 2
tablespoons sunflower
seeds**

Get inspired by sweet strawberries, perky pineapple, creamy bananas, omega-3 fatty acid–rich walnuts, and cool rice milk in this easy, creamy smoothie. Toss in some sunflower seeds for a boost of brain-healthy vitamin E, selenium, and copper.

DIRECTIONS: Combine all the ingredients in a blender and blend from low to high until frosty smooth.

CALORIES: 406, FAT: 8G, CARBS: 85G, PROTEIN: 5G, FIBER: 8G | VITAMIN A: 3%, CALCIUM: 8%, VITAMIN C: 223%, IRON: 9% | ALSO RICH IN MANGANESE.

176 chocolate avocado

½ cup mashed avocado

1 tablespoon raw cacao
   powder

1 cup plain soy milk

2 teaspoons agave
   syrup

¾ cup ice

BOOST IT: **1 teaspoon
raw cacao nibs and/or
1 frozen banana**

Chocolate and avocados might not be the most obvious culinary pairing, but trust me—these two decadent flavors are a match made in smoothie heaven. Avocados are rich in monounsaturated fats for brain health and to aid fat-soluble nutrient absorption.

DIRECTIONS: Combine all the ingredients in a blender and blend from low to high until frosty smooth.

CALORIES: 290, FAT: 15G, CARBS: 30G, PROTEIN: 10G, FIBER: 8G | VITAMIN A: 12%, CALCIUM: 33%, VITAMIN C: 12%, IRON: 13% | ALSO RICH IN RIBOFLAVIN.

177 coconut daydream

2 tablespoons raw walnuts

½ cup vanilla soy milk

2 tablespoons unsweetened dried coconut flakes

½ cup plain soy yogurt

1 frozen banana

½ cup coconut water or coconut milk ice cubes

Pinch of ground cinnamon

BOOST IT: 1 teaspoon raw cacao powder for a chocolate-coconut flavor twist

Take a mini vacation with this mind-soothing smoothie. Dreamy, cool coconut blends with omega-3–rich walnuts and sweet banana. Revel in your post-smoothie-drinking daydream.

DIRECTIONS: Combine the walnuts and soy milk in a blender and blend from low to high until smooth. Add the remaining ingredients and blend from low to high until frosty smooth.

CALORIES: 399, FAT: 17G, CARBS: 55G, PROTEIN: 13G, FIBER: 8G | VITAMIN A: 7%, CALCIUM: 38%, VITAMIN C: 23%, IRON: 15% | ALSO RICH IN MANGANESE.

178 strawberry-banana boost

1 cup frozen strawberries

1 frozen banana

1¼ cups vanilla soy milk

¼ cup ice

BOOST IT: 1 to 2 teaspoons chia seeds

This classic banana-berry soy shake is sure to motivate you to focus on whatever task you face today. Add some chia seeds for a healthy-brain boost of omega-3 fatty acids!

DIRECTIONS: Combine all the ingredients in a blender and blend from low to high until frosty smooth.

CALORIES: 276, FAT: 6G, CARBS: 48G, PROTEIN: 11G, FIBER: 7G | VITAMIN A: 14%, CALCIUM: 41%, VITAMIN C: 158%, IRON: 13%

Strawberry-Banana Boost

179 book of greens

1 cup chopped kale
   leaves

½ cup mashed avocado

½ frozen banana

1 orange, peeled and
   segmented

2 tablespoons raw
   walnuts

1 cup coconut water
   (substitute soy milk
   for a creamier
   version)

½ cup ice

BOOST IT: ¼ cup frozen
mango chunks

Book-smart is in, so read every chance
you get. Browse the front page of your local
newspaper, check out a celeb interview in your
favorite magazine, or download one of those
oh-so-addicting books involving anything from
vampires to magic wands. The perfect afternoon-
read pairing? This green smoothie!

DIRECTIONS: Combine all the ingredients in a blender and
blend from low to high until frosty smooth.

CALORIES: 431, FAT: 21G, CARBS: 58G, PROTEIN: 12G, FIBER: 16G
| VITAMIN A: 217%, CALCIUM: 25%, VITAMIN C: 328%, IRON: 17%
| ALSO RICH IN POTASSIUM AND MANGANESE.

180 silky green

1 cup silken tofu

1 cup soy or rice milk

2 tablespoons mashed
   avocado

1 cup chopped kale
   leaves

1 frozen banana

1 kiwi, peeled

1 to 3 teaspoons maple
   syrup

Salt to taste

½ cup ice

Greens, silky avocado, sweet kiwi, banana, and silken
tofu swirl to create this tofu-infused meal-in-a-glass
blend. Healthy-fat avocado helps nurture brain
function.

DIRECTIONS: Combine all the ingredients in a blender and
blend from low to high until frosty smooth.

BOOST IT: substitute coconut water ice cubes for the
regular ice cubes

CALORIES: 478, FAT: 13G, CARBS: 68G, PROTEIN: 27G,
FIBER: 10G | VITAMIN A: 219%, CALCIUM: 52%, VITAMIN C:
276%, IRON: 30% | ALSO RICH IN POTASSIUM AND MAGNESIUM.

181 brainy avocado green smoothie

½ cup orange juice

½ cup plain soy milk

2 cups chopped kale leaves

¼ cup mashed avocado

1 banana

½ cup ice

BOOST IT: 1 to 2 teaspoons flax oil

This green sweet cooler is loaded with monounsaturated fats, protein, and vitamin C. For a boost of omega-3 fatty acids, add flax oil.

DIRECTIONS: Combine all the ingredients in a blender and blend from low to high until frosty smooth.

CALORIES: 426, FAT: 10G, CARBS: 79G, PROTEIN: 12G, FIBER: 10G | VITAMIN A: 21%, CALCIUM: 43%, VITAMIN C: 64%, IRON: 16% | ALSO RICH IN MANGANESE, POTASSIUM, AND VITAMIN B$_6$.

182 chocolate-covered blueberry brain boost

1 cup frozen blueberries

1 tablespoon raw cacao powder

¾ cup vanilla almond milk

1 frozen banana

2 tablespoons mashed avocado

BOOST IT: 1 teaspoon chia seeds or a spoonful of almond butter

Blueberries, rich in brain-boosting antioxidants, blend with cacao powder to further enhance brain function. Creamy monounsaturated fat–rich avocado smooths out this luscious shake.

DIRECTIONS: Combine all the ingredients in a blender and blend from low to high until frosty smooth.

CALORIES: 259, FAT: 7G, CARBS: 53G, PROTEIN: 5G, FIBER: 10G | VITAMIN A: 11%, CALCIUM: 25%, VITAMIN C: 44%, IRON: 10% | ALSO RICH IN MANGANESE AND VITAMIN E.

Pure Pineapple

183 pure pineapple

2 cups frozen pineapple
  chunks

½ banana

1 cup vanilla soy milk

BOOST IT: **1 teaspoon
chia seeds**

This simple blend of frozen pineapple and soy milk is
a luscious way to get a healthy boost of the digestive
enzyme bromelain. Bromelain, which is found in
pineapple, may help reduce inflammation in the
body, and thus improve digestive function.

DIRECTIONS: Combine all the ingredients in a blender and
blend from low to high until frosty smooth.

**CALORIES: 305, FAT: 5G, CARBS: 61G, PROTEIN: 8G, FIBER: 6G
| VITAMIN A: 4%, CALCIUM: 31%, VITAMIN C: 17%, IRON: 9%**

184 blackberry cream

1 cup vanilla soy yogurt

1 banana

½ frozen banana

½ cup frozen
  blackberries

A few splashes of soy
  milk, as needed

BOOST IT: **splash of
coconut milk**

This creamy pastel purple swirl of soothing bananas,
soy yogurt, and fiber-rich blackberries is a delicious
blend that your tummy will thank you for.

DIRECTIONS: Combine all the ingredients in a blender and
blend from low to high until frosty smooth.

**CALORIES: 365, FAT: 5G, CARBS: 79G, PROTEIN: 10G, FIBER: 11G
| VITAMIN A: 5%, CALCIUM: 38%, VITAMIN C: 51%, IRON: 12%**

Blackberry Cream

185 spa day smoothie

1½ cups fresh or frozen honeydew melon chunks

½ cup chopped cucumber

½ cup plain or vanilla soy yogurt

½ cup coconut water

1 tablespoon chopped fresh mint

BOOST IT: **1 frozen banana for added thickness**

Digestion improves when you are in a relaxed state, so this cool cucumber and honeydew smoothie is here to help in a very delicious way. As you sip these spa day flavors, envision yourself with a facial mask and chilled cucumbers over your eyes—mint, coconut, and melon aromas wafting through the air. Close your eyes and enjoy your spa day smoothie.

DIRECTIONS: Combine all the ingredients in a blender and blend from low to high until frosty smooth.

CALORIES: 202, FAT: 2G, CARBS: 43G, PROTEIN: 6G, FIBER: 5G | VITAMIN A: 4%, CALCIUM: 21%, VITAMIN C: 84%, IRON: 8% | ALSO RICH IN POTASSIUM.

186 papaya-lime sunrise smoothie

2 cups chopped fresh or frozen papaya

2 tablespoons fresh lime juice, plus a pinch of lime zest

1 frozen banana

1 teaspoon maple syrup

½ cup ice

A few splashes of non-dairy milk or coconut water, as needed

BOOST IT: **1 to 2 tablespoons vanilla soy yogurt**

Papaya is the only fruit rich in the digestive enzyme papain—which makes it a super-healthy smoothie ingredient. Papaya produces a silky tropical smoothie. This silky blend is accented with lime and maple.

DIRECTIONS: Combine all the ingredients in a blender and blend from low to high until frosty smooth.

CALORIES: 218, FAT: 1G, CARBS: 55G, PROTEIN: 3G, FIBER: 8G | VITAMIN A: 63%, CALCIUM: 8%, VITAMIN C: 313%, IRON: 3% | ALSO RICH IN POTASSIUM AND VITAMIN B_6.

187 pineapple-ginger enzyme frosty

1½ cups frozen
   pineapple chunks

1 banana

½ teaspoon grated
   fresh ginger

½ cup coconut water

¼ cup ice

BOOST IT: 1 teaspoon
aloe vera juice

This is a light and refreshing blend of fruit and coconut water. Combining enzyme-rich pineapple, spicy-soothing ginger, cool coconut water, and creamy sweet banana is a tropical way to nurture digestion.

DIRECTIONS: Combine all the ingredients in a blender and blend from low to high until frosty smooth.

CALORIES: 247, FAT: 1G, CARBS: 62G, PROTEIN: 4G, FIBER: 8G | VITAMIN A: 4%, CALCIUM: 7%, VITAMIN C: 207%, IRON: 8% | ALSO RICH IN MANGANESE, POTASSIUM, AND VITAMIN B$_6$.

188 green apple pectin perk

1 small green apple,
   cored and chopped

1 cup orange juice

1 frozen banana

½ cup frozen
   strawberries

½ cup ice

BOOST IT: ½ cup vanilla
soy yogurt

Green apples, rich in pectin and fiber, blend with citrus and strawberries here. Cozy up to your favorite smoothie-sipping spot and enjoy this fruity fiber-rich blend. Add soy yogurt for a boost of probiotics.

DIRECTIONS: Combine all the ingredients in a blender and blend from low to high until frosty smooth.

CALORIES: 334, FAT: 1G, CARBS: 83G, PROTEIN: 4G, FIBER: 10G | VITAMIN A: 14%, CALCIUM: 6%, VITAMIN C: 308%, IRON: 7% | ALSO RICH IN POTASSIUM.

189 banana-cashew "milk" shake

¼ cup raw cashews, soaked and drained

¾ cup water

2 frozen bananas

A few pinches of ginger powder or ground cinnamon

1 teaspoon maple syrup (optional)

Pinch of salt

¼ cup ice

BOOST IT: 1 teaspoon chia seeds

I love bananas for their tummy-soothing properties. They are easy to digest, provide a quick boost of energy, and contain potassium and both soluble and insoluble fiber. This ultra creamy "milk" shake is infused with plenty of bananas plus silky soaked cashews. I call this a tummy tamer!

DIRECTIONS: Combine the cashews and water, and maple syrup, if using, in a blender and blend from low to high until creamy. Add the remaining ingredients and blend from low to high until frosty smooth.

CALORIES: 446, FAT: 16G, CARBS: 75G, PROTEIN: 8G, FIBER: 8G | VITAMIN A: 3%, CALCIUM: 6%, VITAMIN C: 34%, IRON: 16% | ALSO RICH IN MANGANESE, POTASSIUM, AND VITAMIN B$_6$.

190 island enzyme blitz

½ cup frozen pineapple chunks

½ cup fresh papaya chunks

1 frozen banana

½ cup orange juice

½ cup soy milk

½ cup coconut water ice cubes

BOOST IT: 1 teaspoon unsweetened dried coconut flakes and/or 1 teaspoon coconut milk

This frosty smoothie is loaded with the fruit enzymes papain and bromelain found in papaya and pineapple. Island-inspired accents—creamy banana, sunny citrus, and coconut water ice cubes— make this a swoon-worthy, island-daydream sort of sip.

DIRECTIONS: Combine all the ingredients in a blender and blend from low to high until frosty smooth.

CALORIES: 300, FAT: 3G, CARBS: 65G, PROTEIN: 8G, FIBER: 8G | VITAMIN A: 28%, CALCIUM: 23%, VITAMIN C: 259%, IRON: 10% | ALSO RICH IN MANGANESE, POTASSIUM, AND VITAMIN B$_6$.

191 spicy radish cooler

¼ cup chopped
    radishes (about 3
    medium radishes)
½ cup coconut water
¼ teaspoon grated
    fresh ginger
½ banana
1 teaspoon agave
    syrup, or to taste
Pinch of salt
½ to 1 cup ice

BOOST IT: 1 teaspoon
aloe vera juice

This radish-infused, frosty-textured cooler may help calm an upset tummy, thanks to the spicy ginger and acid-soothing radishes. For a stronger veggie-radish flavor, omit the banana.

DIRECTIONS: Combine the radishes and coconut water in a blender and blend from low to high until pink and frothy. Add the remaining ingredients and blend from low to high until frosty smooth.

CALORIES: 99, FAT: 1G, CARBS: 23G, PROTEIN: 2G, FIBER: 3G
| VITAMIN A: 1%, CALCIUM: 5%, VITAMIN C: 20%, IRON: 4%
| ALSO RICH IN MAGNESIUM, MANGANESE, AND POTASSIUM.

192 pure banana shake

2 frozen bananas
1 cup vanilla soy milk
    (or substitute rice
    milk)
2 to 3 pinches of
    ground nutmeg (or
    substitute cinnamon)

BOOST IT: 2 tablespoons
raw walnuts plus a
pinch of salt

Keep things simple with this silky-smooth, frosty-cool, pure banana shake—accented by cozy nutmeg and the option of a ruffle of walnuts, rich in omega-3 fatty acids.

DIRECTIONS: Combine all the ingredients in a blender and blend from low to high until frosty smooth.

CALORIES: 310, FAT: 5G, CARBS: 62G, PROTEIN: 10G, FIBER: 7G
| VITAMIN A: 13%, CALCIUM: 31%, VITAMIN C: 34%, IRON: 9%

193 green pineapple paradise

½ cup pineapple juice

½ cup plain soy milk

½ cup frozen mango chunks

½ cup mashed avocado

2 cups chopped spinach

1 frozen banana

½ cup ice

BOOST IT: **1 teaspoon aloe vera juice**

Get back in action with this lively green smoothie. Green spinach and avocado mingle pleasantly with paradise mango, bromelain-rich pineapple juice, and tummy-soothing banana.

DIRECTIONS: Combine all the ingredients in a blender and blend from low to high until frosty smooth.

CALORIES: 406, FAT: 13G, CARBS: 69G, PROTEIN: 9G, FIBER: 12G | VITAMIN A: 134%, CALCIUM: 25%, VITAMIN C: 116%, IRON: 19% | ALSO RICH IN MANGANESE, POTASSIUM, AND VITAMIN B$_6$.

194 cashew chai shake

1 cup brewed chai (from 1 tea bag)

¼ cup raw cashews, soaked and drained

1 frozen banana

1 tablespoon agave syrup or maple syrup

Ground cinnamon, powdered ginger, and/or cayenne to taste

Pinch of salt

½ cup ice

BOOST IT: **½ cup non-dairy yogurt ice cubes for an extra-creamy texture**

Spiced chai tea lattes are a nice substitute for coffee—especially if coffee makes your stomach a bit tense and upset. The cashews make for an ultra-creamy shake.

DIRECTIONS: Combine the tea and cashews in a blender and blend from low to high until smooth. Add the remaining ingredients and blend from low to high until frosty smooth.

CALORIES: 354, FAT: 16G, CARBS: 51G, PROTEIN: 7G, FIBER: 4G | VITAMIN A: 2%, CALCIUM: 4%, VITAMIN C: 17%, IRON: 15%

195 minted matcha tea shake

1 teaspoon matcha powder

2 tablespoons chopped fresh mint (or substitute a few drops of mint extract)

1 cup vanilla soy milk

1½ to 2 frozen bananas

½ cup ice

BOOST IT: 1 teaspoon chia seeds

Craving some digestion-friendly energy? Skip the espresso latte and blend up this creamy, minty matcha smoothie. The flavonoid catechins found in matcha green tea may help reduce inflammation in your body and digestive tract. Matcha induces a Zen-like state of energized relaxation to improve digestion, as stress can greatly interfere with healthy digestion. Bananas also soothe your stomach.

DIRECTIONS: Combine the matcha powder, mint, and soy milk in a blender and blend from low to high until smooth. Add the remaining ingredients and blend from low to high until frosty smooth.

CALORIES: 263, FAT: 5G, CARBS: 49G, PROTEIN: 10G, FIBER: 6G | VITAMIN A: 22%, CALCIUM: 33%, VITAMIN C: 28%, IRON: 16% | ALSO RICH IN POTASSIUM, VITAMIN B$_6$, AND RIBOFLAVIN.

196 pinky papaya

3 cups fresh papaya chunks

1 frozen banana

1 teaspoon grated fresh ginger

1 tablespoon fresh lime juice

1 teaspoon maple syrup

Pinch of salt (optional)

½ cup ice

BOOST IT: 1 teaspoon aloe vera juice

When you pour this soft pink smoothie, it almost slinks out of the blender—silky smooth and tummy-approved. The fresh papaya is rich in the digestive enzyme papain.

DIRECTIONS: Combine all the ingredients in a blender and blend from low to high until frosty smooth.

CALORIES: 269, FAT: 1G, CARBS: 68G, PROTEIN: 4G, FIBER: 10G | VITAMIN A: 78%, CALCIUM: 10%, VITAMIN C: 386%, IRON: 5% | ALSO RICH IN MANGANESE AND POTASSIUM.

197 fab fiber fix

1 cup water

1½ cups chopped kale leaves

1 orange, peeled and segmented

1 banana

3 tablespoons mashed avocado

5 dates, pitted

½ cup ice

BOOST IT: **1 tablespoon chia seeds**

Feeling a bit off your game digestively? Fix it with fiber. This silky, whole food green smoothie may be just what you need to kick things in gear and get back your inner glow!

DIRECTIONS: Combine all the ingredients in a blender and blend from low to high until frosty smooth.

CALORIES: 394, FAT: 6G, CARBS: 88G, PROTEIN: 9G, FIBER: 16G | VITAMIN A: 319%, CALCIUM: 30%, VITAMIN C: 385%, IRON: 18% | ALSO RICH IN MANGANESE, POTASSIUM, AND VITAMIN B$_6$.

198 cran-nana cruiser

1 cup plain soy milk

½ cup vanilla soy yogurt

½ cup frozen cranberries

¼ cup frozen blueberries

1 frozen banana

Sweetener to taste (optional)

½ cup ice

BOOST IT: **1 teaspoon aloe vera juice**

Sweet-tart whole cranberries blend with banana and soy milk for a creamy boost of wellness. Cranberries may help reduce inflammation of the digestive tract because of the presence of antioxidants and flavonoids.

DIRECTIONS: Combine all the ingredients in a blender and blend from low to high until frosty smooth.

CALORIES: 289, FAT: 6G, CARBS: 49G, PROTEIN: 12G, FIBER: 8G | VITAMIN A: 17%, CALCIUM: 44%, VITAMIN C: 34%, IRON: 11% | ALSO RICH IN RIBOFLAVIN.

199 a-peel-ing chai shake

1½ frozen bananas

½ cup brewed chai (using 1 tea bag)

¾ cup vanilla soy milk

1 teaspoon agave syrup

A few pinches of ground cinnamon and cayenne

¼ cup ice

BOOST IT: **make it a chocolate chai with 2 teaspoons raw cacao powder**

Craving a coffee-free stimulating sip? Try this spice-infused creamy chai latte with tummy-soothing, fiber-rich bananas. Chai may be easier on your tummy than coffee yet still provides a boost of energy.

DIRECTIONS: Combine all the ingredients in a blender and blend from low to high until frosty smooth.

CALORIES: 250, FAT: 4G, CARBS: 51G, PROTEIN: 7G, FIBER: 5G | VITAMIN A: 10%, CALCIUM: 24%, VITAMIN C: 26%, IRON: 8% | ALSO RICH IN POTASSIUM, RIBOFLAVIN, AND VITAMIN B$_6$.

200 blueberry pie probiotic shake

¾ cup vanilla soy yogurt ice cubes

¼ cup vanilla soy yogurt

1 cup fresh blueberries

1 banana

2 tablespoons rolled oats

1 teaspoon agave syrup

½ cup ice

BOOST IT: **1 teaspoon chia seeds**

Blueberry pie in a glass, boosted with digestion-helping fiber and probiotics. Soothing soy yogurt blends with sweet blueberries and chia seeds, if you like, to create a thickened texture similar to sweet blueberry pie. Tip: This recipe blends up thick and frosty; you can use all unfrozen yogurt for a silky-textured blend if you prefer.

DIRECTIONS: If using chia seeds, combine them with the ¼ cup of yogurt in your serving glass. Let mixture sit for a minute or two to allow seeds to plump a bit. Then spoon the chia seed yogurt into your blender along with all remaining ingredients and blend from low to high until frosty smooth.

CALORIES: 424, FAT: 5G, CARBS: 92G, PROTEIN: 11G, FIBER: 10G | VITAMIN A: 3%, CALCIUM: 37%, VITAMIN C: 41%, IRON: 13%

Peanut Butter Oat Shake

201 peanut butter oat shake

2 to 3 tablespoons
rolled oats

1 cup vanilla soy milk

1 tablespoon salted
peanut butter

1 to 2 frozen bananas

Maple syrup and
ground cinnamon to
taste

GARNISH: a pinch of
rolled oats, a pinch of
cinnamon, and a drizzle
of maple syrup
(optional)

BOOST IT: 2 to 3
tablespoons soy yogurt

Skip your morning bowl of hot oats for a chilled-
out version. This oat shake is blended with banana,
warm cinnamon, and cozy, comforting peanut butter.
Two frozen bananas give this shake a milkshake-like
texture. Oats and bananas are a perfect healthy-
digestion combo.

DIRECTIONS: Combine the oats and soy milk in a blender
and soak until softened, about one to two minutes. Add
the remaining ingredients and blend from low to high
until frosty smooth. Add garnish, if using.

CALORIES: 443, FAT: 13G, CARBS: 72G, PROTEIN: 15G, FIBER: 9G
| VITAMIN A: 13%, CALCIUM: 32%, VITAMIN C: 34%, IRON: 13%
| ALSO RICH IN VITAMIN B$_6$

202 fiber berry blast

1 cup vanilla soy milk

½ cup frozen
blackberries

½ cup frozen
blueberries

1 frozen banana

1 small orange or
tangerine, peeled

½ cup ice

BOOST IT: 1 teaspoon
chia seeds

Give your digestive system a healthy dose of fruit
fiber with this deep purple, berry-filled, citrus-kick
blend. Add chia seeds for extra fiber and a boost of
omega-3 fatty acids.

DIRECTIONS: Combine all the ingredients in a blender and
blend from low to high until frosty smooth.

CALORIES: 364, FAT: 5G, CARBS: 74G, PROTEIN: 12G, FIBER: 14G
| VITAMIN A: 24%, CALCIUM: 41%, VITAMIN C: 217%, IRON: 12%
| ALSO RICH IN RIBOFLAVIN.

203 the pink pineapple

½ cup frozen
   strawberries
¾ cup frozen pineapple
   chunks
1 frozen banana
1 cup orange juice

BOOST IT: **1 teaspoon
aloe vera juice**

If pineapples were pink, this is what they would taste like: perky-sweet, with berries, banana, and a burst of citrus. Pink pineapple paradise, and bromelain-rich for healthy digestion.

DIRECTIONS: Combine all the ingredients in a blender and blend from low to high until frosty smooth.

CALORIES: 317, FAT: 1G, CARBS: 78G, PROTEIN: 5G, FIBER: 7G | VITAMIN A: 13%, CALCIUM: 6%, VITAMIN C: 418%, IRON: 9% | ALSO RICH IN MANGANESE, POTASSIUM, AND VITAMIN B_6.

204 green ginger zinger

2½ cups honeydew
   melon chunks
1 kiwi, peeled
1 teaspoon grated fresh
   ginger
½ cup ice

BOOST IT: **1 teaspoon
aloe vera juice**

Zingy flavors of kiwi and ginger blend with cool, easy-to-digest melon in this sassy, soothing sip. Try it with frozen melon cubes (plus a splash of coconut water) for a frosty, icy version.

DIRECTIONS: Combine all the ingredients in a blender and blend from low to high until frosty smooth.

CALORIES: 202, FAT: 1G, CARBS: 50G, PROTEIN: 3G, FIBER: 6G | VITAMIN A: 6%, CALCIUM: 6%, VITAMIN C: 245%, IRON: 6% | ALSO RICH IN POTASSIUM AND VITAMIN B_6.

205 sunbeam mango

1 cup frozen mango chunks

1 frozen banana

1 cup vanilla soy milk

2 tablespoons soy yogurt

1 tablespoon unsweetened dried coconut flakes

½ cup ice

BOOST IT: 1 teaspoon spirulina powder

Sip on mango, coconut, and banana flavors as you collapse in your favorite sunbeam and daydream about aqua water, sea breezes, palm trees, and the smell of cocoa butter sunscreen. Go on, take a daydream-filled smoothie break because being relaxed helps ease digestion!

DIRECTIONS: Combine all the ingredients in a blender and blend from low to high until frosty smooth.

CALORIES: 315, FAT: 5G, CARBS: 66G, PROTEIN: 7G, FIBER: 8G | VITAMIN A: 32%, CALCIUM: 25%, VITAMIN C: 94%, IRON: 8% | ALSO RICH IN VITAMIN B$_6$.

206 probiotic purple monkey

1 cup sweetened açaí juice

¾ cup frozen blueberries

½ cup plain soy yogurt

1 frozen banana

½ cup coconut water ice cubes

BOOST IT: 1 teaspoon aloe vera juice

Banana and açaí blend with blueberries and probiotic-rich soy yogurt in this sweet and silly-tastic smoothie. Add a splash of aloe vera juice to boost your blend with tummy-soothing properties.

DIRECTIONS: Combine all the ingredients in a blender and blend from low to high until frosty smooth.

CALORIES: 396, FAT: 3G, CARBS: 91G, PROTEIN: 7G, FIBER: 8G | VITAMIN A: 3%, CALCIUM: 22%, VITAMIN C: 130%, IRON: 9%

207 chia cinna-toast shake

½ cup vanilla soy milk

1 teaspoon chia seeds

1 teaspoon maple syrup

¼ teaspoon ground cinnamon

½ cup soy yogurt ice cubes (or substitute unfrozen soy yogurt)

1 frozen banana

BOOST IT: 1 tablespoon almond butter

This cinnamon-sweet dessert shake is inspired by the cozy simplicity of cinnamon toast. Soy yogurt, chia seeds, and banana give your tummy something to feel good about.

DIRECTIONS: Combine the soy milk, chia seeds, maple syrup, and cinnamon in a blender and blend from low to high until smooth. Add the soy yogurt ice cubes and banana and blend from low to high until frosty smooth.

CALORIES: 270, FAT: 5G, CARBS: 52G, PROTEIN: 9G, FIBER: 6G | VITAMIN A: 7%, CALCIUM: 36%, VITAMIN C: 17%, IRON: 10% | ALSO RICH IN MANGANESE.

208 pink kiss

1 cup vanilla rice milk

½ cup frozen raspberries

½ cup frozen strawberries

1 frozen banana

½ cup ice

BOOST IT: 1 teaspoon chia seeds

Sun-kissed, fiber-rich raspberries and strawberries mingle with vanilla rice milk and a tummy-soothing banana in this totally kissable pink smoothie.

DIRECTIONS: Combine all the ingredients in a blender and blend from low to high until frosty smooth. If using chia seeds, allow them to soak and swell in the rice milk for at least five minutes before blending.

CALORIES: 280, FAT: 3G, CARBS: 65G, PROTEIN: 3G, FIBER: 9G | VITAMIN A: 2%, CALCIUM: 6%, VITAMIN C: 117%, IRON: 8% | ALSO RICH IN MANGANESE.

209 strawberry silk

1½ cups fresh
   strawberries
1 frozen banana
1 cup vanilla soy yogurt
Soy milk, as needed
½ cup ice

BOOST IT: **top with vegan
granola and enjoy via a
spoon**

Swirled fresh strawberries and probiotic-rich soy yogurt make up this soft and creamy soothing banana-berry blend. Probiotics are there for healthy digestion. You may want to use a spoon to enjoy this creamy blend.

DIRECTIONS: Combine all the ingredients in a blender and blend from low to high until frosty smooth.

CALORIES: 376, FAT: 6G, CARBS: 77G, PROTEIN: 12G, FIBER: 10G
| VITAMIN A: 5%, CALCIUM: 47%, VITAMIN C: 229%, IRON: 15%

210 sweet banana kale

1 cup vanilla soy milk
1½ cups chopped kale
   leaves
¼ cup vanilla soy
   yogurt
1 frozen banana
½ cup frozen mango
   chunks
½ cup ice

BOOST IT: **1 teaspoon
chia seeds**

The fluffy, fibrous texture of kale becomes smooth and creamy when blended with soy milk, banana, mango, and probiotic-rich vanilla soy yogurt. This sweet and silky green shake will help keep your digestive system happy.

DIRECTIONS: Combine the soy milk and kale in a blender and blend from low to high until smooth. Add the remaining ingredients and blend from low to high until frosty smooth.

CALORIES: 353, FAT: 6G, CARBS: 67G, PROTEIN: 14G, FIBER: 8G
| VITAMIN A: 333%, CALCIUM: 54%, VITAMIN C: 256%, IRON: 20%
| ALSO RICH IN MANGANESE, POTASSIUM, RIBOFLAVIN, AND
VITAMIN B$_6$.

211 avo-pineapple glow shake

½ cup soy milk

½ cup mashed avocado

1 cup frozen pineapple
chunks

½ cup orange juice

½ cup ice

BOOST IT: **1 teaspoon
chia seeds**

Creamy avocado, rich in monounsaturated fat, blends with spunky frozen pineapple and a hint of sweet citrus in this vibrant shake. Creamy soy milk smooths things out. This smoothie is also delicious with a handful of superfood spinach added.

DIRECTIONS: If using chia seeds, place them in a blender with the soy milk and blend from low to high to incorporate. Let mixture sit in blender for 1 to 2 minutes to allow chia seeds to plump. Add the remaining ingredients and blend from low to high until frosty smooth.

CALORIES: 300, FAT: 13G, CARBS: 43G, PROTEIN: 7G, FIBER: 8G | VITAMIN A: 14%, CALCIUM: 20%, VITAMIN C: 239%, IRON: 9% | ALSO RICH IN MANGANESE.

212 blue chia paradise

1 teaspoon chia seeds

1 cup vanilla soy milk

1 tablespoon raw
walnuts

¾ cup frozen
blueberries

1 frozen banana

½ cup ice

BOOST IT: **1 tablespoon
unsweetened dried
coconut flakes or a
splash of coconut milk**

This paradise-blue smoothie contains a satisfying blend of berries, nuts, banana, soy milk, and chia seeds. Chia seeds are rich in fiber, which may help keep your digestive system moving. Walnuts and chia seeds both contain healthy omega-3 fatty acids.

DIRECTIONS: Combine the chia seeds and soy milk in a blender and blend from low to high to incorporate. Let the mixture sit in the blender for 1 to 2 minutes to allow chia seeds to plump. Add the remaining ingredients and blend from low to high until frosty smooth.

CALORIES: 340, FAT: 11G, CARBS: 53G, PROTEIN: 11G, FIBER: 9G | VITAMIN A: 13%, CALCIUM: 35%, VITAMIN C: 35%, IRON: 12% | ALSO RICH IN RIBOFLAVIN.

213 orange county glow

1 cup vanilla soy milk

1 tablespoon almond butter

1 frozen peeled and segmented orange, plus a pinch of grated orange zest

1 frozen banana

A few pinches of ground cinnamon and/or cayenne (optional)

½ cup coconut water ice cubes

BOOST IT: **2 to 3 tablespoons mashed avocado**

You'll be glowing with glee after sipping this frosty, creamy, almond-citrus creation. Orange County Cali, sip your heart out. Oranges are rich in heart-healthy vitamin C, potassium, and fiber. Add some avocado to boost your smoothie with monounsaturated (healthy!) fats. Healthy fats not only provide flavor and texture but also aid in the absorption of certain nutrients like fat-soluble vitamins A, D, E, and K.

DIRECTIONS: Combine all the ingredients in a blender and blend from low to high until frosty smooth.

CALORIES: 449, FAT: 14G, CARBS: 72G, PROTEIN: 14G, FIBER: 11G | VITAMIN A: 10%, CALCIUM: 21%, VITAMIN C: 188%, IRON: 17% | ALSO RICH IN MANGANESE AND MAGNESIUM.

214 walnut-cacao shake

1¼ cups soy milk

¼ cup raw walnuts

1 tablespoon raw cacao powder

2 frozen bananas

Agave syrup to taste

BOOST IT: **1 tablespoon hemp seeds**

Omega-3 fatty acid–rich walnuts and chocolate swirl into this thick and frosty frozen banana shake. Dessert-approved. Antioxidant-rich dark cacao powder, rich in phytochemical flavonoids, has been shown to improve blood vessel function and help keep your heart healthy.

DIRECTIONS: Combine the walnuts and soy milk in a blender and blend from low to high until smoothed out a bit. Add the remaining ingredients and blend from low to high until frosty smooth.

CALORIES: 484, FAT: 24G, CARBS: 59G, PROTEIN: 18G, FIBER: 9G | VITAMIN A: 13%, CALCIUM: 34%, VITAMIN C: 27%, IRON: 17% | ALSO RICH IN MANGANESE AND POTASSIUM.

215 bella's elixir

¾ cup orange juice

¼ cup plain soy milk

½ cup frozen
blueberries

½ cup frozen
blackberries

½ cup grated beets

½ teaspoon grated
fresh ginger

½ cup coconut water
ice cubes

BOOST IT: **2 tablespoons
soy yogurt**

Deep red beet juice, rich in the phytochemical anthocyanin, is heart-healthy and creates a deep purple-red color for this vibrant, energizing, seductively sweet smoothie. If you have a juicer, you can juice the beets and ginger for easier blending and a silkier texture.

DIRECTIONS: Combine all the ingredients in a blender and blend from low to high until frosty smooth.

CALORIES: 241, FAT: 2G, CARBS: 51G, PROTEIN: 7G, FIBER: 9G
| VITAMIN A: 14%, CALCIUM: 16%, VITAMIN C: 202%, IRON: 13%
| ALSO RICH IN POTASSIUM, MAGNESIUM, AND MANGANESE.

216 chocolate-raspberry shake

1 cup frozen raspberries

1 frozen banana

1 cup vanilla soy milk

1 to 2 tablespoons raw
cacao powder

2 teaspoons raw cacao
nibs (optional)

1 teaspoon agave syrup

BOOST IT: **1 to 2
tablespoons soy yogurt
or mashed avocado**

Rich, dark chocolate swirls with perky, bright, sweet raspberries—this classic dessert flavor pairing is popular for a reason. Sip on some heart-healthy antioxidants and fiber for a guilt-free treat.

DIRECTIONS: Combine all the ingredients in a blender and blend from low to high until frosty smooth.

CALORIES: 350, FAT: 6G, CARBS: 64G, PROTEIN: 12G, FIBER: 17G
| VITAMIN A: 12%, CALCIUM: 34%, VITAMIN C: 91%, IRON: 13%
| ALSO RICH IN MANGANESE AND RIBOFLAVIN.

217 beachy green

1 cup pink grapefruit
  juice
½ cup frozen pineapple
  chunks
1 frozen banana
2 cups chopped
  spinach
½ cup coconut water
  ice cubes

BOOST IT: **1 tablespoon
unsweetened dried
coconut flakes**

Be a beach-blanket baby sipping on a green
smoothie. Pineapple breezes. Salty sunbeam. Aqua
sea-foam waves crawl up toward swaying green
palm trees as far as the eye can see. Heart-healthy
pink grapefruit juice leads this vibrant paradise sip.
Have a healthy beach day, via your smoothie straw.

DIRECTIONS: Combine all the ingredients in a blender and
blend from low to high until frosty smooth.

CALORIES: 254, FAT: 2G, CARBS: 62G, PROTEIN: 6G, FIBER: 9G
| VITAMIN A: 158%, CALCIUM: 13%, VITAMIN C: 244%, IRON: 15%
| ALSO RICH IN MANGANESE, POTASSIUM, VITAMIN B$_6$,
AND MAGNESIUM.

218 purple heart açaí

1 tablespoon açaí
  powder
1 cup vanilla soy milk
½ cup frozen
  blueberries
½ cup frozen
  blackberries
½ frozen banana
1 to 2 tablespoons
  mashed avocado
½ cup ice

BOOST IT: **1 teaspoon
spirulina powder**

Purple power fills each sip of this heart-healthy
smoothie containing blueberries, blackberries, and
açaí berry powder. Healthy fat–rich avocado, creamy
potassium-rich banana, and protein-rich soy milk
swirl this sip into frosty bliss.

DIRECTIONS: Combine the açaí powder and soy milk in a
blender and blend from low to high until smooth. Add
the remaining ingredients and blend from low to high
until frosty smooth.

CALORIES: 272, FAT: 9G, CARBS: 41G, PROTEIN: 10G, FIBER: 10G
| VITAMIN A: 19%, CALCIUM: 34%, VITAMIN C: 63%, IRON: 12%
| ALSO RICH IN RIBOFLAVIN AND MANGANESE.

219 citrus-strawberry fi-burr boost

1 cup frozen orange
    slices

½ cup frozen
    strawberries

¾ cup soy milk

¼ cup coconut water

1 fresh or frozen banana

BOOST IT: **2 to 3
tablespoons mashed
avocado or soy yogurt**

This shake combines frozen whole citrus slices and frozen berries with a creamy banana and heart-healthy soy milk. This blend, rich in fiber, potassium, and antioxidants, is a refreshing healthy-heart sip to crave.

DIRECTIONS: Combine all the ingredients in a blender and blend from low to high until frosty smooth.

CALORIES: 299, FAT: 4G, CARBS: 61G, PROTEIN: 9G, FIBER: 11G | VITAMIN A: 17%, CALCIUM: 33%, VITAMIN C: 250%, IRON: 10% | ALSO RICH IN RIBOFLAVIN AND POTASSIUM.

220 cherry-berry breeze

1 cup cherry juice (or
    pomegranate juice)

½ cup frozen peach
    chunks

½ cup frozen
    raspberries

1 frozen banana

½ cup ice

BOOST IT: **1 teaspoon
flax oil**

Frosty raspberries, peaches, and sweet cherry juice blend into a red swirl of heart-healthy, frosty refreshment. Red pigment fruits like cherries and raspberries are rich in the heart-healthy phytochemical anthocyanin. Add some flax oil for an omega-3 fatty acid boost.

DIRECTIONS: Combine all the ingredients in a blender and blend from low to high until frosty smooth.

CALORIES: 320, FAT: 1G, CARBS: 78G, PROTEIN: 4G, FIBER: 8G | VITAMIN A: 7%, CALCIUM: 5%, VITAMIN C: 53%, IRON: 5% | ALSO RICH IN POTASSIUM.

221 blueberry island kiss

1 cup frozen blueberries

1 frozen banana

1 cup vanilla rice milk

1 to 2 teaspoons unsweetened dried coconut flakes

1 teaspoon maple syrup or agave syrup

½ cup coconut water ice cubes

BOOST IT: 1 teaspoon chia seeds

This simple blueberry, banana, rice milk smoothie is kissed with the gentle flavor of coconut and vanilla. Antioxidant-rich blueberries provide a heart-healthy boost. For more fiber and a boost of omega-3 fatty acids, add chia seeds.

DIRECTIONS: Combine all the ingredients in a blender and blend from low to high until frosty smooth.

CALORIES: 368, FAT: 4G, CARBS: 86G, PROTEIN: 4G, FIBER: 8G | VITAMIN A: 13%, CALCIUM: 35%, VITAMIN C: 45%, IRON: 6% | ALSO RICH IN POTASSIUM.

222 great grape slush

OPTION 1:

1¼ cups red grapes

¾ cup coconut water

1 cup coconut water ice cubes

OPTION 2:

1¼ cups frozen red grapes

1 to 2 cups coconut water

BOOST IT: ½ frozen banana for a creamy accent

This coconut-water-and-grape-infused blend is perfect for cooling off and hydrating your body—the natural way. Grape skins are rich in resveratrol, which may boost heart health and longevity.

DIRECTIONS: Combine the grapes with a splash of liquid in a blender and begin blending on the lowest speed. Add the remaining ingredients and stop blending when you have reached your desired "slush" consistency.

CALORIES: 187, FAT: 1G, CARBS: 41G, PROTEIN: 3G, FIBER: 5G | VITAMIN A: 0%, CALCIUM: 10%, VITAMIN C: 17%, IRON: 7% | ALSO RICH IN MANGANESE, POTASSIUM, AND MAGNESIUM.

223 sweet swoonable spinach

½ cup orange juice

2 cups chopped spinach

1 cup frozen strawberries

1 banana

½ cup ice or coconut water ice cubes

A few splashes of coconut water, as needed

BOOST IT: **1 teaspoon chia seeds**

Spinach is packed with heart-healthy antioxidants, fiber, and minerals. To sweeten the love connection, perky citrus, berries, and a creamy banana get swirled in this totally swoonable sip. Add chia seeds for a heart-healthy boost of fiber and omega-3 fatty acids.

DIRECTIONS: Combine the orange juice, spinach, and chia seeds, if using, in a blender and blend from low to high until smooth. If including chia seeds, leave to plump for a couple of minutes. Add the remaining ingredients and blend from low to high until frosty smooth.

CALORIES: 228, FAT: 1G, CARBS: 54G, PROTEIN: 6G, FIBER: 8G | VITAMIN A: 176%, CALCIUM: 14%, VITAMIN C: 304%, IRON: 20% | ALSO RICH IN MANGANESE, POTASSIUM, VITAMIN B$_6$, AND MAGNESIUM.

224 big bright orange sunbeam

1 medium orange, peeled and segmented, plus a pinch of zest

1 cup coconut water

½ cup frozen mango chunks

1 cup frozen peach chunks

1 fresh or frozen banana

BOOST IT: **1 teaspoon flax oil**

This vitamin C–, potassium-, and fiber-infused smoothie is bursting with golden, heart-healthy orange, peach, and mango. Glow from the inside out with this sweet, vibrant smoothie. Oranges have been shown to reduce blood pressure and aid in healthy cholesterol. Potassium-rich foods like coconut water are good for the heart.

DIRECTIONS: Combine the orange and coconut water in a blender and blend from low to high until smooth. Add the remaining ingredients and blend until frosty smooth.

CALORIES: 357, FAT: 2G, CARBS: 87G, PROTEIN: 7G, FIBER: 14G | VITAMIN A: 33%, CALCIUM: 16%, VITAMIN C: 247%, IRON: 10% | ALSO RICH IN POTASSIUM AND VITAMIN B$_6$.

225 love frenzy raspberry shake

¼ cup raw pistachios,
   soaked and drained
1 cup vanilla soy milk
1 cup frozen raspberries
1 frozen banana
Pinch of salt

BOOST IT: **1 tablespoon
raw cacao powder and
agave syrup to taste**

This swoon-worthy berry shake will have you in
a pistachio-raspberry love frenzy! Heart-healthy
soy milk adds a silky, alluring texture as it blends
with the healthy fat–containing and copper-rich
pistachios. Plenty of cholesterol-helping fiber in
each sweet sip. Add a boost of cacao powder for
a chocolate-covered berry spin.

DIRECTIONS: Combine the pistachios, soy milk, and cacao
powder, if using, in a blender and blend from low to high
until smooth. Add the remaining ingredients and blend
from low to high until frosty smooth.

CALORIES: 447, FAT: 19G, CARBS: 58G, PROTEIN: 16G,
FIBER: 15G | VITAMIN A: 16%, CALCIUM: 37%, VITAMIN C: 74%,
IRON: 20% | ALSO RICH IN MANGANESE AND VITAMIN B$_6$.

226 cinnamon-fudge shake

1 heaping tablespoon
   raw cacao powder
½ cup vanilla soy
   yogurt
½ cup vanilla soy milk
2 frozen bananas
3 to 4 pinches of
   ground cinnamon
Sweetener to taste
   (optional)

BOOST IT: **1 teaspoon
almond or peanut
butter**

Heart-healthy raw cacao powder meets creamy soy
yogurt, warming cinnamon, and sweet potassium-
rich bananas in this Fudgsicle-inspired shake. Add
some nut butter for a boost of protein and
decadence!

DIRECTIONS: Combine all the ingredients in a blender and
blend from low to high until frosty smooth.

CALORIES: 405, FAT: 6G, CARBS: 88G, PROTEIN: 11G, FIBER: 10G
| VITAMIN A: 8%, CALCIUM: 36%, VITAMIN C: 34%, IRON: 14%

227 rainforest green smoothie

1 tablespoon goji
   berries

½ cup coconut water

2 to 3 raw Brazil nuts

1 cup chopped kale
   leaves

1 fresh or frozen banana

1 cup frozen mango
   chunks

½ cup ice

Splash of soy milk
   (optional)

BOOST IT: 1 to 2
teaspoons açaí powder
and/or 1 teaspoon
shredded coconut

Step inside a tropical rain forest with this exotic blend of vitamin A–rich goji berries, sweet mango, coconut water, and selenium-rich Brazil nuts. Plus a dose of superfood kale to give it some green power!

DIRECTIONS: Combine the goji berries and coconut water in a blender and soak for 10 minutes to soften the berries. Add the Brazil nuts and blend from low to high until smoothed out a bit. Add the remaining ingredients and blend until frosty smooth.

CALORIES: 360, FAT: 9G, CARBS: 71G, PROTEIN: 7G, FIBER: 10G
| VITAMIN A: 267%, CALCIUM: 16%, VITAMIN C: 236%, IRON: 14%
| ALSO RICH IN POTASSIUM AND VITAMIN B$_6$.

228 choco-berry almond shake

1½ frozen bananas

1 cup vanilla soy milk

½ cup frozen
   strawberries

1 tablespoon raw cacao
   powder

1 tablespoon almond
   butter

½ cup ice

BOOST IT: 1 teaspoon raw
cacao nibs

Like a chocolate-covered strawberry in a glass, this dessert-approved banana, berry, chocolate, almond butter shake is a nutrient-infused way to satisfy your sweet tooth. Add cacao nibs for even more heart-healthy antioxidants per sip.

DIRECTIONS: Combine all the ingredients in a blender and blend from low to high until frosty smooth.

CALORIES: 403, FAT: 15G, CARBS: 61G, PROTEIN: 13G, FIBER: 9G
| VITAMIN A: 12%, CALCIUM: 37%, VITAMIN C: 96%, IRON: 16%
| ALSO RICH IN RIBOFLAVIN.

229 simple spinach

2 cups chopped
   spinach

1 cup soy milk

1 frozen banana

3 to 4 pinches of
   cayenne

Salt to taste

½ cup ice

BOOST IT: 1 orange,
peeled and segmented
(fresh or frozen)

This super-simple blend of spinach, soy milk, banana, and stimulating cayenne is a very nice way to boost your leafy green intake for the day. Add sweetness and fiber by tossing in an orange too!

DIRECTIONS: Combine all the ingredients in a blender and blend from low to high until frosty smooth.

CALORIES: 219, FAT: 5G, CARBS: 37G, PROTEIN: 10G, FIBER: 5G | VITAMIN A: 124%, CALCIUM: 37%, VITAMIN C: 45%, IRON: 17% | ALSO RICH IN MANGANESE, POTASSIUM, AND VITAMIN B$_6$.

230 chocolate-avocado ob-seed-sion

¾ to 1 cup vanilla soy
   milk

1 frozen banana

½ cup mashed avocado

2 tablespoons raw
   pumpkin seeds

1 tablespoon raw cacao
   powder

1 to 2 teaspoons agave
   syrup, or to taste

¼ cup ice

BOOST IT: 1 teaspoon raw
cacao nibs

Dark chocolate and healthy fat–rich avocado meet mineral-rich pumpkin seeds in this heart-healthy blend. It's a creamy and rich dessert-approved shake. Chill your avocado flesh before adding it for a slightly thicker shake texture.

DIRECTIONS: Combine all the ingredients in a blender and blend from low to high until frosty smooth.

CALORIES: 449, FAT: 24G, CARBS: 52G, PROTEIN: 15G, FIBER: 11G | VITAMIN A: 15%, CALCIUM: 33%, VITAMIN C: 30%, IRON: 27% | ALSO RICH IN MAGNESIUM.

231 chocolate-banana s'mores freeze

1 cup chocolate soy
  milk ice cubes

1 cup chocolate soy
  milk

1 frozen banana

BOOST IT: **1 teaspoon
chia seeds**

TOPPINGS

2 tablespoons crushed
  vegan graham
  crackers

1 teaspoon raw cacao
  nibs (optional)

A few pinches of
  ground cinnamon

1 or 2 vegan
  marshmallows

This vegan marshmallow–topped, graham-cracker-sprinkled shake is a frosty treat to enjoy all year long—no campfire needed. You can make your own chocolate soy milk by adding cacao powder and sweetener to vanilla soy milk. Add chia seeds for an omega-3 fatty acid boost.

DIRECTIONS: Combine all the ingredients in a blender and blend from low to high until frosty smooth. Pour into a glass and add the toppings.

CALORIES: 401, FAT: 7G, CARBS: 76G, PROTEIN: 10G, FIBER: 7G | VITAMIN A: 18%, CALCIUM: 51%, VITAMIN C: 17%, IRON: 16% | ALSO RICH IN RIBOFLAVIN.

232 pink-hearted power

1 cup pink grapefruit
  juice

½ cup frozen
  strawberries

½ cup frozen
  raspberries

1 frozen banana

½ cup coconut water
  ice cubes

BOOST IT: **1 teaspoon
flax oil**

Pink power fills this frosty, zesty-sweet berry-citrus smoothie. Each pink sip is infused with heart-healthy antioxidants from citrus and berries, potassium-rich coconut water ice cubes, and an option for heart-healthy flax oil.

DIRECTIONS: Combine all the ingredients in a blender and blend from low to high until frosty smooth.

CALORIES: 395, FAT: 6G, CARBS: 89G, PROTEIN: 5G, FIBER: 14G | VITAMIN A: 46%, CALCIUM: 9%, VITAMIN C: 233%, IRON: 11% | ALSO RICH IN MANGANESE.

I Heart Chocolate Shake

233 i heart chocolate shake

1 cup vanilla soy milk

1 tablespoon agave syrup

Pinch of ground cinnamon

1 to 2 tablespoons raw cacao powder

2 frozen bananas

¼ cup ice

GARNISH: **sliced banana**

BOOST IT: **1 tablespoon almond or peanut butter and/or a scoop of raw cacao nibs**

Hooray! Studies show that dark chocolate can help your heart. So feel good about adding this raw cacao shake to your day. This chocolate lover's dessert smoothie is a guilt-free treat.

DIRECTIONS: Combine the soy milk, agave, cinnamon, and cacao powder in a blender and blend from low to high until smooth. Add the remaining ingredients and blend from low to high until frosty smooth.

CALORIES: 406, FAT: 6G, CARBS: 82G, PROTEIN: 12G, FIBER: 10G | VITAMIN A: 13%, CALCIUM: 34%, VITAMIN C: 34%, IRON: 17% | ALSO RICH IN MANGANESE AND VITAMIN B$_6$.

234 summer haze

2 cups watermelon chunks

½ cup frozen strawberries

1 small peach, pitted and sliced

1 tablespoon orange or lime juice

½ cup coconut water ice cubes

BOOST IT: **1 tablespoon chopped fresh mint**

Sip on the flavors of summer in this light and frosty blend of potassium-rich melon, coconut water ice cubes, cool frozen strawberries, and a sweet juicy peach. Add some mint to this cooler for ultra refreshment. The potassium helps support your heart. Use frozen watermelon for a frosty take on this recipe: Omit the ice and add splashes of coconut water to blend.

DIRECTIONS: Combine all the ingredients in a blender and blend from low to high until frosty smooth.

CALORIES: 174, FAT: 1G, CARBS: 42G, PROTEIN: 4G, FIBER: 6G | VITAMIN A: 45%, CALCIUM: 8%, VITAMIN C: 134%, IRON: 13% | ALSO RICH IN MANGANESE, POTASSIUM, AND MAGNESIUM.

235 green meadow kiwi cooler

1 cup coconut water

2 kiwis, peeled

2 tablespoons mashed
avocado

1 banana

1 cup chopped kale or
spinach leaves

½ cup ice

BOOST IT: 1 small orange,
peeled and segmented

This light and lovely green cooler contains fresh kiwis, creamy avocado, superfood greens, and a sweet banana, all blended into a frosty blur with chilled potassium-rich coconut water. Potassium is crucial to keeping your heart healthy. Boost this smoothie's whole food fiber by adding an orange; fiber is important for keeping healthy cholesterol levels.

DIRECTIONS: Combine all the ingredients in a blender and blend from low to high until frosty smooth.

CALORIES: 323, FAT: 5G, CARBS: 69G, PROTEIN: 9G, FIBER: 13G | VITAMIN A: 314%, CALCIUM: 26%, VITAMIN C: 466%, IRON: 18% | ALSO RICH IN MANGANESE, MAGNESIUM, POTASSIUM, AND VITAMIN B_6.

236 apple-walnut pie shake

⅓ cup vanilla soy milk

1 small apple, cored and
chopped

2 to 3 tablespoons raw
walnuts

1 tablespoon rolled oats

1 tablespoon maple syrup

2 to 3 pinches of ground
cinnamon or apple pie
spice

1 frozen banana

⅔ cup vanilla soy
milk ice cubes
(or substitute liquid
soy milk)

This cozy, creamy shake is apple pie–inspired with fiber-rich apples, omega-3–rich walnuts, cinnamon, maple syrup, and a dose of heart-healthy rolled oats. Add some soy yogurt for a creamy accent.

DIRECTIONS: Combine the soy milk, apple, walnuts, oats, maple syrup, and cinnamon in a blender and blend from low to high until smooth. Add the remaining ingredients and blend from low to high until frosty smooth.

BOOST IT: 2 to 3 tablespoons soy yogurt

CALORIES: 452, FAT: 14G, CARBS: 74G, PROTEIN: 13G, FIBER: 10G | VITAMIN A: 13%, CALCIUM: 35%, VITAMIN C: 29%, IRON: 14% | ALSO RICH IN MANGANESE.

237 two-minute strawberry-chocolate "milk" shake

1 cup vanilla soy milk

1 tablespoon raw cacao powder

½ cup frozen strawberries

1½ frozen bananas

2 teaspoons agave syrup, or to taste

BOOST IT: **1 tablespoon peanut butter**

Two minutes is all it takes to blend up this thick, creamy shake filled with the craveable flavors of strawberry, banana, and chocolate. Cacao powder is rich in heart-healthy antioxidants, so feel good about satisfying your chocolate cravings. For an extra-thick shake, add another ½ frozen banana or reduce the soy milk by ¼ cup.

DIRECTIONS: Combine the soy milk and cacao in a blender and blend from low to high until smooth. Add the remaining ingredients and blend from low to high until frosty smooth.

CALORIES: 336, FAT: 5G, CARBS: 67G, PROTEIN: 10G, FIBER: 7G | VITAMIN A: 12%, CALCIUM: 33%, VITAMIN C: 96%, IRON: 11% | ALSO RICH IN RIBOFLAVIN.

238 cherry-kiwi kiss

1 cup fresh cherries, pitted

½ cup frozen strawberries

1 kiwi, peeled

¾ cup coconut water

½ cup ice

BOOST IT: **2 to 3 tablespoons vanilla soy yogurt**

Kiss me, I'm a cherry frosty! This ravishing red blend of antioxidant-rich fresh cherries, potassium-rich coconut water, and vitamin C–filled kiwi is a refreshing sip to revive your day. And yes, all that cherry pitting is worth it for the fresh cherry flavor in each sip!

DIRECTIONS: Combine all the ingredients in a blender and blend from low to high until frosty smooth.

CALORIES: 194, FAT: 1G, CARBS: 45G, PROTEIN: 5G, FIBER: 9G | VITAMIN A: 3%, CALCIUM: 10%, VITAMIN C: 210%, IRON: 8% | ALSO RICH IN POTASSIUM.

Cherry-Kiwi Kiss

239 pb oat bar

1 cup vanilla soy milk

1 frozen banana

2 tablespoons peanut butter

2 tablespoons rolled oats

1 teaspoon maple syrup

1 teaspoon raw cacao nibs (optional)

A few pinches of ground cinnamon

¼ cup ice

BOOST IT: ½ teaspoon flax seeds

If you love the nutty, rustic flavor of a peanut butter granola bar, you will love this earthy smoothie blend of peanut butter, oats, banana, and creamy soy milk. Heart-healthy ingredients galore, including fiber-rich oats, an option for antioxidant-rich cacao, and potassium-rich banana.

DIRECTIONS: Combine all the ingredients in a blender and blend from low to high until frosty smooth.

CALORIES: 371, FAT: 13G, CARBS: 52G, PROTEIN: 14G, FIBER: 7G | VITAMIN A: 12%, CALCIUM: 34%, VITAMIN C: 17%, IRON: 14%

240 heart of green

½ to 1 cup water, soy milk, or coconut water

1 cup chopped spinach

1 cup chopped kale or chard leaves

½ cup frozen mango chunks

1 frozen banana

2 tablespoons mashed avocado

½ cup ice

BOOST IT: ½ cup fresh or frozen grapes

Your heart will love this super-green smoothie accented with creamy sweet mango and banana. Swoon over the bright green color as you fall in love with greens with each sweet sip.

DIRECTIONS: Combine all the ingredients in a blender and blend from low to high until frosty smooth.

CALORIES: 232, FAT: 4G, CARBS: 50G, PROTEIN: 6G, FIBER: 8G | VITAMIN A: 305%, CALCIUM: 16%, VITAMIN C: 213%, IRON: 16% | ALSO RICH IN MANGANESE, POTASSIUM, VITAMIN B₆, AND MAGNESIUM.

241 fresh strawberry-peach potassium

1 cup fresh strawberries

1 cup frozen peach chunks

1 frozen banana

1 cup soy milk

½ cup ice

Drizzle of maple syrup (optional)

BOOST IT: **2 to 3 tablespoons vanilla soy yogurt**

Heart-healthy potassium infuses your body as you sip on this fresh strawberry, peach, banana, and soy smoothie.

DIRECTIONS: Combine all the ingredients in a blender and blend from low to high until frosty smooth.

CALORIES: 317, FAT: 5G, CARBS: 82G, PROTEIN: 11G, FIBER: 10G | VITAMIN A: 23%, CALCIUM: 34%, VITAMIN C: 177%, IRON: 13% | ALSO RICH IN POTASSIUM.

242 basil-blueberry cream

1 cup frozen blueberries

1 frozen banana

1 cup vanilla soy milk

1 to 2 tablespoons chopped fresh basil leaves

½ cup ice

BOOST IT: **2 to 3 tablespoons vanilla soy yogurt**

Heart-healthy blueberries, rich in antioxidants and fiber, swirl with fresh basil and creamy banana and heart-healthy soy for a soothing sweet smoothie.

DIRECTIONS: Combine all the ingredients in a blender and blend from low to high until frosty smooth.

CALORIES: 290, FAT: 5G, CARBS: 56G, PROTEIN: 10G, FIBER: 8G | VITAMIN A: 18%, CALCIUM: 33%, VITAMIN C: 42%, IRON: 14% | ALSO RICH IN RIBOFLAVIN.

Frozen Cantaloupe Infatuation

243 frozen cantaloupe infatuation

3 cups frozen cantaloupe chunks

½ cup coconut water

½ banana

BOOST IT: **1 tablespoon chopped fresh mint**

When I first tasted this frosty, cool, peach-colored smoothie, I fell in love. Pure infatuation. A cantaloupe lover's dream! Give your heart a dose of love at first sip with this golden cantaloupe smoothie. This tall sweet glass is rich in vitamin A and low in calories.

DIRECTIONS: Combine all the ingredients in a blender and blend from low to high until frosty smooth.

CALORIES: 234, FAT: 1G, CARBS: 56G, PROTEIN: 5G, FIBER: 7G | VITAMIN A: 317%, CALCIUM: 7%, VITAMIN C: 300%, IRON: 8% | ALSO RICH IN MAGNESIUM, POTASSIUM, AND VITAMIN B$_6$.

244 raspberry freeze

¾ cup frozen raspberries

¼ cup frozen watermelon chunks (or substitute more raspberries)

½ cup apple cider or juice

½ cup vanilla soy milk

1 frozen banana

Sweetener to taste (optional)

BOOST IT: **2 to 3 tablespoons vanilla soy yogurt**

Sip this pink blend and freeze those facial lines with the help of antioxidant-rich raspberries. Turn up the pink power with the addition of some frosty low-calorie watermelon and a little sweet apple juice. Creamy frozen banana thickens this luscious blend. Add some soy yogurt for a creamy boost of protein and probiotics.

DIRECTIONS: Combine all the ingredients in a blender and blend from low to high until frosty smooth.

CALORIES: 273, FAT: 3G, CARBS: 59G, PROTEIN: 6G, FIBER: 10G | VITAMIN A: 11%, CALCIUM: 19%, VITAMIN C: 64%, IRON: 11% | ALSO RICH IN MANGANESE.

245 pineapple shake shake shake

1½ cups frozen pineapple chunks

1 cup orange juice

1 frozen banana

3 tablespoons vanilla soy yogurt

½ cup ice

Drizzle of maple syrup for topping (optional)

BOOST IT: **3 pinches of cayenne**

Vibrant, enzyme-rich pineapple leads the way in this antioxidant-rich smoothie. Grab your dance partner and shake, shake, shake. Exercise and healthy eating is a tried-and-true way to stay feeling forever young. And sipping on this perky pineapple blend is sure to make you feel energized for some exercise! Add cayenne for a boost of heat.

DIRECTIONS: Combine all the ingredients in a blender and blend from low to high until frosty smooth. Top with maple syrup if you like.

CALORIES: 368, FAT: 2G, CARBS: 89G, PROTEIN: 6G, FIBER: 7G | VITAMIN A: 14%, CALCIUM: 14%, VITAMIN C: 409%, IRON: 10% | ALSO RICH IN MANGANESE AND VITAMIN B_6.

246 matcha ginger an-tea-oxidant shake

1 teaspoon matcha
    powder

1 cup vanilla soy milk

2 frozen bananas

3 to 5 pinches of ginger
    powder

Agave syrup to taste

½ cup ice

BOOST IT: **1 tablespoon
raw walnuts**

Matcha and ginger flavors swirl together in this frosty green tea shake. Green tea is antioxidant-infused to neutralize free radicals that contribute to the aging process.

DIRECTIONS: Combine all the ingredients in a blender and blend from low to high until frosty smooth.

CALORIES: 318, FAT: 5G, CARBS: 63G, PROTEIN: 11G, FIBER: 8G | VITAMIN A: 13%, CALCIUM: 32%, VITAMIN C: 35%, IRON: 11% | ALSO RICH IN POTASSIUM.

247 chocolate-almond "milk" shake

1 cup water

Pinch of salt

4 to 5 tablespoons raw
    almonds, soaked and
    drained

1 tablespoon raw cacao
    powder

2 teaspoons agave
    syrup

1 frozen banana

½ cup ice

BOOST IT: **make it a
cacao chip shake by
adding 1 to 2 teaspoons
raw cacao nibs**

Superfood almonds and antioxidant-rich cacao blend with banana and agave for a homemade almond "milk" shake. Frosty chocolate swoon. Add more anti-aging power by including superfood cacao nibs.

DIRECTIONS: Combine the water, salt, and almonds in a blender and blend from low to high until smooth. For a silkier texture, strain the almond pulp and return to the blender. Add the remaining ingredients and blend until frosty smooth.

CALORIES: 297, FAT: 13G, CARBS: 45G, PROTEIN: 8G, FIBER: 8G | VITAMIN A: 2%, CALCIUM: 9%, VITAMIN C: 17%, IRON: 10% | ALSO RICH IN RIBOFLAVIN.

248 protein pom-berry shake

1 cup pomegranate
  juice
1 frozen banana
½ cup frozen
  blueberries
½ cup frozen
  strawberries
1 scoop vegan protein
  powder

BOOST IT: 1 to 2
teaspoons hemp seeds

Antioxidant-rich pomegranate juice swirls and whirls with frosty berries and a scoop of protein powder. This deep red blend will have you feeling feisty! Protein helps maintain lean muscle mass, and as muscle burns more calories than fat and provides strength, you will want to keep a good amount of it on your body!

DIRECTIONS: Combine all the ingredients in a blender and blend from low to high until frosty smooth.

CALORIES: 449, FAT: 3G, CARBS: 87G, PROTEIN: 23G, FIBER: 6G
| VITAMIN A: 2%, CALCIUM: 13%, VITAMIN C: 99%, IRON: 9%

249 lime-in-the-coconut shake

½ cup coconut water
¼ cup coconut milk (or
  substitute soy milk)
1 frozen banana
¼ cup fresh lime juice,
  plus a pinch of zest
½ cup fresh young
  coconut meat
  (or substitute
  1 tablespoon
  unsweetened dried
  coconut flakes)
½ cup ice

BOOST IT: splash of
coconut milk (optional)

Lime, banana, and plenty of coconut! This ultra-creamy, tropical blend is potassium-rich and hydrating. Cool coconut, reminiscent of an island getaway, helps reduce your stress, and we all know stress can greatly speed up the aging process!

DIRECTIONS: Combine all the ingredients in a blender and blend from low to high until frosty smooth.

CALORIES: 423, FAT: 28G, CARBS: 46G, PROTEIN: 5G, FIBER: 10G
| VITAMIN A: 2%, CALCIUM: 6%, VITAMIN C: 58%, IRON: 15%
| ALSO RICH IN MANGANESE, POTASSIUM, AND MAGNESIUM.

Lime-in-the-Coconut Shake

250 peach-cantaloupe skin soother

2 cups fresh cantaloupe chunks

¾ cup frozen peach chunks

1 frozen banana

½ cup coconut water ice cubes

BOOST IT: 1 teaspoon aloe vera juice

Juicy-sweet peaches and fresh cantaloupe can help your skin reclaim its youthful glow from the inside out, as these fruits are rich in the antioxidant vitamins A and C.

DIRECTIONS: Combine all the ingredients in a blender and blend from low to high until frosty smooth.

CALORIES: 284, FAT: 1G, CARBS: 69G, PROTEIN: 6G, FIBER: 9G | VITAMIN A: 221%, CALCIUM: 7%, VITAMIN C: 227%, IRON: 9% | ALSO RICH IN POTASSIUM AND VITAMIN B$_6$.

251 grape-banana freeze

1½ cups frozen red grapes

½ frozen banana

2 tablespoons fresh lemon juice

About ¼ cup coconut water or water, as needed

BOOST IT: 1 teaspoon aloe vera juice

Eating grapes is a delicious way to infuse your day with vibrant free-radical-fighting antioxidants like resveratrol. Choose red grapes because their dark purple skins contain more purple plant polyphenol power.

DIRECTIONS: Combine the grapes, banana, and lemon juice in a blender and blend from low to high until thick; reduce the speed to low and slowly pour in enough coconut water or water to reach your desired texture.

CALORIES: 240, FAT: 1G, CARBS: 58G, PROTEIN: 4G, FIBER: 5G | VITAMIN A: 7%, CALCIUM: 2%, VITAMIN C: 77%, IRON: 8%

Grape-Banana Freeze

252 matcha-cado

¾ cup plain soy milk

½ avocado

1 frozen banana

¼ cup orange juice

1 teaspoon matcha
powder

½ cup ice

BOOST IT: **1 cup chopped
kale or spinach leaves**

This creamy, frothy blend of soy, avocado, and matcha—swirled with citrus and sweet banana—is a delicious whole food way to satisfy your caffeine craving. Matcha green tea is rich in anti-aging antioxidants. Add kale or spinach for more free-radical-fighting power! Toss in an extra frozen banana for a sweeter, thicker drink.

DIRECTIONS: Combine all the ingredients in a blender and blend from low to high until frosty smooth.

CALORIES: 369, FAT: 18G, CARBS: 48G, PROTEIN: 9G, FIBER: 11G | VITAMIN A: 14%, CALCIUM: 25%, VITAMIN C: 86%, IRON: 10%

253 timeless grapefruit

1 cup pink grapefruit
juice

1 frozen banana

½ cup frozen
strawberries

2 kiwis, peeled

Agave syrup or maple
syrup, if needed

½ cup ice

BOOST IT: **2 to 3
tablespoons soy yogurt**

It is easy being timeless when you are sipping on a smoothie loaded with this much free-radical-fighting vitamin C from perky pink grapefruit, kiwi, and strawberries. Add a drizzle of agave or maple syrup if your grapefruit juice is on the tart side of sweet.

DIRECTIONS: Combine all the ingredients in a blender and blend from low to high until frosty smooth.

CALORIES: 294, FAT: 2G, CARBS: 73G, PROTEIN: 5G, FIBER: 12G | VITAMIN A: 47%, CALCIUM: 10%, VITAMIN C: 454%, IRON: 7% | ALSO RICH IN POTASSIUM AND VITAMIN B$_6$.

254 l.a. green smoothie

2 cups chopped kale leaves

½ cup fresh or frozen grapes

½ cup orange juice

½ cup coconut water (or substitute soy milk)

1 fresh or frozen banana

½ cup ice

BOOST IT: 2 tablespoons mashed avocado

In the City of Angels, residents of all ages love kale salads, coconut water, green juice, and Mexican food. Now you can get all the spunk of L.A. in each frosty sip of this green smoothie. Add in avocado for a boost of healthy fats.

DIRECTIONS: Combine all the ingredients in a blender and blend from low to high until frosty smooth.

CALORIES: 281, FAT: 2G, CARBS: 65G, PROTEIN: 8G, FIBER: 8G | VITAMIN A: 419%, CALCIUM: 24%, VITAMIN C: 396%, IRON: 18% | ALSO RICH IN MANGANESE, MAGNESIUM, POTASSIUM, AND VITAMIN B$_6$.

255 green tea–lemonade melon frosty

½ cup cold green tea

2 cups frozen watermelon chunks (other varieties of melon work too)

1 frozen banana

2 tablespoons fresh lemon juice

2 teaspoons maple syrup

BOOST IT: 1 teaspoon chia seeds

This super-refreshing blend of frozen watermelon, lemon, and green tea is a fantastic way to sip on some antioxidants. Feel forever young with this lemonade-inspired frosty.

DIRECTIONS: Combine all the ingredients in a blender and blend from low to high until frosty smooth.

CALORIES: 239, FAT: 1G, CARBS: 61G, PROTEIN: 3G, FIBER: 5G | VITAMIN A: 36%, CALCIUM: 4%, VITAMIN C: 82%, IRON: 7% | ALSO RICH IN MANGANESE, POTASSIUM, AND VITAMIN B$_6$.

256 matcha glow

1 cup vanilla soy milk

1 frozen banana

1 cup frozen honeydew melon chunks

1 teaspoon matcha powder

BOOST IT: **1 scoop vanilla vegan protein powder**

Antioxidant-rich melon-matcha smoothies are a welcome treat on a busy, blurry day. Frosty honeydew swirls with banana and vanilla soy milk. Pastel green matcha bliss. Swoon. Matcha is Zen-mood-inducing to help combat stress, which can contribute to the aging process. Add a scoop of protein powder to help build or maintain muscle mass.

DIRECTIONS: Combine all the ingredients in a blender and blend from low to high until frosty smooth.

CALORIES: 266, FAT: 5G, CARBS: 50G, PROTEIN: 10G, FIBER: 5G | VITAMIN A: 13%, CALCIUM: 32%, VITAMIN C: 68%, IRON: 9% | ALSO RICH IN RIBOFLAVIN, VITAMIN B$_6$, AND POTASSIUM.

257 saving-grace green smoothie

½ cup orange juice

½ cup plain soy milk

2 cups chopped kale leaves

½ avocado

½ cup fresh or frozen blueberries

1 kiwi, peeled

½ cup chopped pear or grapes (optional)

½ cup coconut water ice cubes

BOOST IT: **1 to 2 teaspoons flax seeds or flax oil**

We have all slipped off track and let wellness slide—giving sleep, exercise, stress management, and healing foods a backseat—causing wear and tear on our bodies. One way to get back on track in a jiffy is through healing green foods. This sweet green smoothie will fill your cells with optimism for a more well future. Share with a friend to spread wellness inspiration. Add flax seeds or oil for an omega-3 boost.

DIRECTIONS: Combine all the ingredients in a blender and blend from low to high until frosty smooth.

CALORIES: 491, FAT: 19G, CARBS: 77G, PROTEIN: 14G, FIBER: 18G | VITAMIN A: 427%, CALCIUM: 42%, VITAMIN C: 528%, IRON: 25% | ALSO RICH IN MANGANESE.

258 golden goji glow

½ cup coconut water

2 tablespoons goji berries

½ cup orange juice

1 frozen banana

1 cup frozen mango or pineapple chunks

½ cup ice

BOOST IT: 1 to 2 teaspoons unsweetened dried coconut flakes

This tropical blend is dedicated to my mother, who just loves her goji berries. Those tart, sweet, perky-pink dried berries really do blend nicely in a frosty smoothie. And they are loaded with forever-young nutrients like fiber and vitamins C and A.

DIRECTIONS: Combine the coconut water and goji berries in a blender and soak until the berries soften up a bit, about 10 minutes. Add the remaining ingredients and blend from low to high until frosty smooth.

CALORIES: 336, FAT: 2G, CARBS: 82G, PROTEIN: 4G, FIBER: 9G | VITAMIN A: 100%, CALCIUM: 10%, VITAMIN C: 209%, IRON: 11% | ALSO RICH IN POTASSIUM AND VITAMIN B$_6$.

259 california sunrise: pistachio-strawberry

1 cup vanilla soy milk

1 cup frozen strawberries

1 frozen banana

3 tablespoons raw pistachios, soaked and drained

2 teaspoons agave syrup

½ cup ice

BOOST IT: 1 teaspoon chia seeds

Glow at any age with this silky pistachio smoothie reminiscent of a glowing sunrise along the California coast. Antioxidant-rich berries and mineral-rich pistachios blend with creamy banana and soy to help you feel youthful. Add chia seeds for an omega-3 and fiber boost.

DIRECTIONS: Combine all the ingredients in a blender and blend from low to high until frosty smooth.

CALORIES: 460, FAT: 16G, CARBS: 71G, PROTEIN: 16G, FIBER: 10G | VITAMIN A: 5%, CALCIUM: 12%, VITAMIN C: 160%, IRON: 20% | ALSO RICH IN MANGANESE AND VITAMIN B$_6$.

260 super "c" citrus blitz

1 cup coconut water

1 orange, peeled and segmented (fresh or frozen)

½ grapefruit, peeled and segmented

½ cup frozen strawberries

1 banana

½ cup ice

BOOST IT: 1 teaspoon flax oil

Super "C" your day with this whole food blend of citrus and berries, like sipping on a frosty-sweet fruit salad. Trade your fork for a straw. Add some flax oil for an omega-3 boost.

DIRECTIONS: Combine all the ingredients in a blender and blend from low to high until frosty smooth.

CALORIES: 301, FAT: 1G, CARBS: 73G, PROTEIN: 6G, FIBER: 13G | VITAMIN A: 34%, CALCIUM: 17%, VITAMIN C: 334%, IRON: 9% | ALSO RICH IN MANGANESE, POTASSIUM, VITAMIN B$_6$, AND MAGNESIUM.

261 banana split smoothie

SMOOTHIE BASE

½ cup soy milk

1 tablespoon almond butter

1 frozen banana

½ cup frozen watermelon chunks (or more banana)

TOPPINGS

½ cup sliced banana

2 squeezes of vegan chocolate syrup

1 teaspoon chopped raw walnuts

2 tablespoons soy whipped topping

Pinch of ground cinnamon

1 cherry

There's nothing like a childhood dessert to make you feel young at heart! This banana split smoothie should make you feel like a kid again at first sip.

DIRECTIONS: Blend the base ingredients from low to high until frosty smooth. Fill a glass halfway with the smoothie; top with most of the banana slices and a squeeze of syrup. Add the rest of the smoothie and banana, and more syrup. Crown with the rest of the toppings.

BOOST IT: 1 tablespoon raw cacao powder

CALORIES: 412, FAT: 23G, CARBS: 46G, PROTEIN: 11G, FIBER: 5G | VITAMIN A: 15%, CALCIUM: 25%, VITAMIN C: 29%, IRON: 13%

Banana Split Smoothie

262 hip hemp-chocolate shake

1 cup water

2 to 3 tablespoons raw hemp seeds

Pinch of salt

1 tablespoon raw cacao powder

1½ frozen bananas

2 tablespoons almond butter

A few pinches of ground cinnamon

Agave syrup to taste

½ cup ice

BOOST IT: ½ cup mashed avocado

You'll feel hip sipping this rich chocolate-almond hemp shake. Bananas, cacao, and creamy almond butter fuel this sassy strengthening smoothie. Cacao is rich in free-radical-fighting antioxidants, and hemp seeds provide complete vegan protein to help you maintain healthy muscle mass at any age. Add silky avocado for a boost of healthy fats.

DIRECTIONS: Combine the water, hemp seeds, and salt in a blender and blend from low to high until the mixture becomes opaque white and ultra-creamy. Strain out the hemp pulp if you like. Add the remaining ingredients and blend from low to high until frosty smooth.

CALORIES: 457, FAT: 27G, CARBS: 50G, PROTEIN: 13G, FIBER: 8G | VITAMIN A: 2%, CALCIUM: 12%, VITAMIN C: 26%, IRON: 22% | ALSO RICH IN MANGANESE AND MAGNESIUM.

263 rad raspberry

½ cup orange juice

½ cup coconut water or soy milk

1 to 2 cups chopped Swiss chard

1 cup frozen raspberries

1 frozen banana

½ cup ice

BOOST IT: 1 teaspoon chia seeds

This refreshing blend of raspberries, citrus, banana, and chard greens will have you feeling super-radical. In a free-radical-fighting sort of way.

DIRECTIONS: Combine the orange juice, coconut water, and chard in a blender and blend from low to high until smooth. Add the remaining ingredients and blend from low to high until frosty smooth.

CALORIES: 281, FAT: 2G, CARBS: 61G, PROTEIN: 6G, FIBER: 14G | VITAMIN A: 95%, CALCIUM: 12%, VITAMIN C: 215%, IRON: 17% | ALSO RICH IN MANGANESE, POTASSIUM, VITAMIN B_6, AND MAGNESIUM.

264 poolside peach

1 large peach, pitted and sliced

½ cup frozen pineapple chunks

1 frozen banana

¾ cup orange juice

½ cup coconut water ice cubes

BOOST IT: 1 teaspoon chia seeds

Take a break from stress and make this your afternoon: Lounge poolside, or wherever your favorite chill spot is, frosty drink in hand, drenched in sunshine. Stress can contribute to the aging process, so take a few long, deep breaths and sink into your spot while you enjoy this hydrating drink, with plenty of vitamin C, fiber, and potassium in each sip. Add chia seeds, rich in omega-3 fatty acids and fiber, for even more "forever young" nutrients.

DIRECTIONS: Combine all the ingredients in a blender and blend from low to high until frosty smooth.

CALORIES: 308, FAT: 2G, CARBS: 74G, PROTEIN: 5G, FIBER: 8G | VITAMIN A: 19%, CALCIUM: 7%, VITAMIN C: 255%, IRON: 9% | ALSO RICH IN MANGANESE, POTASSIUM, AND VITAMIN B$_6$.

265 classy cooler

1 cup coconut water

½ cup diced cucumber

½ cup chopped watercress

½ cup grated carrot

1 small green apple, cored and chopped

½ cup ice

BOOST IT: 3 pinches of cayenne and/or 1 teaspoon grated fresh ginger

This classy blend of veggies and fruit is a sweet way to fuel your body with healthful free-radical-fighting nutrients. Plenty of skin-soothing vitamin A in each sip. Add some cayenne or ginger to liven things up.

DIRECTIONS: Combine all the ingredients in a blender and blend from low to high until frosty smooth.

CALORIES: 157, FAT: 1G, CARBS: 37G, PROTEIN: 3G, FIBER: 8G | VITAMIN A: 202%, CALCIUM: 11%, VITAMIN C: 35%, IRON: 7% | ALSO RICH IN MANGANESE, POTASSIUM, VITAMIN B$_6$, MAGNESIUM, AND RIBOFLAVIN.

266 the golden apricot

3 small apricots (or 2 large), pitted

1 cup orange juice, plus a pinch of orange zest

½ cup frozen peach chunks

1 frozen banana

½ cup ice

BOOST IT: 1 tablespoon raw walnuts

Golden fuzzy-skinned apricots and peaches blend into a brilliant frosty smoothie loaded with antioxidants to keep your skin glowing.

DIRECTIONS: Combine all the ingredients in a blender and blend from low to high until frosty smooth.

CALORIES: 383, FAT: 14G, CARBS: 52G, PROTEIN: 16G, FIBER: 9G
| VITAMIN A: 12%, CALCIUM: 33%, VITAMIN C: 17%, IRON: 18%
| ALSO RICH IN POTASSIUM.

267 limes over laser

3 tablespoons fresh lime juice

1 tablespoon chopped fresh mint

3 kiwis, peeled (if frozen, chopped)

1 frozen banana

½ cup coconut water

½ cup ice

BOOST IT: 1 teaspoon flax oil

Forget about laser and Botox, and grab some limes. And kiwis. And mint. And chug this antioxidant-rich sip. This free-radical-fighting smoothie is a much more enjoyable way to take care of yourself from the inside out.

DIRECTIONS: Combine all the ingredients in a blender and blend from low to high until frosty smooth.

CALORIES: 281, FAT: 2G, CARBS: 69G, PROTEIN: 5G, FIBER: 12G
| VITAMIN A: 11%, CALCIUM: 13%, VITAMIN C: 399%, IRON: 12%
| ALSO RICH IN MANGANESE, POTASSIUM, AND VITAMIN B$_6$.

268 super skin soother

1 cup carrot juice

½ cup chopped cucumber

½ cup chopped spinach

½ cup frozen peach chunks

½ cup coconut water ice cubes

BOOST IT: **1 teaspoon aloe vera juice**

This light and frosty fruit-meets-veggie sip is loaded with skin-soothing minerals and antioxidants.

DIRECTIONS: Combine all the ingredients in a blender and blend from low to high until frosty smooth.

CALORIES: 112, FAT: 1G, CARBS: 26G, PROTEIN: 4G, FIBER: 6G | VITAMIN A: 402%, CALCIUM: 9%, VITAMIN C: 34%, IRON: 8% | ALSO RICH IN MANGANESE, POTASSIUM, VITAMIN B$_6$, AND MAGNESIUM.

269 sassy southern citrus peach

1 cup frozen peach chunks

1 cup orange juice

1 frozen banana

½ cup ice

BOOST IT: **2 to 3 pinches cayenne or cinnamon**

Filled with skin-loving antioxidants, this swirled citrus sip will help you feel sassy.

DIRECTIONS: Combine all the ingredients in a blender and blend from low to high until frosty smooth.

CALORIES: 283, FAT: 1G, CARBS: 69G, PROTEIN: 5G, FIBER: 6G | VITAMIN A: 23%, CALCIUM: 5%, VITAMIN C: 242%, IRON: 7% | ALSO RICH IN POTASSIUM.

270 frozen kiwi-basil kiss

1 frozen peeled and segmented medium grapefruit

2 kiwis, peeled

1 banana

¼ cup water or coconut water

2 to 3 tablespoons chopped fresh basil, plus more for garnish

½ cup ice

BOOST IT: 1 cup chopped spinach

This zesty sweet green smoothie is rich in collagen-building vitamin C. The bright kiwi and frosty frozen grapefruit flavors mesh perfectly with the creamy sweet banana and basil.

DIRECTIONS: Combine all the ingredients in a blender and blend from low to high until frosty smooth. Top with basil.

CALORIES: 246, FAT: 1G, CARBS: 60G, PROTEIN: 5G, FIBER: 10G | VITAMIN A: 84%, CALCIUM: 11%, VITAMIN C: 339%, IRON: 10% | ALSO RICH IN MANGANESE, POTASSIUM, AND VITAMIN B$_6$.

271 farm-stand cooler

1 cup fresh blueberries

¾ cup orange juice

1 banana

1 cup chopped kale leaves

½ cup ice

BOOST IT: 1 teaspoon flax oil

Grab some organic blueberries, ruffled kale, and freshly squeezed orange juice from a farm stand or market and blend this simple, sweet, frosty green cooler. Each sweet green sip is rich in fresh and fruity antioxidants. Add flax oil for a boost of omega-3 fatty acids. Freeze your fresh fruit before blending for a thicker smoothie-like texture.

DIRECTIONS: Combine all the ingredients in a blender and blend from low to high until frosty smooth.

CALORIES: 305, FAT: 2G, CARBS: 74G, PROTEIN: 6G, FIBER: 9G | VITAMIN A: 217%, CALCIUM: 13%, VITAMIN C: 330%, IRON: 12% | ALSO RICH IN MANGANESE, POTASSIUM, AND VITAMIN B$_6$.

272 forever-fabulous green shake

½ cup orange juice

½ cup water

2 cups chopped spinach

¼ cup plain soy yogurt

1 frozen banana

½ cup frozen strawberries

½ cup ice

BOOST IT: **2 or 3 raw Brazil nuts**

Antioxidant-rich greens and fruit blend with creamy soy yogurt in this sweet green shake that makes you feel forever young (and fabulous) from the inside out. Selenium-rich Brazil nuts give an anti-aging boost. Toss in another banana for a thicker blend.

DIRECTIONS: Combine the orange juice, water, spinach, yogurt, and nuts, if using, in a blender and blend from low to high until smooth. Add the remaining ingredients and blend from low to high until frosty smooth.

CALORIES: 242, FAT: 2G, CARBS: 56G, PROTEIN: 6G, FIBER: 7G | VITAMIN A: 119%, CALCIUM: 18%, VITAMIN C: 219%, IRON: 16% | ALSO RICH IN MANGANESE, POTASSIUM, VITAMIN B$_6$, AND MAGNESIUM.

273 coconut-ginger-brazil shake

4 or 5 raw Brazil nuts

1 cup vanilla soy milk

1½ frozen bananas

1 orange, peeled and segmented, plus a pinch of zest

1 teaspoon unsweetened dried coconut flakes

A few pinches of ginger powder

½ cup coconut water ice cubes

This creamy cool shake is loaded with selenium-rich, anti-aging Brazil nuts, tropical banana, and a hint of vibrant orange, ginger, and exotic coconut. Add chia seeds for a healthy boost of fiber and omega-3 fatty acids.

DIRECTIONS: Combine the Brazil nuts and soy milk in a blender and blend from low to high until smooth. Add the remaining ingredients and blend from low to high until frosty smooth.

BOOST IT: **1 teaspoon chia seeds**

CALORIES: 482, FAT: 16G, CARBS: 75G, PROTEIN: 14G, FIBER: 12G | VITAMIN A: 21%, CALCIUM: 41%, VITAMIN C: 194%, IRON: 12%

274 ageless açaí cacao

1 cup vanilla soy milk

¼ cup plain soy yogurt

2 frozen bananas

1 tablespoon raw cacao powder

2 to 3 teaspoons açaí powder

1 teaspoon agave syrup (optional)

½ cup ice

BOOST IT: **2 teaspoons raw cacao nibs**

Rich cacao and açaí are the perfect antioxidant-rich pairing. This dessert-approved shake is cool and creamy with a dark chocolate–purple color. Add cacao nibs for even more anti-aging antioxidants.

DIRECTIONS: Combine all the ingredients in a blender and blend from low to high until frosty smooth.

CALORIES: 426, FAT: 10G, CARBS: 79G, PROTEIN: 12G, FIBER: 10G | VITAMIN A: 21%, CALCIUM: 43%, VITAMIN C: 64%, IRON: 16% | ALSO RICH IN POTASSIUM.

275 happy banana

2 frozen bananas

1½ tablespoons peanut butter

1 cup vanilla rice milk (or substitute any variety plant milk)

2 to 3 pinches of ground cinnamon

BOOST IT: **2 tablespoons rolled oats**

Bananas make me happy. Bananas and peanut butter make me really happy! You too? Bananas provide creamy sweetness, plus potassium and fiber to make you feel good from the inside out—all packed inside an easy-open peel. Sip some happiness via this thick milkshake-like peanut butter–banana shake. Add some rustic rolled oats to further boost blood sugar–regulating fiber and help stimulate mood-lifting serotonin.

DIRECTIONS: Combine all the ingredients in a blender and blend from low to high until frosty smooth.

CALORIES: 482, FAT: 15G, CARBS: 83G, PROTEIN: 11G, FIBER: 8G | VITAMIN A: 3%, CALCIUM: 4%, VITAMIN C: 36%, IRON: 8% | ALSO RICH IN POTASSIUM.

276 chocolate-chia cheer shake

1 cup vanilla soy milk

1½ frozen bananas

1 tablespoon salted peanut butter

1 teaspoon chia seeds

1 teaspoon agave syrup, or to taste

1 tablespoon raw cacao powder

2 to 3 pinches of ground cinnamon

BOOST IT: **1 teaspoon raw cacao nibs**

Give me a C, H . . . ! You will be cheering as your chia seeds, cacao powder, and peanut butter swirl and dance in your blender to create this thick and frosty dessert-approved shake. Cacao has been known to boost mood, and chia seeds are rich in mood-helping omega-3 fatty acids and blood sugar–regulating fiber.

DIRECTIONS: Combine all the ingredients in a blender and blend from low to high until frosty smooth.

CALORIES: 410, FAT: 15G, CARBS: 62G, PROTEIN: 15G, FIBER: 10G | VITAMIN A: 12%, CALCIUM: 36%, VITAMIN C: 26%, IRON: 15%

277 perky pumpkin-seed pear

1½ cups sliced fresh or frozen pear

1 cup chopped spinach

1 frozen banana

3 tablespoons raw pumpkin seeds, soaked and drained

½ cup coconut water

½ cup ice

BOOST IT: 1 teaspoon grated fresh ginger

Perk up with sweet pear and mineral-rich pumpkin seeds. Magnesium is known as the mood-boosting mineral—and pumpkin seeds and coconut water are two delicious sources of it!

DIRECTIONS: Combine all the ingredients in a blender and blend from low to high until frosty smooth.

CALORIES: 415, FAT: 13G, CARBS: 75G, PROTEIN: 11G, FIBER: 14G | VITAMIN A: 61%, CALCIUM: 10%, VITAMIN C: 54%, IRON: 32% | ALSO RICH IN MANGANESE AND MAGNESIUM.

278 orchard bliss

½ cup apple cider or fresh-pressed apple juice

1 cup frozen peach chunks

1 orange, peeled and segmented

1 frozen banana

2 tablespoons vanilla soy yogurt

1 teaspoon grated fresh ginger

½ cup ice

BOOST IT: 1 teaspoon chia seeds

This orchard-fresh blend of peaches and apple cider is accented with creamy banana and perky citrus. One sip and you'll feel transported to a lush orchard, blue sky above you and birds singing all around. Add chia seeds for mood-boosting omega-3 fatty acids and extra fiber.

DIRECTIONS: Combine all the ingredients in a blender and blend from low to high until frosty smooth.

CALORIES: 316, FAT: 1G, CARBS: 79G, PROTEIN: 5G, FIBER: 10G | VITAMIN A: 21%, CALCIUM: 10%, VITAMIN C: 285%, IRON: 8% | ALSO RICH IN POTASSIUM.

279 woo-hoo watermelon

1 cup soy milk

1½ cups frozen
watermelon chunks

½ cup frozen pineapple
chunks

1 frozen banana

BOOST IT: 1 to 3 pinches
of cayenne

This light and frosty watermelon shake—a blend
of sweet summer watermelon, frozen pineapple,
and banana—will make you shout "Woo-hoo!"
Really, it will! Add some spicy cayenne to further
perk things up.

DIRECTIONS: Combine all the ingredients in a blender and
blend from low to high until frosty smooth.

CALORIES: 312, FAT: 5G, CARBS: 62G, PROTEIN: 10G, FIBER: 6G
| VITAMIN A: 38%, CALCIUM: 33%, VITAMIN C: 110%, IRON: 12%
| ALSO RICH IN MANGANESE AND RIBOFLAVIN.

280 light-hearted lavender melon frosty

2 cups frozen
honeydew melon
chunks

½ cup Lavender
Lemonade (recipe
follows)

½ banana

This relaxing, mood-lifting blend of lavender and
vibrant citrus swirls with frosty melon for an arctic
infusion of sassy, smooth, and sweet.

DIRECTIONS: Combine all the ingredients in a blender and
blend from low to high until frosty smooth.

BOOST IT: 1 teaspoon chia seeds

Lavender Lemonade   *Makes about 4 cups; refrigerate leftovers*

3 tablespoons culinary
lavender buds

1 cup boiling water

¾ cup fresh lemon juice

4 to 5 tablespoons
organic vegan sugar,
maple syrup, or
agave syrup

2 cups chilled water

DIRECTIONS: Steep the lavender buds in the boiling water
for 15 minutes. Strain the buds and pour the lavender
water into a pitcher; stir in the lemon juice and sugar until
the sugar is dissolved. Stir in the chilled water.

CALORIES FOR SMOOTHIE: 246, FAT: 1G, CARBS: 63G,
PROTEIN: 3G, FIBER: 5G | VITAMIN A: 4%, CALCIUM: 3%,
VITAMIN C: 134%, IRON: 5% | ALSO RICH IN POTASSIUM
AND VITAMIN B$_6$.

281 pineapple-cacao paradise

1 tablespoon raw cacao powder

1 cup vanilla soy milk

½ cup frozen pineapple chunks

1 frozen banana

2 teaspoons agave syrup or maple syrup (optional)

½ cup ice

BOOST IT: 1 to 2 teaspoons unsweetened dried coconut flakes

Two very blissful ingredients: pineapple and chocolate. But together? In a smoothie? Oh, yes! The sunny-sweet pineapple accents the rich cacao in a mood-boosting sort of way that rivals the ever-popular flavor of chocolate-covered strawberries. Add more ice or another frozen banana for a thicker texture.

DIRECTIONS: Combine all the ingredients in a blender and blend from low to high until frosty smooth.

CALORIES: 299, FAT: 6G, CARBS: 59G, PROTEIN: 10G, FIBER: 7G | VITAMIN A: 12%, CALCIUM: 33%, VITAMIN C: 79%, IRON: 12% | ALSO RICH IN MANGANESE AND RIBOFLAVIN.

282 green your mood

1 cup chopped kale leaves

1 cup chopped romaine lettuce (or another green of choice)

½ cup chopped apple

1 banana

½ cup green grapes

½ cup coconut water (or substitute soy milk for a creamier texture)

1 tablespoon fresh lemon juice

Sweetener to taste (optional)

½ cup ice

Put on a green mood. What is a green mood, you ask? It is that happy, energized feeling you get after you guzzle green smoothies or juice! Crave it! This nutrient-dense green smoothie nurtures your body to keep you feeling good from the inside out.

DIRECTIONS: Combine all the ingredients in a blender and blend from low to high until frosty smooth.

BOOST IT: 1 teaspoon grated fresh ginger

CALORIES: 232, FAT: 1G, CARBS: 56G, PROTEIN: 6G, FIBER: 9G | VITAMIN A: 215%, CALCIUM: 15%, VITAMIN C: 177%, IRON: 12% | ALSO RICH IN MAGNESIUM, MANGANESE, POTASSIUM, AND VITAMIN B$_6$.

283 orangetastic morning

2 small oranges, peeled (fresh or frozen)

1 frozen banana

1 kiwi, peeled

¾ cup vanilla soy milk

½ cup ice

BOOST IT: **2 to 3 tablespoons mashed avocado**

Wake up ready to start your day with a big citrus-inspired smile on your face—this feel-good blend of oranges, banana, kiwi, and vanilla soy milk will usher in some a.m. glee. The fiber in the whole oranges and healthy fat in the avocado help slow down the release of energy, which may help regulate your blood sugar and prevent a cranky mood.

DIRECTIONS: Combine all the ingredients in a blender and blend from low to high until frosty smooth.

CALORIES: 421, FAT: 4G, CARBS: 92G, PROTEIN: 11G, FIBER: 15G | VITAMIN A: 27%, CALCIUM: 41%, VITAMIN C: 461%, IRON: 10% | ALSO RICH IN POTASSIUM.

284 mom's peach pie

½ cup vanilla rice milk

2 peaches, pitted and roughly chopped

1 frozen banana

1 tablespoon rolled oats

1 tablespoon raw walnuts

3 pinches of ground cinnamon

½ cup ice

1 teaspoon maple syrup (optional)

BOOST IT: **make it à la mode—add a scoop of vegan vanilla coconut milk ice cream**

Cozy and sweet, just like Mom, this peach pie smoothie will boost your mood and energize your body. Oats help boost serotonin, while walnuts add omega-3 fatty acids. Fiber and healthy fats help stabilize your blood sugar as you sip.

DIRECTIONS: Combine all the ingredients in a blender and blend from low to high until frosty smooth.

CALORIES: 310, FAT: 7G, CARBS: 62G, PROTEIN: 6G, FIBER: 7G | VITAMIN A: 14%, CALCIUM: 4%, VITAMIN C: 40%, IRON: 8% | ALSO RICH IN MANGANESE.

Mom's Peach Pie

285 macadamia-banana daydream

1 cup vanilla soy milk

3 tablespoons raw macadamia nuts

1½ frozen bananas

2 teaspoons agave syrup

2 teaspoons unsweetened dried coconut flakes

¼ cup ice

BOOST IT: **splash of coconut milk**

Daydream of your favorite happy place (or person) as you sip this paradise blend of bananas, coconut, soy milk, and crunchy, buttery macadamia nuts. Macadamias are rich in mood-helping magnesium and copper, and the fats in the nuts help regulate your blood sugar as your sip. Blood-sugar spikes and crashes can make you feel moody!

DIRECTIONS: Combine the soy milk and macadamia nuts in a blender and blend from low to high until smooth. Add the remaining ingredients and blend from low to high until frosty smooth.

CALORIES: 492, FAT: 25G, CARBS: 63G, PROTEIN: 11G, FIBER: 8G | VITAMIN A: 12%, CALCIUM: 34%, VITAMIN C: 28%, IRON: 15% | ALSO RICH IN MANGANESE.

286 grapefruit glee

1 large pink grapefruit, peeled and segmented

½ cup vanilla rice milk

1½ frozen bananas

1 teaspoon maple syrup

½ cup ice

BOOST IT: **1 tablespoon raw walnuts**

GARNISH: **2 tablespoons fresh blueberries**

Pink vitamin C–filled grapefruit is a happiness-inducing ingredient. Blend this zingy flavor with creamy banana, rice milk, and a garnish of fresh blueberries for a simple sip to lighten your mood. Boost with walnuts for added mood-helping omega-3 fatty acids.

DIRECTIONS: Combine all the ingredients in a blender and blend from low to high until frosty smooth. Garnish with the blueberries—they will float on top and you can eat them as you sip!

CALORIES: 297, FAT: 2G, CARBS: 73G, PROTEIN: 3G, FIBER: 7G | VITAMIN A: 31%, CALCIUM: 5%, VITAMIN C: 94%, IRON: 4% | ALSO RICH IN VITAMIN B$_6$.

287 spunky spirulina-blueberry

1 cup frozen blueberries

1 frozen banana

½ to 1 teaspoon
  spirulina powder

1 cup vanilla soy milk

1 teaspoon agave syrup

½ cup ice

BOOST IT: **1 tablespoon
pumpkin seeds**

Feeding your body an abundance of healthy nutrients makes you feel alive, well, and happy. Taking a dose of nutrient-dense spirulina (green algae) is an easy way to inspire that feel-good bliss. Blueberries perfectly pair with creamy banana. This is also delicious with frozen papaya in place of berries. Add pumpkin seeds for a boost of mood-helping magnesium.

DIRECTIONS: Combine all the ingredients in a blender and blend from low to high until frosty smooth.

CALORIES: 351, FAT: 5G, CARBS: 69G, PROTEIN: 12G, FIBER: 9G | VITAMIN A: 13%, CALCIUM: 33%, VITAMIN C: 41%, IRON: 15% | ALSO RICH IN RIBOFLAVIN.

288 green me up, scotty!

½ cup soy milk

½ cup coconut water

2 cups chopped
  spinach or kale leaves

½ cup frozen grapes

1 frozen banana

2 tablespoons chopped
  fresh mint

½ cup ice

BOOST IT: **1 teaspoon
chia seeds**

OK, I promise I'm not a Trekkie, but this cooling, frosty blend of sweet greens paired with soothing mint feels like the space-age way to lighten your mood and transport your body to wellness. Add some futuristic (sort of) chia seeds for an added boost of mood-helping omega-3 fatty acids.

DIRECTIONS: Combine the soy milk, coconut water, and spinach in a blender and blend from low to high until smooth. Add the remaining ingredients and blend from low to high until frosty smooth.

CALORIES: 227, FAT: 3G, CARBS: 48G, PROTEIN: 8G, FIBER: 7G | VITAMIN A: 129%, CALCIUM: 28%, VITAMIN C: 56%, IRON: 24%

289 vanilla pumpkin pleasure shake

1 cup vanilla soy milk ice cubes

½ cup 100% pumpkin puree ice cubes

¼ cup vanilla soy milk (or soy creamer or coconut milk for a richer shake)

1 teaspoon pumpkin pie spice

2 tablespoons maple syrup or agave syrup, or to taste

A few pinches of salt

BOOST IT: 1 teaspoon flax oil

This seasonal smoothie swirls pumpkin pie flavors into frosty bliss. Frozen pumpkin puree makes for a frosty shake-like sip. A boost of omega-3–rich flax oil will further enhance your lifted mood. For a more decadent shake, substitute coconut milk ice cubes for the soy milk ice cubes.

DIRECTIONS: Combine all the ingredients in a blender and blend from low to high until frosty smooth.

CALORIES: 279, FAT: 5G, CARBS: 50G, PROTEIN: 10G, FIBER: 4G | VITAMIN A: 292%, CALCIUM: 44%, VITAMIN C: 8%, IRON: 14% | ALSO RICH IN MANGANESE.

290 fresh strawberry smile

1 cup fresh strawberries

1 cup vanilla rice milk (or substitute soy milk)

1 frozen banana

½ cup coconut water ice cubes

BOOST IT: 1 tablespoon almond butter

GARNISH: fresh mint leaves

Fresh strawberries are sure to make anyone smile. Especially when blended with cool rice milk and banana and garnished with soothing mint leaves. Refresh your mood with each sip. Add almond butter for a boost of mood-managing magnesium and copper.

DIRECTIONS: Combine all the ingredients in a blender and blend from low to high until frosty smooth.

CALORIES: 294, FAT: 3G, CARBS: 67G, PROTEIN: 4G, FIBER: 7G | VITAMIN A: 2%, CALCIUM: 8%, VITAMIN C: 165%, IRON: 8% | ALSO RICH IN MANGANESE.

Vanilla Pumpkin Pleasure Shake

291 magnesium magic

1 cup soy milk

2 cups chopped spinach

3 tablespoons pumpkin seeds, soaked and drained

½ cup frozen peach chunks

1 frozen banana

½ cup coconut water ice cubes

BOOST IT: **2 or 3 raw Brazil nuts**

Magnesium is known as the feel-good mineral. Well, this green smoothie is packed with magnesium-rich pumpkin seeds and spinach. A smoothie that may turn your mood around? Now that is quite an amazing magic trick.

DIRECTIONS: Combine the soy milk, spinach, pumpkin seeds, and Brazil nuts, if using, and blend from low to high until smooth. Add the remaining ingredients and blend from low to high until frosty smooth.

CALORIES: 415, FAT: 16G, CARBS: 54G, PROTEIN: 18G, FIBER: 9G | VITAMIN A: 132%, CALCIUM: 41%, VITAMIN C: 60%, IRON: 41% | ALSO RICH IN MAGNESIUM, MANGANESE, POTASSIUM, RIBOFLAVIN, AND PHOSPHORUS.

292 blissful blackberry-walnut

1 cup frozen blackberries

3 tablespoons raw walnuts

1¼ cups vanilla soy milk

1 frozen banana

2 pinches of ginger powder or cayenne

¼ cup ice

BOOST IT: **2 tablespoons rolled oats**

Blackberries remind me of summertime, and that always puts me in a good mood. This frosty blend of berries, walnuts, banana, and soy—with a spicy accent of ginger or cayenne—will have you feeling all summery too. Add some rustic oats to help boost serotonin.

DIRECTIONS: Combine all the ingredients in a blender and blend from low to high until frosty smooth.

CALORIES: 438, FAT: 19G, CARBS: 54G, PROTEIN: 18G, FIBER: 14G | VITAMIN A: 20%, CALCIUM: 44%, VITAMIN C: 68%, IRON: 19% | ALSO RICH IN MANGANESE AND RIBOFLAVIN.

293 sweet green glee

½ cup soy milk

¼ cup orange juice

1 tablespoons pumpkin seeds, soaked and drained

2 cups chopped spinach

½ cup green grapes

½ banana

1 tablespoon hemp seeds (optional)

3 tablespoons mashed avocado

½ cup ice

BOOST IT: 2 teaspoons flax seed oil

This frothy green smoothie is a mood-lifting elixir for sure! Each sip is filled with superfood spinach, banana, perky-sweet grapes, mineral- and tryptophan-rich seeds, and healthy fat–rich avocado. A few splashes of sunny orange juice and creamy soy milk, and blend it all into liquid green smoothie bliss.

DIRECTIONS: Combine the soy milk, orange juice, and pumpkin seeds in a blender and blend from low to high until smooth. Add the remaining ingredients and blend from low to high until frosty smooth.

CALORIES: 311, FAT: 14G, CARBS: 39G, PROTEIN: 12G, FIBER: 7G | VITAMIN A: 121%, CALCIUM: 23%, VITAMIN C: 96%, IRON: 25% | ALSO RICH IN MAGNESIUM AND MANGANESE.

294 lemonade stand

1 cup lemonade

½ cup frozen strawberries

½ cup frozen peach chunks

½ banana

½ cup ice

BOOST IT: 1 teaspoon aloe vera juice

A lot of us have many happy childhood memories of running our very own lemonade stand. Well, this happy blend of cheerful lemonade, strawberries, peaches, and banana will remind you how far you've come in life—and how sweetly satisfying lemonade can be!

DIRECTIONS: Combine all the ingredients in a blender and blend from low to high until frosty smooth.

CALORIES: 208, FAT: 1G, CARBS: 53G, PROTEIN: 2G, FIBER: 4G | VITAMIN A: 7%, CALCIUM: 3%, VITAMIN C: 105%, IRON: 6%

295 sunflower butter bliss

1 cup vanilla soy milk

2 tablespoons sunflower butter

2 frozen bananas

1 teaspoon maple syrup

¼ cup ice

BOOST IT: **1 tablespoon rolled oats**

Sunflower butter is rich and creamy and filled with such nutrients as protein, iron, mood-regulating magnesium, and healthy fats. This banana-based shake may help put you in a sunny mood. Add complex-carbohydrate oats to help boost serotonin.

DIRECTIONS: Combine all the ingredients in a blender and blend from low to high until frosty smooth.

CALORIES: 443, FAT: 20G, CARBS: 60G, PROTEIN: 14G, FIBER: 9G | VITAMIN A: 12%, CALCIUM: 34%, VITAMIN C: 26%, IRON: 15%

296 strawberry-banana-peach shake

1 cup vanilla soy milk

1½ frozen bananas

½ cup frozen strawberries

½ cup frozen peach chunks

BOOST IT: **1 to 2 tablespoons raw walnuts and/or 1 tablespoon rolled oats**

Let this light pink blend of strawberries, vanilla soy milk, peaches, and banana wrap you in a blanket of bliss. This sweet smoothie blends up thick and creamy. Add magnesium-rich walnuts and/or complex carbohydrate–rich oats to further boost your mood.

DIRECTIONS: Combine all the ingredients in a blender and blend from low to high until frosty smooth.

CALORIES: 314, FAT: 5G, CARBS: 62G, PROTEIN: 11G, FIBER: 8G | VITAMIN A: 18%, CALCIUM: 33%, VITAMIN C: 106%, IRON: 11% | ALSO RICH IN POTASSIUM AND VITAMIN B$_6$.

297 purple paradise açaí

1 cup açaí juice
¼ cup vanilla soy milk
1 cup frozen blueberries
½ frozen banana
½ cup coconut water ice cubes

BOOST IT: **1 teaspoon unsweetened dried coconut flakes**

Crashing waves. Beach towel. Palm trees. Flip-flops. But where is the frosty beverage for your hand? Right here! Grab this cool purple blend of creamy açaí, tropical banana, soy, and sweet blueberries and head to paradise with each sip. Give your mood the paradise island treatment.

DIRECTIONS: Combine all the ingredients in a blender and blend from low to high until frosty smooth.

CALORIES: 333, FAT: 5G, CARBS: 72G, PROTEIN: 6G, FIBER: 8G | VITAMIN A: 15%, CALCIUM: 14%, VITAMIN C: 72%, IRON: 7%

298 kiwi perk-up

1 cup chopped spinach
½ cup orange juice
2 to 3 kiwis, peeled (if frozen, chopped)
1 frozen banana
½ cup chopped fresh parsley
½ cup ice

BOOST IT: **1 teaspoon flax oil**

Perky-sweet kiwis, with their vibrant green color, plentiful amounts of vitamin C, and zesty aroma, are a naturally mood-lifting fruit. Blend them with citrus and greens and smile as you sip. Add some flax oil for a boost of mood-balancing omega-3 fatty acids.

DIRECTIONS: Combine the spinach and orange juice in a blender and blend from low to high until smooth. Add the remaining ingredients and blend from low to high until frosty smooth.

CALORIES: 318, FAT: 2G, CARBS: 78G, PROTEIN: 7G, FIBER: 12G | VITAMIN A: 117%, CALCIUM: 17%, VITAMIN C: 553%, IRON: 22% | ALSO RICH IN POTASSIUM, MAGNESIUM, AND VITAMIN B$_6$.

Strawberry-Banana-Peach Shake

299 green ginger lift

2 cups chopped Swiss
chard or spinach

1 cup carrot juice

½ cup chopped apple
or pear

2 tablespoons fresh
lemon juice

1 teaspoon grated fresh
ginger

½ cup ice

BOOST IT: 1 teaspoon
aloe vera juice

Watch out, free radicals! Superfood greens blend with carrot juice and ginger for a supercharged sweet green juice you can feel good about chugging. Taking care of yourself is an instant mood-lifter!

DIRECTIONS: Combine all the ingredients in a blender and blend from low to high until frosty smooth.

CALORIES: 126, FAT: 1G, CARBS: 28G, PROTEIN: 4G, FIBER: 4G | VITAMIN A: 789%, CALCIUM: 8%, VITAMIN C: 89%, IRON: 11% | ALSO RICH IN MANGANESE, POTASSIUM, AND MAGNESIUM.

300 "c" breeze kiwi frosty

½ cup coconut water

3 or 4 frozen peeled
and chopped kiwis

1 banana

2 tablespoons fresh
lime juice

Drizzle of agave syrup
(optional)

BOOST IT: 2 to 3
tablespoons mashed
avocado

This frosty kiwi, lime, and banana smoothie has an uplifting flavor and is loaded with vitamin C. Add avocado for some mood-boosting omega-3 fatty acids.

DIRECTIONS: Combine all the ingredients in a blender and blend from low to high until frosty smooth.

CALORIES: 321, FAT: 2G, CARBS: 79G, PROTEIN: 6G, FIBER: 14G | VITAMIN A: 7%, CALCIUM: 15%, VITAMIN C: 507%, IRON: 9% | ALSO RICH IN POTASSIUM AND VITAMIN B_6.

301 lively lime-avocado-blackberry

1½ cups fresh
   blackberries

½ cup mashed avocado

1 tablespoon agave
   syrup

¾ cup coconut water

1 tablespoon fresh lime
   juice, plus a few
   pinches of zest

½ to 1 cup ice

BOOST IT: **1 teaspoon
apple cider vinegar**

Juicy fresh blackberries swirl with creamy avocado, lime juice, and coconut water in this antioxidant-rich fresh berry blend. Antioxidants help your body neutralize free radicals that could make you feel worn down and not as lively and cheerful as you'd like.

DIRECTIONS: Combine all the ingredients in a blender and blend from low to high until frosty smooth.

CALORIES: 312, FAT: 12G, CARBS: 51G, PROTEIN: 6G, FIBER: 18G | VITAMIN A: 12%, CALCIUM: 12%, VITAMIN C: 103%, IRON: 13% | ALSO RICH IN POTASSIUM AND MANGANESE.

302 pumpkin seed pleasure

3 tablespoons pumpkin
   seeds, soaked and
   drained

1 cup soy milk

Pinch of salt

¼ cup mashed avocado

1½ frozen bananas

½ cup ice

BOOST IT: **1 cup chopped
spinach**

Silky avocado, nutty pumpkin seeds, and creamy bananas swirl into a pleasurable green smoothie to lift your mood from the inside out. Magnesium, found in pumpkin seeds, may help with balancing your mood. Add superfood spinach for even more feel-good vitamins and minerals.

DIRECTIONS: Combine the pumpkin seeds, soy milk, salt, and avocado in a blender and blend from low to high until smooth. Add the remaining ingredients and blend from low to high until frosty smooth.

CALORIES: 487, FAT: 21G, CARBS: 60G, PROTEIN: 20G, FIBER: 7G | VITAMIN A: 58%, CALCIUM: 10%, VITAMIN C: 31%, IRON: 20% | ALSO RICH IN MAGNESIUM.

303 feel-good guava

½ cup frozen pineapple chunks

½ cup frozen mango chunks

1 cup 100% guava juice

1 frozen banana

½ cup coconut water ice cubes

BOOST IT: **2 teaspoons unsweetened dried coconut flakes and/or a pinch of orange zest**

No matter where you are, what the weather is, or how bad your day is going, this guava, pineapple, mango, and banana smoothie is your first-class ticket to your very own paradise island. Hop on board and feel your mood lift. If you can't find guava juice, use apple, orange, or pineapple juice, or non-dairy milk for a creamy spin on this tropical sip.

DIRECTIONS: Combine all the ingredients in a blender and blend from low to high until frosty smooth.

CALORIES: 340, FAT: 1G, CARBS: 85G, PROTEIN: 3G, FIBER: 9G | VITAMIN A: 15%, CALCIUM: 5%, VITAMIN C: 222%, IRON: 10% | ALSO RICH IN MANGANESE.

304 simple citrus-berry pleasure

1 cup frozen strawberries

1 frozen banana

1 cup orange juice

½ cup ice

BOOST IT: **1 tablespoon raw walnuts**

Vibrant vitamin C–filled orange juice and cheerful strawberries combine with banana in this simple, sweet pink smoothie. Add walnuts for some mood-boosting magnesium.

DIRECTIONS: Combine all the ingredients in a blender and blend from low to high until frosty smooth.

CALORIES: 263, FAT: 1G, CARBS: 63G, PROTEIN: 4G, FIBER: 6G | VITAMIN A: 12%, CALCIUM: 6%, VITAMIN C: 365%, IRON: 8% | ALSO RICH IN POTASSIUM, MANGANESE, AND VITAMIN B$_6$.

305 spicy green cold crusher

1 cup orange juice

½ cup frozen peach chunks

½ cup chopped green bell pepper

1 cup chopped spinach

1 banana

2 to 3 pinches of cayenne

½ cup ice

BOOST IT: **1 teaspoon flax oil**

Vitamin C and a hint of stimulating cayenne pack some immunity-enhancing power into this citrus green smoothie.

DIRECTIONS: Combine all the ingredients in a blender and blend from low to high until frosty smooth.

CALORIES: 272, FAT: 1G, CARBS: 65G, PROTEIN: 5G, FIBER: 7G | VITAMIN A: 106%, CALCIUM: 8%, VITAMIN C: 346%, IRON: 12% | ALSO RICH IN POTASSIUM AND VITAMIN B$_6$.

306 pink superstar

1 cup pink grapefruit juice

¼ cup mashed avocado

½ cup frozen peach chunks

1 cup frozen strawberries

1 frozen banana

½ cup ice

BOOST IT: **2 to 3 tablespoons soy yogurt**

Feel like an energized wellness-filled superstar with this smoothie rich in vitamin C from creamy peaches, sweet strawberries, and vibrant pink grapefruit juice and boosted with omega-3 fatty acids from the avocado. Add soy yogurt for some immunity-boosting probiotics.

DIRECTIONS: Combine all the ingredients in a blender and blend from low to high until frosty smooth.

CALORIES: 320, FAT: 6G, CARBS: 69G, PROTEIN: 4G, FIBER: 12G | VITAMIN A: 51%, CALCIUM: 7%, VITAMIN C: 254%, IRON: 9%

307 green-kick wellness cooler

½ cup coconut water

2 tablespoons fresh lemon juice

1 cup chopped spinach

½ cup chopped fresh watercress or parsley

½ cup green grapes

½ cup frozen mango chunks

½ cup ice

2 to 3 pinches of cayenne

BOOST IT: 1 teaspoon grated fresh ginger

This light and spicy green smoothie may help you calm a cold or soothe a tired, weary body. This smoothie is rich in potassium to help you stay hydrated. Beat the "I don't feel so hot" blues with a swig of this whole food green drink. Try it with frozen grapes and frozen lemon juice ice cubes for a frostier blend.

DIRECTIONS: Combine all the ingredients in a blender and blend from low to high until frosty smooth.

CALORIES: 124, FAT: 1G, CARBS: 30G, PROTEIN: 3G, FIBER: 4G | VITAMIN A: 81%, CALCIUM: 10%, VITAMIN C: 96%, IRON: 8% | ALSO RICH IN POTASSIUM, MANGANESE, AND MAGNESIUM.

308 green apple fixer

¾ cup orange juice

1 banana

½ cup frozen peaches

1 kiwi, peeled

½ cup chopped green apple

2 to 3 pinches of cayenne and/or 1 teaspoon grated fresh ginger

BOOST IT: 2 tablespoons mashed avocado

This whole food green smoothie blended with sassy green apple, vibrant orange juice, creamy banana, kiwi, and peach is a delicious and natural way to help fix what ails you. Boost with omega-3 fatty acids by adding some silky avocado.

DIRECTIONS: Combine all the ingredients in a blender and blend from low to high until frosty smooth.

CALORIES: 297, FAT: 2G, CARBS: 73G, PROTEIN: 5G, FIBER: 8G | VITAMIN A: 16%, CALCIUM: 6%, VITAMIN C: 303%, IRON: 7% | ALSO RICH IN POTASSIUM.

Peachy-Keen Shake

309 peachy-keen shake

1 cup frozen peach chunks

½ cup freshly squeezed orange juice

½ cup vanilla soy milk

½ cup frozen cantaloupe chunks (or substitute coconut water ice cubes)

1 frozen banana

1 to 3 pinches of cayenne (optional)

BOOST IT: **2 to 3 tablespoons soy yogurt**

Feel peachy keen with this luscious blend of peaches, soy milk, banana, and citrus. No need for ice—frozen potassium-rich cantaloupe makes this blend extra frosty!

DIRECTIONS: Combine all the ingredients in a blender and blend from low to high until frosty smooth.

CALORIES: 304, FAT: 3G, CARBS: 66G, PROTEIN: 8G, FIBER: 7G | VITAMIN A: 75%, CALCIUM: 19%, VITAMIN C: 187%, IRON: 9% | ALSO RICH IN POTASSIUM.

310 cold smasher citrus smoothie

½ cup orange juice

½ cup grapefruit juice

1 cup frozen strawberries

1 frozen banana

3 pinches of cayenne

2 to 3 tablespoons vanilla soy yogurt

½ cup ice

BOOST IT: **1 teaspoon grated fresh ginger**

Stuck with a clumsy cold weighing you down—one that keeps lingering and won't go away? Vibrant citrus, spicy cayenne, and C-filled berries may help you finally smash it!

DIRECTIONS: Combine all the ingredients in a blender and blend from low to high until frosty smooth.

CALORIES: 290, FAT: 2G, CARBS: 68G, PROTEIN: 6G, FIBER: 8G | VITAMIN A: 34%, CALCIUM: 15%, VITAMIN C: 328%, IRON: 9% | ALSO RICH IN POTASSIUM, MANGANESE, AND VITAMIN B_6.

311 mango-avocado immunity

1 cup frozen mango
    chunks

1 cup orange juice

½ cup mashed avocado

1 frozen banana

1 to 3 pinches of
    cayenne

½ cup ice

BOOST IT: 1 or 2 raw
Brazil nuts

Creamy avocado blends with vitamin C–rich mango and citrus. Toss in a few Brazil nuts to add a dose of selenium, a mineral that keeps your immune system strong.

DIRECTIONS: Combine all the ingredients in a blender and blend from low to high until frosty smooth.

CALORIES: 441, FAT: 12G, CARBS: 87G, PROTEIN: 5G, FIBER: 12G | VITAMIN A: 41%, CALCIUM: 6%, VITAMIN C: 312%, IRON: 8% | ALSO RICH IN POTASSIUM AND VITAMIN B$_6$.

312 ginger-mango mega "c"

1 cup orange juice

1 cup frozen mango
    chunks

1 kiwi, peeled

½ cup fresh
    strawberries

1 teaspoon grated fresh
    ginger

½ cup ice

BOOST IT: a few pinches
of cayenne

This mango, strawberry, citrus, and kiwi smoothie is a super way to drink your vitamin C and nurture your immune system. It includes a boost of stimulating fresh ginger too!

DIRECTIONS: Combine all the ingredients in a blender and blend from low to high until frosty smooth.

CALORIES: 295, FAT: 2G, CARBS: 71G, PROTEIN: 4G, FIBER: 7G | VITAMIN A: 37%, CALCIUM: 9%, VITAMIN C: 471%, IRON: 8% | ALSO RICH IN POTASSIUM.

313 pink power immunity

1¼ cups grapefruit juice

½ cup frozen
strawberries

½ cup frozen
raspberries

1½ fresh or frozen
bananas

½ cup ice

A few pinches of
cayenne (optional)

BOOST IT: 1 teaspoon
flax seeds

Power up with pink! This frosty blend of antioxidant-rich grapefruit, raspberries, strawberries, and creamy banana can have you feeling fabulous in a flash. Get ready for some *zing* in your step!

DIRECTIONS: Combine all the ingredients in a blender and blend from low to high until frosty smooth.

CALORIES: 305, FAT: 2G, CARBS: 76G, PROTEIN: 5G, FIBER: 13G | VITAMIN A: 55%, CALCIUM: 7%, VITAMIN C: 288%, IRON: 8% | ALSO RICH IN POTASSIUM, MANGANESE, AND VITAMIN B$_6$.

314 orange-cranberry-burst frosty

1 cup cranberry juice

½ cup orange juice

1 fresh or frozen banana

About 1 cup ice

BOOST IT: 1 teaspoon
grated fresh ginger

Sweet orange juice, rich in the antioxidant vitamin C, blends with sweet-tart cranberry juice in this uplifting blend of ice and fruit. Antioxidants can help keep your body healthy and prevent illness. Staying well hydrated also helps keep your immune system performing at its best.

DIRECTIONS: Combine all the ingredients in a blender and blend from low to high until frosty smooth.

CALORIES: 301, FAT: 1G, CARBS: 74G, PROTEIN: 2G, FIBER: 3G | VITAMIN A: 6%, CALCIUM: 3%, VITAMIN C: 120%, IRON: 3%

315 frosty green melon

½ cup orange juice

¼ cup water

1 cup chopped spinach, chard, or kale

1 cup frozen honeydew melon chunks

1 banana

BOOST IT: 2 tablespoons vanilla soy yogurt

This sweet green blend of melon, banana, citrus, and spinach is a cooling way to give your immune system a boost.

DIRECTIONS: Combine the orange juice, water, and spinach in a blender and blend from low to high until smooth. Add the remaining ingredients and blend from low to high until frosty smooth.

CALORIES: 229, FAT: 1G, CARBS: 56G, PROTEIN: 4G, FIBER: 5G | VITAMIN A: 52%, CALCIUM: 5%, VITAMIN C: 189%, IRON: 8% | ALSO RICH IN POTASSIUM AND VITAMIN B$_6$.

316 frozen tangerine

2 frozen large seedless tangerines, segmented

1 banana

½ cup vanilla soy milk

2 teaspoons maple syrup

½ cup ice

BOOST IT: 2 to 3 pinches of ground cinnamon and cayenne

Take two frozen tangerines and call me in the morning. This vitamin C–filled blend of whole frozen fruit is a delicious way to boost immunity.

DIRECTIONS: Combine all the ingredients in a blender and blend from low to high until frosty smooth.

CALORIES: 300, FAT: 3G, CARBS: 68G, PROTEIN: 7G, FIBER: 6G | VITAMIN A: 57%, CALCIUM: 20%, VITAMIN C: 188%, IRON: 10%

317 chard immunity charger

2 cups chopped Swiss chard

2 tablespoons fresh lemon juice

1 teaspoon grated fresh ginger

1 banana

1 tablespoon almond butter

1 to 2 teaspoons maple syrup

½ cup water

½ cup ice

BOOST IT: **1 teaspoon flax seeds**

This frothy blend of chard, banana, stimulating ginger, lemon, and almond butter will charge you up in no time with the help of vitamins A and C, a boost of copper, and magnesium from the almond butter.

DIRECTIONS: Combine all the ingredients in a blender and blend from low to high until frosty smooth.

CALORIES: 245, FAT: 10G, CARBS: 40G, PROTEIN: 5G, FIBER: 5G | VITAMIN A: 90%, CALCIUM: 10%, VITAMIN C: 77%, IRON: 13% | ALSO RICH IN MAGNESIUM, MANGANESE, AND VITAMIN B$_6$.

318 peach-hemp healer

1 tablespoon hemp seeds

1 cup orange juice

½ cup frozen peach chunks

½ cup plain soy yogurt

1 frozen banana

2 to 3 pinches of cayenne

½ cup ice

BOOST IT: **1 tablespoon raw walnuts**

Sweet peaches and antioxidant-rich orange juice blend with probiotic soy yogurt and hemp seeds rich with omega-3 and protein. Spicy cayenne warms and boosts immunity.

DIRECTIONS: Combine the hemp seeds and orange juice in a blender and blend from low to high until smooth. Add the remaining ingredients and blend from low to high until frosty smooth.

CALORIES: 381, FAT: 6G, CARBS: 77G, PROTEIN: 10G, FIBER: 6G | VITAMIN A: 21%, CALCIUM: 21%, VITAMIN C: 234%, IRON: 14%

Chia Cream Citrus

319 chia cream citrus

1½ cups frozen orange slices

1 banana

½ cup vanilla soy milk

¼ cup coconut water

1 teaspoon chia seeds

BOOST IT: **1 to 2 teaspoons unsweetened dried coconut flakes or a splash of coconut milk**

Frozen oranges, vanilla soy milk, chia seeds, and banana blend into this cool, sweet smoothie. Add some coconut flakes or coconut milk for a tropical accent. Plenty of immune system–boosting vitamin C in each sip!

DIRECTIONS: Combine all the ingredients in a blender and blend from low to high until frosty smooth.

CALORIES: 317, FAT: 5G, CARBS: 69G, PROTEIN: 9G, FIBER: 12G
| VITAMIN A: 19%, CALCIUM: 30%, VITAMIN C: 259%, IRON: 9%
| ALSO RICH IN POTASSIUM.

320 walnut-ginger cookie

1¼ cups vanilla soy milk

3 dates, pitted, or a splash of maple syrup

2 tablespoons rolled oats

3 tablespoons raw walnuts

1 frozen banana

3 pinches of ground cinnamon

¼ teaspoon ginger powder

BOOST IT: **a few drops of vanilla extract**

Cookies always make me feel a little better—especially a cookie loaded with healthy walnuts and fiber-rich oats. Cookie goodness is crammed into each sip of this frosty dessert shake. Tip: Soak the walnuts overnight in water for a smoother blend.

DIRECTIONS: Combine the soy milk, dates, oats, and walnuts in a blender and blend from low to high until smooth. Add the remaining ingredients and blend from low to high until frosty smooth.

CALORIES: 486, FAT: 20G, CARBS: 65G, PROTEIN: 18G, FIBER: 9G
| VITAMIN A: 14%, CALCIUM: 42%, VITAMIN C: 18%, IRON: 17%

321 pineapple-papaya allergy fighter

1 cup fresh pineapple chunks

1 cup fresh or frozen papaya chunks

1 frozen banana

½ cup orange juice

½ cup ice

BOOST IT: **2 to 3 pinches of cayenne and/or 1 teaspoon grated fresh ginger**

Fruit enzymes from papaya and pineapple may help fight your seasonal allergies naturally. This tropical smoothie, rich in antioxidants, helps give your body a healthy boost.

DIRECTIONS: Combine all the ingredients in a blender and blend from low to high until frosty smooth.

CALORIES: 293, FAT: 1G, CARBS: 73G, PROTEIN: 4G, FIBER: 8G | VITAMIN A: 39%, CALCIUM: 7%, VITAMIN C: 388%, IRON: 6% | ALSO RICH IN POTASSIUM, MANGANESE, AND VITAMIN B$_6$.

322 green-tea chia recharge

2 tablespoons chia seeds

1 cup vanilla soy milk

1 to 2 teaspoons matcha powder

1 teaspoon grated fresh ginger or ¼ teaspoon ginger powder

1 frozen banana

1 tablespoon maple syrup

½ cup ice

BOOST IT: **½ cup frozen watermelon for a frosty, thick texture**

Recharge your cells with this ginger-flavored matcha green tea shake blended with plump superfood chia seeds and potassium-rich banana. Antioxidant power in every green tea–filled sip. For a thicker shake, reduce the soy milk or toss in another frozen banana.

DIRECTIONS: In a blender, soak the chia seeds in the soy milk for at least one to two minutes or until they have plumped and become gel-like. Add the remaining ingredients and blend from low to high until frosty smooth.

CALORIES: 336, FAT: 9G, CARBS: 54G, PROTEIN: 14G, FIBER: 12G | VITAMIN A: 12%, CALCIUM: 40%, VITAMIN C: 20%, IRON: 18% | ALSO RICH IN RIBOFLAVIN.

323 pineapple-kiwi-mint immunity

½ cup orange juice

¼ cup plain soy milk

2 kiwis, peeled

½ cup fresh or frozen pineapple chunks

1 cup chopped kale leaves

1 banana

¼ cup green grapes

1 tablespoon chopped fresh mint

½ cup coconut water ice cubes

Bromelain- and enzyme-rich pineapple, vitamin C–filled kiwi and citrus, banana, grapes, and soothing mint swirl together in this antioxidant-rich blend of green deliciousness. Plus, it's loaded with immunity-boosting vitamins A and C. Try it with frozen grapes, kiwi, and/or banana for a frostier blend.

DIRECTIONS: Combine all the ingredients in a blender and blend from low to high until frosty smooth.

BOOST IT: **2 to 3 tablespoons soy yogurt**

CALORIES: 397, FAT: 4G, CARBS: 90G, PROTEIN: 10G, FIBER: 12G | VITAMIN A: 217%, CALCIUM: 22%, VITAMIN C: 557%, IRON: 18% | ALSO RICH IN POTASSIUM, MANGANESE, AND VITAMIN B$_6$.

324 walnut "milk" shake

2 to 3 tablespoons raw walnuts

1 cup vanilla soy milk or rice milk

1 frozen banana

A few pinches of ground cinnamon and ginger powder

2 teaspoons maple syrup

½ cup ice

BOOST IT: **2 teaspoons raw cacao powder**

Cool, creamy soy or rice milk blends with omega-3–rich walnuts in this banana-infused feel-good shake that's smooth and sweet with accents of vanilla and cinnamon. Omega-3 fatty acids and cacao powder boost your immunity. For a thicker texture, reduce the liquid by ¼ cup and add an additional frozen banana or more walnuts.

DIRECTIONS: Combine the walnuts, cacao powder, if using, and soy milk in a blender and blend from low to high until thickened. Add the remaining ingredients and blend from low to high until frosty smooth.

CALORIES: 330, FAT: 13G, CARBS: 45G, PROTEIN: 10G, FIBER: 5G | VITAMIN A: 12%, CALCIUM: 33%, VITAMIN C: 17%, IRON: 11% | ALSO RICH IN RIBOFLAVIN.

325 "feel super!" superfood smoothie

1 cup soy milk

1 cup chopped spinach

2 teaspoons açaí powder (optional)

1 tablespoon raw walnuts

1 cup frozen blueberries

1 frozen banana

½ cup coconut water ice cubes

BOOST IT: **1 teaspoon chia seeds and/or 1 teaspoon flax oil**

"Sick? I never get sick! I always feel super!" That's what you may be saying if you include this superfood smoothie in your weekly routine. Rich in antioxidants to ward off illness and keep you feeling super from the inside out, this sweet green smoothie combining blueberries, spinach, walnuts, and banana may be just what the doctor ordered.

DIRECTIONS: Combine the soy milk, spinach, açaí powder, if using, and walnuts in a blender and blend from low to high until smooth. Add the remaining ingredients and blend from low to high until frosty smooth.

CALORIES: 404, FAT: 13G, CARBS: 64G, PROTEIN: 13G, FIBER: 10G | VITAMIN A: 77%, CALCIUM: 40%, VITAMIN C: 90%, IRON: 20% | ALSO RICH IN MANGANESE AND VITAMIN B$_6$.

326 fizzy ginger-berry cooler

½ cup orange juice

½ cup frozen strawberries

1 cup naturally sweetened ginger ale

½ cup ice

BOOST IT: **2 to 3 pinches of cayenne**

Ginger ale over ice is a classic feel-better drink. I've added in a few fruity accents and ice to make this favorite fizzy beverage a feel-good cooler.

DIRECTIONS: Combine the orange juice and strawberries in a blender and blend from low to high until smooth. Add the remaining ingredients and blend from low to high until frosty smooth.

CALORIES: 162, FAT: 1G, CARBS: 39G, PROTEIN: 1G, FIBER: 2G | VITAMIN A: 5%, CALCIUM: 4%, VITAMIN C: 174%, IRON: 8%

327 super-spicy beet sipper

¼ cup grated beets

½ cup coconut water

1 cup chopped cucumber

1 cup chopped arugula

3 to 4 pinches of cayenne

½ cup ice

BOOST IT: **1 to 2 cloves raw garlic**

This spicy veggie blend should perk your immune system up quite a bit! Sweet red beets and cayenne blend with cool cucumber and greens. For extra spiciness and immunity power, add a garlic clove or two. If you have a juicer, you can juice the beets instead of grating them.

DIRECTIONS: Combine all the ingredients in a blender and blend from low to high until frosty smooth.

CALORIES: 74, FAT: 1G, CARBS: 16G, PROTEIN: 4G, FIBER: 4G | VITAMIN A: 19%, CALCIUM: 10%, VITAMIN C: 21%, IRON: 8% | ALSO RICH IN POTASSIUM, MANGANESE, VITAMIN B$_6$, PHOSPHORUS, RIBOFLAVIN, AND MAGNESIUM.

328 blue pineapple zing shake

½ cup frozen pineapple chunks

1 cup frozen blueberries

1 frozen banana

¾ cup pineapple juice

Pinch of cayenne (optional)

BOOST IT: **2 to 3 tablespoons soy yogurt**

Rich in antioxidants and bromelain, this blueberry, banana, and pineapple smoothie is a perky-sweet wellness treat for your immune system. It's got a thick, frosty texture and a nice dose of vitamin C.

DIRECTIONS: Combine all the ingredients in a blender and blend from low to high until frosty smooth.

CALORIES: 326, FAT: 1G, CARBS: 82G, PROTEIN: 4G, FIBER: 8G | VITAMIN A: 4%, CALCIUM: 5%, VITAMIN C: 134%, IRON: 8% | ALSO RICH IN MANGANESE AND VITAMIN B$_6$.

329 pink pear

1 pear, cored and chopped

½ cup frozen strawberries

1 cup vanilla soy yogurt

1 frozen banana

½ teaspoon grated fresh ginger

½ cup ice

BOOST IT: **1 teaspoon flax oil**

This probiotic-rich creamy pink smoothie will give your digestive system a boost—and that helps out your immune system! Spicy ginger also boosts immunity.

DIRECTIONS: Combine all the ingredients in a blender and blend from low to high until frosty smooth.

CALORIES: 388, FAT: 5G, CARBS: 86G, PROTEIN: 10G, FIBER: 11G | VITAMIN A: 2%, CALCIUM: 39%, VITAMIN C: 98%, IRON: 12%

330 banana-pineapple sunbeam

¾ cup pineapple juice

1 frozen banana

1 small fresh peach, pitted and sliced

½ cup frozen strawberries

½ cup ice

BOOST IT: **1 teaspoon flax oil**

Sunny pineapple juice blends with creamy banana, strawberries, and a juicy sweet peach. This oasis of vibrant fruit will infuse your body with immune system–strengthening vitamin C. Add some flax oil for extra immune-boosting power.

DIRECTIONS: Combine all the ingredients in a blender and blend from low to high until frosty smooth.

CALORIES: 258, FAT: 1G, CARBS: 64G, PROTEIN: 3G, FIBER: 6G | VITAMIN A: 7%, CALCIUM: 5%, VITAMIN C: 128%, IRON: 8% | ALSO RICH IN MANGANESE, POTASSIUM, AND VITAMIN B$_6$.

331 twilight berry blend

1¼ cups vanilla soy milk

2 teaspoons açaí powder

½ cup frozen blackberries

½ cup frozen blueberries

1 frozen banana

Sweetener to taste (optional)

½ cup ice

BOOST IT: 1 teaspoon raw cacao nibs or cacao powder

This deep purple smoothie is a moody-delicious blend of berries, açaí, and soy milk. Add a scoop of cacao nibs or powder for extra antioxidants and dark chocolate flavor. Antioxidant-rich berries help strengthen your immune system.

DIRECTIONS: Combine the soy milk, açaí powder, and cacao nibs, if using, in a blender and blend from low to high until smooth. Add the remaining ingredients and blend from low to high until frosty smooth.

CALORIES: 340, FAT: 9G, CARBS: 56G, PROTEIN: 12G, FIBER: 10G | VITAMIN A: 26%, CALCIUM: 43%, VITAMIN C: 84%, IRON: 15%

332 summertime nectarine squeeze

2 nectarines, pitted and chopped

1 banana

½ cup orange juice

1 cup frozen strawberries

½ cup coconut water ice cubes

BOOST IT: ¼ cup vanilla soy yogurt

Celebrate the natural beauty of summertime with this fresh nectarine smoothie. This smoothie is loaded with immune system–boosting vitamin C and feel-good fiber.

DIRECTIONS: Combine all the ingredients in a blender and blend from low to high until frosty smooth.

CALORIES: 355, FAT: 2G, CARBS: 85G, PROTEIN: 7G, FIBER: 12G | VITAMIN A: 27%, CALCIUM: 9%, VITAMIN C: 292%, IRON: 13% | ALSO RICH IN MANGANESE AND POTASSIUM.

333 two-ingredient tropical shake

2 frozen bananas

1½ cups fresh pineapple chunks

BOOST IT: **1 peeled and chopped kiwi for more vitamin C**

When you are in a hurry for a creamy immunity boost, grab these two ingredients and blend up this exotic sweet shake. It's thick and frosty, full of tropical flavor. Pineapple is rich in immunity-boosting vitamin C and the digestive enzyme bromelain. If you're not using a high-speed blender, you may need to add a few splashes of liquid—try non-dairy milk, orange juice, or pineapple juice.

DIRECTIONS: Combine all the ingredients in a blender and blend from low to high until frosty smooth.

CALORIES: 326, FAT: 1G, CARBS: 84G, PROTEIN: 4G, FIBER: 9G | VITAMIN A: 6%, CALCIUM: 4%, VITAMIN C: 219%, IRON: 7% | ALSO RICH IN MANGANESE AND VITAMIN B$_6$.

334 "seedy" watermelon frosty

2 cups frozen watermelon chunks

2 tablespoons fresh lemon juice

1 teaspoon chia seeds

½ cup coconut water

1 banana

BOOST IT: **handful of fresh strawberries**

This cute-looking frosty is perfect for summer because it looks like a slice of watermelon, seeds and all. Only those sneaky "seeds" are actually superfood chia seeds! Watermelon is rich in potassium to keep you hydrated, chia seeds give you an omega-3 boost, and the vitamin C in lemon juice boosts your immune system.

DIRECTIONS: Combine all the ingredients in a blender and blend from low to high until frosty smooth.

CALORIES: 250, FAT: 3G, CARBS: 59G, PROTEIN: 5G, FIBER: 7G | VITAMIN A: 36%, CALCIUM: 8%, VITAMIN C: 86%, IRON: 10% | ALSO RICH IN POTASSIUM AND VITAMIN B$_6$.

335 rosy cheeks delight

1 cup carrot juice

1 cup frozen
   strawberries

1 frozen banana

½ cup coconut water
   ice cubes

BOOST IT: **a few pinches
of ground turmeric or
a scoop of vanilla soy
yogurt**

Antioxidant-rich berries and carrot juice will flood
your cheeks with a warm rosy-peach glow. All that
free-radical-fighting vitamin C provides a beauty
burst from the inside out. Potassium-rich coconut
water and banana help hydrate your skin. Make the
carrot juice yourself if you have a juicer; otherwise,
use store-bought carrot juice.

DIRECTIONS: Combine all the ingredients in a blender and
blend from low to high until frosty smooth.

**CALORIES: 244, FAT: 1G, CARBS: 56G, PROTEIN: 5G, FIBER: 8G
| VITAMIN A: 702%, CALCIUM: 10%, VITAMIN C: 188%, IRON: 9%
| ALSO RICH IN MANGANESE, POTASSIUM, AND VITAMIN B$_6$.**

336 green goddess grapefruit

1 cup chopped spinach

1 cup chopped kale
   leaves

½ cup green grapes

1 cup grapefruit juice

1 frozen banana

½ cup coconut water
   ice cubes

BOOST IT: **2 to 3
tablespoons mashed
avocado**

Grapefruit is a super anti-aging ingredient because
it is rich in free-radical-fighting vitamin C and
lycopene. This green goddess blend of citrus and
greens offers up a rejuvenating sip for you to enjoy.

DIRECTIONS: Combine the spinach, kale, grapes, and
grapefruit juice in a blender and blend from low to high
until smooth. Add the remaining ingredients and blend
from low to high until frosty smooth.

**CALORIES: 273, FAT: 2G, CARBS: 65G, PROTEIN: 7G, FIBER: 9G
| VITAMIN A: 307%, CALCIUM: 19%, VITAMIN C: 305%, IRON: 16%
| ALSO RICH IN MANGANESE, POTASSIUM, MAGNESIUM, AND
VITAMIN B$_6$.**

Ravishing Raspberry

337 ravishing raspberry

½ cup fresh raspberries

2 frozen bananas

1 cup vanilla soy yogurt

¼ cup ice

TOPPING: **a couple of fresh raspberries or 2 tablespoons vegan granola or chopped nuts, plus 1 teaspoon flax oil (optional)**

Grab a spoon for this frosty, thick frozen yogurt–like blend. Creamy soy yogurt blends with frozen bananas and sweet raspberries; add some crunch by topping your shake with crunchy nuts or vegan granola.

DIRECTIONS: Combine all the ingredients in a blender and blend from low to high until frosty smooth. Top with the raspberries or granola and serve with a spoon. If using the flax oil, drizzle it over the top.

CALORIES: 493, FAT: 8G, CARBS: 101G, PROTEIN: 13G, FIBER: 14G | VITAMIN A: 3%, CALCIUM: 39%, VITAMIN C: 61%, IRON: 16% | ALSO RICH IN MANGANESE AND POTASSIUM.

338 pretty pink bananaberry

1½ frozen bananas

1 cup fresh raspberries or other berry

1 cup vanilla soy milk

2 teaspoons agave syrup

½ cup ice

BOOST IT: **2 to 3 tablespoons vanilla soy yogurt**

Pretty fresh pink raspberries swirl with potassium-rich banana and soy for a sweet antioxidant-rich treat. Bananas are also rich in soluble and insoluble fiber, and fiber is important for keeping your digestive tract healthy at any age!

DIRECTIONS: Combine all the ingredients in a blender and blend from low to high until frosty smooth.

CALORIES: 364, FAT: 5G, CARBS: 74G, PROTEIN: 10G, FIBER: 14G | VITAMIN A: 13%, CALCIUM: 35%, VITAMIN C: 79%, IRON: 14% | ALSO RICH IN MANGANESE AND RIBOFLAVIN.

339 strawberry-melon cooler

1½ cups fresh watermelon chunks

1 cup fresh strawberries

½ cup diced cucumber

1 tablespoon chopped fresh mint

½ cup coconut water ice cubes

BOOST IT: 1 to 3 tablespoons fresh lime juice

This potassium-rich, skin-soothing blend of watermelon, mint, cucumber, and berries will help keep your skin hydrated and looking supple. Strawberries are an excellent source of the antioxidant vitamin C.

DIRECTIONS: Combine all the ingredients in a blender and blend from low to high until frosty smooth.

CALORIES: 148, FAT: 1G, CARBS: 35G, PROTEIN: 4G, FIBER: 6G | VITAMIN A: 32%, CALCIUM: 9%, VITAMIN C: 180%, IRON: 13% | ALSO RICH IN MANGANESE, POTASSIUM, AND MAGNESIUM.

340 apricot glow

1¼ cups vanilla rice milk

3 apricots, pitted

½ cup frozen peach chunks

½ frozen banana

½ cup coconut water ice cubes

1 to 2 teaspoons maple syrup (optional)

BOOST IT: 1 tablespoon raw walnuts

Sweet summer apricots and creamy vanilla rice milk create a silky sweet smoothie to give your skin that hydrated apricot glow. Apricots are a good source of the antioxidant vitamins A and C and potassium; add some nutty walnuts for a boost of omega-3 fatty acids and magnesium.

DIRECTIONS: Combine all the ingredients in a blender and blend from low to high until frosty smooth.

CALORIES: 309, FAT: 4G, CARBS: 68G, PROTEIN: 4G, FIBER: 6G | VITAMIN A: 47%, CALCIUM: 8%, VITAMIN C: 43%, IRON: 8%

Mango Majesty

341 mango majesty

1 cup fresh mango chunks

¼ cup orange juice (or soy or coconut milk for a creamier version)

½ cup frozen pineapple chunks

1 frozen banana

½ cup ice

BOOST IT: **1 to 2 tablespoons fresh lime juice, plus a pinch of zest**

Silky fresh mango, rich in skin-glowing vitamin A, spins with luscious banana, frosty pineapple, and vibrant orange juice for an island-inspired, antioxidant-rich smoothie to crave!

DIRECTIONS: Combine all the ingredients in a blender and blend from low to high until frosty smooth.

CALORIES: 279, FAT: 1G, CARBS: 71G, PROTEIN: 3G, FIBER: 7G | VITAMIN A: 30%, CALCIUM: 4%, VITAMIN C: 207%, IRON: 5% | ALSO RICH IN POTASSIUM AND VITAMIN B$_6$.

342 cucumber-melon skin soother

1 cup diced cucumber

3 tablespoons fresh lime juice

1 teaspoon maple syrup

½ cup coconut water

2 cups frozen honeydew melon chunks

BOOST IT: **1 teaspoon aloe vera juice**

Hydrate your skin with this soothing melon-cucumber frosty with an accent of lime. Honeydew melon and coconut water are excellent sources of potassium, to help your skin stay hydrated and supple.

DIRECTIONS: Combine all the ingredients except the melon in a blender and blend from low to high until smooth. Add the melon and blend from low to high until frosty smooth.

CALORIES: 190, FAT: 1G, CARBS: 47G, PROTEIN: 4G, FIBER: 5G | VITAMIN A: 6%, CALCIUM: 8%, VITAMIN C: 135%, IRON: 7% | ALSO RICH IN POTASSIUM, MAGNESIUM, AND VITAMIN B$_6$.

343 hot date shake

4 dates, pitted and
roughly chopped

2 tablespoons raw
pecans

1¼ cups vanilla soy milk

1 frozen banana

3 pinches of ground
cinnamon

1 to 2 pinches of
cayenne

½ cup ice

BOOST IT: a scoop of
coconut milk ice cream
for a dessert version

Look at you! You are a hot date for sure. So blend
up a bevie to match! Sweet dates, rich nutty pecans,
and spices make up this sweet-treat date-banana
shake. Those pecans are a good source of thiamine,
copper, magnesium, and manganese.

DIRECTIONS: Combine the dates, pecans, and soy milk in
a blender and blend from low to high until smoothed a
bit. Add the remaining ingredients and blend from low to
high until frosty smooth.

CALORIES: 420, FAT: 15G, CARBS: 84G, PROTEIN: 12G, FIBER: 9G
| VITAMIN A: 18%, CALCIUM: 42%, VITAMIN C: 18%, IRON: 14%
| ALSO RICH IN RIBOFLAVIN.

344 apples and oranges beauty sipper

1 cup chopped apple

1 orange, peeled and
segmented

1 banana

½ cup frozen peach
chunks

1 cup chopped spinach

½ to 1 cup coconut
water

½ cup ice

BOOST IT: 1 tablespoon
aloe vera juice

Everyone loves everyday apples and oranges,
and they are perfect for achieving a healthy glow.
This whole food smoothie sipper combines crunchy
apples, fiber-rich skins and all, plus vibrant vitamin
C–filled oranges. Some superfood spinach gives an
added beauty boost!

DIRECTIONS: Combine all the ingredients in a blender and
blend from low to high until frosty smooth.

CALORIES: 312, FAT: 1G, CARBS: 77G, PROTEIN: 6G, FIBER: 14G
| VITAMIN A: 73%, CALCIUM: 15%, VITAMIN C: 217%, IRON: 11%
| ALSO RICH IN POTASSIUM AND VITAMIN B$_6$.

345 secret garden honeydew shake

2 cups chopped
   spinach

1¼ cups plain soy milk

1½ cups frozen
   honeydew melon
   chunks

1 frozen banana

BOOST IT: 1 tablespoon
chopped fresh mint

This frosty, sweet soy shake made with honeydew melon and banana has a secret: it is loaded with superfood spinach. Use less milk for a thicker shake.

DIRECTIONS: Combine the spinach and soy milk in a blender and blend from low to high until smooth. Add the remaining ingredients and blend from low to high until frosty smooth.

CALORIES: 336, FAT: 6G, CARBS: 62G, PROTEIN: 13G, FIBER: 8G | VITAMIN A: 129%, CALCIUM: 46%, VITAMIN C: 122%, IRON: 21% | ALSO RICH IN MAGNESIUM, POTASSIUM, RIBOFLAVIN, AND VITAMIN B$_6$.

346 24 "carrot" gold

1 cup fresh carrot juice

¼ cup vanilla soy
   yogurt

½ cup frozen mango
   chunks

½ cup frozen peach
   chunks

½ frozen banana

½ cup ice

BOOST IT: a few pinches
of cayenne or grated
fresh ginger

Drinking carrot juice is one of the easiest (and most delicious) ways to infuse your body with a serious dose of vitamin A. This creamy, hydrating carrot juice smoothie includes sweet peaches, banana, and mango to give you a 24 "carrot" gold glow.

DIRECTIONS: Combine all the ingredients in a blender and blend from low to high until frosty smooth.

CALORIES: 253, FAT: 2G, CARBS: 58G, PROTEIN: 6G, FIBER: 6G | VITAMIN A: 719%, CALCIUM: 15%, VITAMIN C: 81%, IRON: 6%

347 grapevine glow

1 cup frozen red grapes

1 cup pomegranate
juice

1 banana (optional)

¾ cup coconut water
ice cubes

BOOST IT: **2 teaspoons
aloe vera juice**

Red grapes swirl with pomegranate juice for
a red-glow frosty filled with feel-beautiful nutrients.
This icy blend is a refreshing sip on a hot day or after
a workout session. Grape skins are rich in the free-
radical-fighting, anti-aging antioxidant resveratrol.
Including the banana adds potassium, sweetness,
and fiber.

DIRECTIONS: Combine all the ingredients in a blender and
blend from low to high until frosty smooth.

**CALORIES: 399, FAT: 1G, CARBS: 95G, PROTEIN: 5G, FIBER: 7G
| VITAMIN A: 6%, CALCIUM: 7%, VITAMIN C: 54%, IRON: 9%**

348 peachy cream skin soother

1 cup vanilla soy milk

2 peaches, pitted and
chopped

1 frozen banana

½ cup vanilla soy
yogurt

3 pinches of ground
cinnamon

1 tablespoon maple
syrup

½ cup ice

BOOST IT: **1 tablespoon
rolled oats and/or raw
walnuts**

Want a peaches-and-cream glow to your skin?
Give this juicy peach soy-milk shake a whirl: Fresh
peaches and creamy soy blend with cinnamon and
maple flavors. Peaches are a good source of the
antioxidant vitamins A and C.

DIRECTIONS: Combine all the ingredients in a blender and
blend from low to high until frosty smooth.

**CALORIES: 424, FAT: 7G, CARBS: 82G, PROTEIN: 14G, FIBER: 9G
| VITAMIN A: 24%, CALCIUM: 52%, VITAMIN C: 39%, IRON: 16%**

349 frozen green oasis

1 cup chopped frozen
   cucumber
1 cup frozen green
   grapes
1 cup coconut water
Drizzle of agave syrup
Pinch of salt (optional)

BOOST IT: 2 teaspoons
aloe vera juice

This green blend of frozen grapes and cucumbers
and coconut water will leave you—and your skin—
feeling hydrated and glowing.

DIRECTIONS: Combine all the ingredients in a blender and
blend from low to high until frosty smooth.

CALORIES: 123, FAT: 1G, CARBS: 28G, PROTEIN: 3G, FIBER: 4G
| VITAMIN A: 4%, CALCIUM: 9%, VITAMIN C: 21%, IRON: 7%
| ALSO RICH IN MANGANESE, POTASSIUM, AND MAGNESIUM.

350 surf's-up peach shake

1½ cups frozen peach
   chunks
1 frozen banana
½ cup pineapple juice
½ cup 100% guava juice
1 teaspoon
   unsweetened dried
   coconut flakes
½ cup ice

BOOST IT: splash of
coconut milk

Those surfer boys and girls always have that sun-
kissed healthy glow about them. And this tropical
blend of banana, pineapple, coconut, and guava will
give you that island look by fighting plenty of free
radicals as you sip.

DIRECTIONS: Combine all the ingredients in a blender and
blend from low to high until frosty smooth.

CALORIES: 337, FAT: 2G, CARBS: 82G, PROTEIN: 4G, FIBER: 8G
| VITAMIN A: 18%, CALCIUM: 4%, VITAMIN C: 116%, IRON: 10%
| ALSO RICH IN MANGANESE.

351 orange glow frosty

1 cup freshly squeezed orange juice

1 fresh or frozen banana

About 1 cup coconut water ice cubes

BOOST IT: ¼ cup grated carrot or a splash of carrot juice

Vitamin C–rich freshly squeezed orange juice is vibrant and refreshing when served in frosty form. This free-radical-fighting frosty is simple and sweet with a hint of creamy banana.

DIRECTIONS: Combine the orange juice, banana, and carrot, if using, in a blender and blend from low to high, adding ice a scoop at a time until you reach your desired iciness.

CALORIES: 262, FAT: 1G, CARBS: 61G, PROTEIN: 5G, FIBER: 6G | VITAMIN A: 11%, CALCIUM: 9%, VITAMIN C: 233%, IRON: 8% | ALSO RICH IN POTASSIUM, MAGNESIUM, AND VITAMIN B_6.

352 pretty in purple

1¼ cups vanilla soy milk

1 cup frozen blueberries

1 teaspoon açaí powder

1 frozen banana

½ cup ice

1 teaspoon agave syrup

BOOST IT: ½ teaspoon spirulina powder

You'll need a pretty purple outfit to match this pretty purple smoothie—and the pretty pink glow on your face as you sip in plenty of pretty purple antioxidants.

DIRECTIONS: Combine all the ingredients in a blender and blend from low to high until frosty smooth.

CALORIES: 332, FAT: 7G, CARBS: 59G, PROTEIN: 11G, FIBER: 8G | VITAMIN A: 20%, CALCIUM: 40%, VITAMIN C: 56%, IRON: 13% | ALSO RICH IN RIBOFLAVIN.

353 pretty in potassium

1½ cups fresh
   cantaloupe chunks

1 banana

½ cup strawberries

½ cup coconut water
   ice cubes

BOOST IT: **1 to 2
tablespoons fresh
lime juice**

Melon is an excellent low-calorie source of the electrolyte potassium, and you need a steady intake of electrolytes to help your skin stay hydrated and glowing. Try this sweet and refreshing cantaloupe cooler for a natural beauty lift. Use frozen strawberries and banana if you want a frostier blend.

DIRECTIONS: Combine all the ingredients in a blender and blend from low to high until frosty smooth.

CALORIES: 230, FAT: 1G, CARBS: 56G, PROTEIN: 5G, FIBER: 8G | VITAMIN A: 160%, CALCIUM: 7%, VITAMIN C: 236%, IRON: 8% | ALSO RICH IN MANGANESE, POTASSIUM, MAGNESIUM, AND VITAMIN B$_6$.

354 apple orchard skin soother

½ cup apple cider
   or fresh-pressed
   apple juice

2 tablespoons fresh
   lemon juice

1 banana

2 cups chopped
   spinach

½ cup chopped parsley

½ cup chopped
   cucumber

½ cup ice

BOOST IT: **1 teaspoon
grated fresh ginger**

Sweet apple cider, tart lemon, and an option for fresh ginger perk up a slew of nutrient-dense greens, including spinach, cool cucumber, and zesty parsley, in this soothing green cooler.

DIRECTIONS: Combine all the ingredients in a blender and blend from low to high until frosty smooth.

CALORIES: 203, FAT: 1G, CARBS: 50G, PROTEIN: 5G, FIBER: 6G | VITAMIN A: 166%, CALCIUM: 13%, VITAMIN C: 139%, IRON: 25% | ALSO RICH IN MANGANESE, POTASSIUM, MAGNESIUM, AND VITAMIN B$_6$.

355 chocolate peanut butter cup

1½ tablespoons peanut butter

1½ tablespoons raw cacao powder

1 cup vanilla soy milk

¼ cup vanilla soy yogurt

1½ frozen bananas

¼ cup ice

BOOST IT: 1 teaspoon raw cacao nibs

Lets face it: Happiness makes you look beautiful from the inside out. And I think everyone gets giddy indulging their craving for peanut butter and chocolate. Cacao is rich in antioxidants, so you can feel good about treating yourself. Reduce the soy milk by ¼ cup for a thicker shake.

DIRECTIONS: Combine all the ingredients in a blender and blend from low to high until frosty smooth.

CALORIES: 470, FAT: 19G, CARBS: 54G, PROTEIN: 20G, FIBER: 10G | VITAMIN A: 12%, CALCIUM: 41%, VITAMIN C: 26%, IRON: 17%

356 peachy breezy boost

½ cup frozen peach chunks

½ cup fresh strawberries

¾ cup freshly squeezed orange juice, plus a pinch of zest

¼ cup plain soy milk

1 banana

½ cup coconut water ice cubes

BOOST IT: 1 tablespoon flax seeds

This beauty-boost blend of soft berries and citrus is like sipping on a summer breeze. Vitamin C–infused peaches, fresh strawberries, and orange juice flavor each sip—and help crush free radicals.

DIRECTIONS: Combine all the ingredients in a blender and blend from low to high until frosty smooth.

CALORIES: 293, FAT: 2G, CARBS: 66G, PROTEIN: 7G, FIBER: 8G | VITAMIN A: 17%, CALCIUM: 15%, VITAMIN C: 257%, IRON: 10% | ALSO RICH IN POTASSIUM.

Peachy Breezy Boost

357 frozen avocado sunbeam

½ avocado

1 cup orange juice

1 frozen banana

½ cup coconut water ice cubes

Pinch of salt

BOOST IT: ¼ cup frozen mango chunks

Avocado and orange swirl together for a creamy smoothie that soothes and adds vibrancy to your skin and mood. Healthy fat–rich avocado nurtures your skin from the inside out.

DIRECTIONS: Combine all the ingredients in a blender and blend from low to high until frosty smooth.

CALORIES: 400, FAT: 16G, CARBS: 65G, PROTEIN: 6G, FIBER: 12G | VITAMIN A: 14%, CALCIUM: 7%, VITAMIN C: 245%, IRON: 10% | ALSO RICH IN VITAMIN B$_6$.

358 plum-fection frosty

3 plums, pitted

½ cup frozen blueberries

1 frozen banana

½ cup coconut water ice cubes

BOOST IT: drizzle of maple syrup

This refreshing summertime sip is a cool way to embrace plum season. Purple plums and blueberries are rich in free-radical-fighting antioxidants.

DIRECTIONS: Combine all the ingredients in a blender and blend from low to high until frosty smooth.

CALORIES: 260, FAT: 1G, CARBS: 65G, PROTEIN: 4G, FIBER: 9G | VITAMIN A: 16%, CALCIUM: 5%, VITAMIN C: 65%, IRON: 7% | ALSO RICH IN MANGANESE, POTASSIUM, AND VITAMIN B$_6$.

359 creamy vanilla-orange shake

¾ cup freshly squeezed orange juice, plus a pinch of zest

¾ cup vanilla soy yogurt

1 frozen banana

½ cup frozen peach chunks

½ cup ice

BOOST IT: 1 tablespoon raw walnuts

Vanilla soy yogurt blends with vibrant freshly squeezed orange, peaches, and banana here. Vitamin C helps neutralize free radicals with each creamy citrus sip; add walnuts for a boost of omega-3 fatty acids.

DIRECTIONS: Combine all the ingredients in a blender and blend from low to high until frosty smooth.

CALORIES: 354, FAT: 4G, CARBS: 79G, PROTEIN: 9G, FIBER: 7G | VITAMIN A: 14%, CALCIUM: 30%, VITAMIN C: 181%, IRON: 11%

360 pretty peach frozen green tea

1 cup unsweetened iced green tea

1 fresh peach, pitted and chopped

2 tablespoons fresh lemon juice

½ teaspoon grated fresh ginger

Agave syrup to taste

¾ cup ice or coconut water ice cubes

BOOST IT: 1 tablespoon chopped fresh mint

If you love sipping green tea for an antioxidant and energy boost, try this frozen green tea blended with accents of fresh peach, lemon, and ginger.

DIRECTIONS: Combine all the ingredients in a blender and blend from low to high until frosty smooth.

CALORIES: 46, FAT: 0G, CARBS: 12G, PROTEIN: 1G, FIBER: 2G | VITAMIN A: 7%, CALCIUM: 1%, VITAMIN C: 34%, IRON: 1% | ALSO RICH IN POTASSIUM.

361 spa day blackberry

1 cup frozen
  blackberries

1 cup chopped fresh or
  frozen cucumber

1 cup coconut water

1 frozen banana

1 teaspoon agave syrup
  (optional)

½ cup ice

BOOST IT: **2 teaspoons
aloe vera juice**

Have a spa beauty day via your smoothie with this creamy sweet blend of antioxidant-rich blackberries and hydrating coconut water. Soothing cucumber is added to the blend; save a couple of slices to place on your eyes for a post-smoothie puffy-eye treatment.

DIRECTIONS: Combine all the ingredients in a blender and blend from low to high until frosty smooth.

CALORIES: 249, FAT: 2G, CARBS: 59G, PROTEIN: 6G, FIBER: 14G | VITAMIN A: 10%, CALCIUM: 13%, VITAMIN C: 82%, IRON: 12% | ALSO RICH IN MANGANESE, POTASSIUM, MAGNESIUM, AND VITAMIN B$_6$.

362 vivacious vanilla-berry-almond shake

1 cup frozen
  strawberries

1 frozen banana

1 cup vanilla soy milk

1 tablespoon almond
  butter

2 teaspoons maple
  syrup

½ cup ice

BOOST IT: **1 tablespoon
hemp seeds**

Creamy vanilla soy milk blends with sweet strawberries, banana, and nutty almond butter in this energizing smoothie that simply makes you feel all aglow inside! Add hemp seeds for a protein boost.

DIRECTIONS: Combine all the ingredients in a blender and blend from low to high until frosty smooth.

CALORIES: 387, FAT: 14G, CARBS: 58G, PROTEIN: 12G, FIBER: 8G | VITAMIN A: 12%, CALCIUM: 38%, VITAMIN C: 158%, IRON: 15% | ALSO RICH IN MANGANESE AND RIBOFLAVIN.

363 sweet carrot and greens

1 cup fresh carrot juice

1 orange or tangerine, peeled and segmented

¾ cup frozen mango chunks

1 cup chopped spinach

1 cup chopped kale leaves

½ cup ice

BOOST IT: 1 teaspoon grated ginger

Infuse your cells with a serious boost of free-radical-fighting antioxidant vitamins A and C via this carrot, mango, and greens cooler. Boost with some fresh ginger for a spicy kick.

DIRECTIONS: Combine all the ingredients in a blender and blend from low to high until frosty smooth.

CALORIES: 277, FAT: 1G, CARBS: 64G, PROTEIN: 7G, FIBER: 10G | VITAMIN A: 990%, CALCIUM: 25%, VITAMIN C: 393%, IRON: 15% | ALSO RICH IN MANGANESE, THIAMINE, AND VITAMIN B$_6$.

364 kale-banana beautiful

2 cups chopped kale leaves

1 cup orange juice

½ cup frozen mango chunks

1 frozen banana

1 kiwi, peeled

½ cup ice

BOOST IT: 1 tablespoon almond butter

This antioxidant-rich blend of greens and fruit is an easy way to give your body a beauty boost. Perky kiwi and sweet mango combine with superfood kale in this sunny green smoothie.

DIRECTIONS: Combine the kale and orange juice in a blender and blend from low to high until smooth. Add the remaining ingredients and blend from low to high until frosty smooth.

CALORIES: 384, FAT: 2G, CARBS: 91G, PROTEIN: 9G, FIBER: 10G | VITAMIN A: 437%, CALCIUM: 25%, VITAMIN C: 647%, IRON: 19% | ALSO RICH IN MANGANESE, POTASSIUM, AND VITAMIN B$_6$.

365 gorgeous guava-banana shake

1 cup 100% guava juice

2 frozen bananas

1 to 2 tablespoons fresh lime juice, plus a pinch of zest

¼ cup coconut water ice cubes

BOOST IT: **splash of coconut water or 1 teaspoon unsweetened dried coconut flakes**

This tropical pink blend of guava juice, lime, and bananas will leave you feeling exotic, groovy, and gorgeous—glowing from the inside out. Which way to the beach?

DIRECTIONS: Combine all the ingredients in a blender and blend from low to high until frosty smooth.

CALORIES: 334, FAT: 1G, CARBS: 85G, PROTEIN: 3G, FIBER: 8G | VITAMIN A: 3%, CALCIUM: 1%, VITAMIN C: 142%, IRON: 7% | ALSO RICH IN POTASSIUM AND VITAMIN B$_6$.

RESOURCES

Online

Amazon.com: Specialty superfood
ingredients, tools, and more

CrateAndBarrel.com: Tools

NavitasNaturals.com:
Superfood powders

OneLuckyDuck.com: Tools and
superfood ingredients

SunFood.com: Ingredients

SurLaTable.com: Tools

Target.com: Tools

VitaminShoppe.com: Ingredients

Vitamix.com and Blendtec.com:
High-speed blenders

Williams-Sonoma.com: Specialty
high-speed blenders,
smoothie-making tools,
and more

Offline

Local natural food stores:
Basic ingredients

National chains like Whole Foods
and Trader Joe's and more
mainstream grocery store
chains: Basic ingredients

Kathy's website

Healthy-Happy-Life.com: Vegan
recipes, advice, and smoothie
inspiration

ACKNOWLEDGMENTS

Always first. Thank you to my husband for loving me forever, and for inspiring me to always follow my dreams and nurture my happiness. Thank you for drinking and swooning over each and every smoothie I placed in front of you. And for letting me fill our kitchen with a mountain of bananas, stuff our freezer with fruit, and buy just about every smoothie glass under the sun. And thanks for being my farmers' market schlepper.

Thank you to my mom and dad, who instilled in me a passion for farmers' markets, backyard fruit trees, and California sunshine. And thanks for teaching me that life (stress and all) is better when you learn to laugh and smile with ease. To my brilliant forever best friend—my sister, Chrissy, and her RC&K—thank you for your love, fun, and energy!

To my girlfriends, old and new, thank you for all the joy and love. And to my wide circle of blog friends, some of whom I have never met in person but already know I love and adore. Thanks to the entire big, beautiful, compassionate, and inspiring vegan community.

Thank you, Gena, for your foreword, and your advice and friendship! I feel blessed to have met you.

A huge thanks to my awesome agent, Holly. And to all the talented folks at Penguin Group and Avery—William, Marisa, and more—you are all rock stars and magic makers to me.

Thank you to all my Healthy-Happy-Life.com readers and followers. It is through your virtual friendship, community, and constant support that I have found the inspiration and strength to bring my vegan recipes and photos to the world.

Last, to my kitty, Nelly, who has been by my side (or on my lap or desk) since 2001—I always say that I rescued you from a shelter—but, really, thank you for rescuing me. Purr.

INDEX

ABOUT THE AUTHOR

KATHY PATALSKY is a writer and photographer who grew up in Santa Cruz, California, where her passion for wellness, cooking, art, writing, sunshine, and smoothies began.

She graduated from American University in Washington, D.C., with a bachelor of science in health promotion. A few years out of college, she ventured wholeheartedly into the world of blogging, writing, and photography—and her ideal career was born. Patalsky's celebrated vegan recipe blog, Healthy-Happy-Life.com, is filled with creative recipes, photos, and vegan inspiration. She tweets from @lunchboxbunch.

Her recipe and photography work have been featured in *VegNews Magazine*, *Zooey Magazine*, *Foodista Best of Blogs Cookbook*, and *ThinkFood Cookbook*; in the PCRM iPhone App; on Babble.com, Meatless Monday.org, TheKitchn.com, BlogHer.com, and Saveur.com; and elsewhere.

Patalsky is thankful to have lived (and sipped smoothies) in a variety of inspiring cities with her husband and her cat, Nelly—including New York City, Los Angeles, and Washington, D.C.